"This book provides solid foundation in a critically important area of emergency management. Knox & Haupt present a compelling guide for ensuring optimal outcomes when working with diverse populations in crises. It should be on every emergency planner's desk, and consulted regularly!"

John J. Kiefer, *Ph.D., Professor and Director,*
MPA Program, University of New Orleans

"*Cultural Competency for Emergency and Crisis Management* addresses two major goals of professionals and professors in the disaster field: increased understanding of social vulnerability and improved instruction relating to the scholarship of teaching and learning. Knox, Haupt and the other authors of this book do a wonderful job providing the context for their cases along with other useful materials to facilitate in-class exercises. This book will increase comprehension among students and ultimately improve the performance in emergency management."

David A. McEntire, *Ph.D., Dean, College of Health and*
Public Service, Utah Valley University

"Knox and Haupt have put together an excellent resource for faculty wishing to add coverage of cultural competency in their emergency management courses. The chapters provide case studies illustrating why cultural competency is important in situations ranging from managing active shooter incidents in schools, to accommodating the homeless during wildfire evacuations, autistic children in disasters, and religious minorities in emergency shelters. There are also chapters on teaching preparedness to vulnerable populations and dealing with cultural issues in an Ebola outbreak in a refugee camp and delivering disaster relief in Syria. The case studies include discussion questions and assessment tools."

William L. Waugh, *Professor Emeritus,*
Georgia State University

Cultural Competency for Emergency and Crisis Management

Disasters are complex and dynamic events that test emergency and crisis professionals and leaders – even the most ethical ones. Within all phases of emergency management, disasters highlight social vulnerabilities that require culturally competent practices. The lack of culturally respectable responses to diverse populations underscores the critical need for cultural competency education and training in higher education and practice. Using a case study approach that is both adaptable and practical, this textbook is an accessible and essential guide on what makes teaching effective in emergency and crisis management.

Key Features

- ♦ An in-depth understanding of cultural competence makes it well suited for teaching effectively in emergency preparedness
- ♦ Expert guidance from leading authorities ensures a fresh perspective in various aspects of emergency and crisis management
- ♦ National and international emergency and crisis management case studies containing ground rules, a scenario, roles/actors, guiding questions, facilitator questions, and resources
- ♦ Pedagogy and andragogy theories that drive design and implementation
- ♦ Pre- and post-tests for each case study allow faculty and trainers to empirically measure the participants' learning outcomes
- ♦ Short case study structure can be easily implemented in a course as a group discussion, group assignment, or individual assignment

With unparalleled resources to reach every participant and facilitator, *Cultural Competency for Emergency and Crisis Management* offers educators a roadmap for successfully engaging participants in various aspects of cultural competency knowledge, skills, and abilities.

Claire Connolly Knox, Ph.D., is an associate professor and the director of the Master of Emergency and Crisis Management program in the School of Public Administration at the University of Central Florida. Her research interests include environmental vulnerability and disaster response, environmental policy and management, Habermas Critical Theory, and the scholarship of teaching and learning. She has published in multiple journals, including *Public Administration Review, Coastal Management Journal, Disaster Prevention and Management, Journal of Environmental Policy and Planning, Environmental Politics, Administration & Society, Journal of Emergency Management*, and *Journal of Public Affairs Education*. She is Chair of ASPA's Section on Emergency and Crisis Management, associate editor for Emergency Management for *Public Administration Review*, and editorial board member for the *International Journal of Security, Preparedness and Resilience Education*, and she is the past chair for FEMA's Scholarship of Teaching and Learning special interest group. She has won multiple awards for her research and teaching, including the 2015 Florida Emergency Preparedness Association's Gary Arnold for her dedication to improving Florida's emergency management community through higher education.

Brittany "Brie" Haupt, Ph.D., is an assistant professor at Virginia Commonwealth University. Her previous educational achievements contributed to developing her passion for increasing her cultural competency and becoming trained in diversity education and multiculturalism, as well as intercultural dialogue and community development. Her research interests include cultural competency, emergency management communication, community resilience, and competency-based education. She has published in *Public Administration Review*; *Journal of Public Affairs Education*; *Disaster Prevention and Management*; *Risk, Hazards, & Crisis in Public Policy*; *Journal of Emergency Management*; and the *Frontiers in Communication* section on disaster communications. In addition, she has presented at the American Society for Public Administration, the Association for Public Policy Analysis and Management, Public Administration Research conferences, as well as presented for the Federal Emergency Management Agency on a case study created for diversity education–related training. Her professional efforts were acknowledged through selection as the American Society for Public Administration's Founders Fellow in 2017, as well as an International Scholar Workshop participant in Chennai, India.

Cultural Competency for Emergency and Crisis Management

Concepts, Theories and
Case Studies

Edited by Claire Connolly Knox
and Brittany "Brie" Haupt

Routledge
Taylor & Francis Group

NEW YORK AND LONDON

First published 2020
by Routledge
52 Vanderbilt Avenue, New York, NY 10017

and by Routledge
2 Park Square, Milton Park, Abingdon, Oxon, OX14 4RN

Routledge is an imprint of the Taylor & Francis Group, an informa business

Library of Congress Cataloging-in-Publication Data
A catalog record for this book has been requested

ISBN: 978-0-367-32181-9 (hbk)
ISBN: 978-0-367-32183-3 (pbk)
ISBN: 978-0-367-32188-8 (ebk)

Typeset in Palatino
by Apex CoVantage, LLC

Visit the eResources: www.routledge.com/9780367321833

First and foremost, we dedicate this book to the "Others."

To Charles and Adele Connolly, who always believed in me; Michael Knox, who is my rock; and Sarah Camille, who is my light in this world – Claire Connolly Knox

To my family and friends who picked me up, dusted me off, and pushed me forward when closed-minded people and societal barriers knocked me down – Brittany "Brie" Haupt

Contents

Illustrations

Figures

Tables

Preface

Why This Book?

As an Emergency Management Homeland Security program director for ten years, I would receive (and ask for) feedback from professionals in the community, especially those hosting interns or who had recently hired students. Along with the good news, they shared critiques about students' ability to handle diversity-related issues or their inability to interact with individuals with special needs. Or would have a blind spot in considering these populations during planning and training exercises. It was not all of our students, but enough to raise some concerns. In addition, I was observing related discussions in the classroom that aligned with the feedback from the practitioners. They asked how much cultural competence training the students were receiving before graduating. I asked them how much cultural competence training practitioners receive before applying for their certified emergency manager credentials. One trainer told me, "Diversity is one or two slides in a series of training sessions." Other trainers confirmed this and struggled to add material because they lacked case studies specific to emergency and crisis management.

We found the problem: an assumption that the other was doing it. This left our students – the next generation of emergency and crisis managers and staff – as well as existing practitioners lacking cultural competency skills, knowledge, and abilities.

That is when I got to work. After reviewing the program's curriculum map, I found some elements of cultural competency included in one or two classes, but nothing measurable. First, I created an advisory board consisting of practitioners from all sectors and levels of government to ensure regular communications. Second, I worked with faculty to write a program-specific diversity statement and identify core courses to introduce, teach, and reinforce measurable cultural competency skills, abilities, and knowledge throughout the program. Finally, I worked with Brie to create a diversity case study for one of the core courses. The results of our longitudinal analysis of this case study were published in *Disaster Prevention and Management: An International Journal* (discussed further in Chapter 4).

We then facilitated our case studies at the Federal Emergency Management Agency's Higher Education Symposium, International Association of Fire Chiefs Annual Meeting, and the Governor's Hurricane Conference, and we received feedback that practitioners needed this training as well. Emergency and management academic program directors who responded to the open-ended questions of our 2018 national survey specifically stated the need for case studies, scenarios, and exercises to use in a classroom and online setting. There was a need for a cultural competency case study book specific to the discipline and profession of emergency and crisis management. Existing books on the market were geared for public administration, public health officials, or first responders. While helpful, they did not fully capture the complex and dynamic aspects of emergency and crisis management.

Our Backgrounds

Brie's Story

Growing up, I was always on the sidelines. Although I seemed to make friends easily and was sought out for my advice and empathetic listening skills, I was also the one who had to grow up faster than the rest. Each new life event exposed harsh realities and discrimination. For a long time, I tried to assimilate into my environments and not be seen as "that chick" or "the one who is not <insert identity group> enough." It was not until my undergraduate years that a supervisor pointed out that the experiences I had gave me a unique viewpoint and skillset in life. I was a Connector. Although I could not imagine what it was like being a part of certain groups, I had other experiences that allowed me to form relationships and to empower others. It was through her mentorship that I realized I wanted to be an advocate and challenge others to understand how their identity not only impacts who they are but those around them.

My personal and professional experience regarding facilitation began during my graduate years and focused on workshops related to LGBTTQQIAAP,[1] racial, and gender identity dialogues, National Coalition Building Institute, individuals with disabilities, and intercultural communication dialogues. Within each of these facilitations, I soon became aware that my abilities to connect with participants relied heavily on personal experiences, and the idea of "success" was an illusion. Each workshop was a mystery, with some individuals who were actively disengaged or some being triggered by the topics. It was through these facilitations I saw a range of emotional breakdowns, angry storm-outs, breakthroughs, and "a-ha" moments. In addition, some participants would tell me how much they appreciated the dialogue and were impressed with my skills, while others would tell me that they learned nothing.

The analogy I soon became comfortable with was the invisible backpack. It was a concept developed by Peggy McIntosh (1989) and focused on unpacking white privilege. What I garnered from this analogy and translated into practice is that each of us wears this invisible backpack. Inside is all of our life experiences and the identities we carry with us every day. In many instances, we subconsciously remove this backpack whenever we face uncomfortable situations and choose to ignore or detach from ourselves because the idea or potential to unpack our identities is too much to process. In other instances, we become aware of what we carry around and may soon come to try to understand how these identities impact who we are as well as those with whom we interact. In some circumstances, we have grown intimately aware of this backpack and the ones that others carry. This realization leads to an ability to engage in conversations surrounding cultural identities and the impact they have in our professional and personal lives.

Understanding the intersection of diverse identities and how they affect practice has led me down the path of developing my own cultural competency and determining when practice is impacted negatively because of completely disregarding cultural implications. To exemplify this a bit more, I share experiences from two different environments and the cultural dialogues that permeated practice. The first is when I worked for a Historically Black College/University (HBCU). I was the first white woman hired in the department and was met with a range of acceptance and rejection. Some were not fazed by my appearance, and others questioned my choice from the beginning. Regardless, the question I received the most was: "Why are you here?" Some were genuinely curious as to why a white woman would choose to work at an HBCU, and others were cautious because of their own, mostly negative, experiences with white individuals. Race became a daily conversation during my time at this institution, and it was not to be ignored.

One of the more significant situations occurred during a student leadership conference when a student created a nickname for me of "White Chocolate Mocha." It did not take long for students, and some staff, to follow suit. When I questioned the student who coined the nickname and those surrounding this individual, they stated that I was not white. It floored me because I cannot tan even if I try. What soon surfaced through the dialogue was that I was not a representation of a stereotypical white woman, and the nickname made the students more comfortable with me because I no longer challenged their ideology.

Variations of this experience continued throughout my time – some positive and some negative – but every day it was a conversation or just stating how my racial identity affected interactions to being called a racist by irate students in conduct hearings. What seemed to surprise some of my colleagues and students was my ability to connect to individuals despite my race. Per a friend's request, I presented at a couple of conferences about my experience working at an HBCU and what being white came to mean. During question-and-answer sessions of these presentations, a black woman approached me and said, "I wish more white people would do what you did so they would get it." This comment has stayed with me for years. Essentially, she wished for individuals with a racial majority identity to put themselves in positions that would help them understand what it means to be a minority.

Although this comment was meant to denote appreciation of my willingness to engage in the dialogue and step outside my comfort zone, I was dismayed. For years, my identity as being white was considered a detriment. I was always the white chick in diversity education or the white chick at the HBCU or the white chick that was never white enough. My abilities were always in question because of being viewed as a white woman who innately was not a diverse individual. The accumulation of all these experiences led to my truly questioning whether I was on the right path, and I had to process my identity development repeatedly. Yet, it became the validation I needed to continue advocating for cultural competence, because, although I felt dismayed, I also recollected experiences in which individuals appreciated my authentic, honest desire to listen, understand who they are, and validate their experiences. It is a mantra I repeat to myself with every interaction – Listen, Understand, and Validate – LUV others. This was cemented even more when I entered my doctoral program and researched common themes that surfaced in my personal and professional life concerning cultural competence, diverse communities, the impact of communication, and human resilience. My mentor and friend, Dr. Claire Connolly Knox, called upon my experience and background when we decided to generate a cultural competence–related case study for a disaster response and recovery course.

Claire's Story

Three distinct personal experiences impacted who I am as a facilitator. Starting with my childhood, I attended a dance studio on the other side of town that was a block from my grandmother's house. I was the only white child in the all-black studio. As the "other," I was made fun of for how I talked, my hair, and my body shape, along with other random things. This experience made me realize, even as a child, that I was different; it began my path of self-reflection. This "othering" experience has stayed with me; as an adult, I gravitate to those perceived as "other" in my environmental justice volunteer work.

The second experience was being a woman in a male-dominated science profession when I began my career with the federal government. Very few women were working at the federal science center in the early 2000s. The majority of women employed were located in the technical writing department located in a different part of the facility. In the science wings of the building, the male culture was so strong you could taste it in the air. This was before the #MeToo movement and the public discussion about discrimination against women in the workplace. I struggled with multiple unethical behaviors that left a lasting impression on me. A few examples include unwelcome comments about feminine hygiene and body parts; being denied leave for a medical appointment while the men's leave was unquestioned and granted; and being required to work late without compensation when the men did not. When I reached out to the other few women at the facility to confirm my experiences, they quickly recommended that I not say anything; this is how it always was. With men as supervisors and the facility director, they were blind to changes of the status quo. After another incident, I stood up for myself and the other woman in our department and filed a formal complaint, which cost me my job. My father was furious with me, and he told me to "just deal with it." However, I knew deep down that if I had not stood up for myself and those women, I would have quit shortly thereafter. This gave me more motivation to pursue graduate school.

After graduation, I entered academia where the discrimination I experienced was more subtle than with the federal government. As a woman with a Ph.D., I am regularly addressed as Ms. or by my first name by students or in school-, college-, and university-level committee meetings, while the men are addressed as Dr. so and so. After ten years at the university, I lost count of how many meetings I had attended in which one or more of the women were addressed this way. Following the Pulse Nightclub mass shooting incident, a national radio show host interviewed me and a male colleague. We both have doctorates, but throughout the 20-minute interview, he was addressed as *Dr. X* and described as an *expert* in x, y, and z. Meanwhile, I was addressed by my *first name* and described as *teaching* x, y, and z. Luckily, it was not a live recording, so at the end of the interview, I thanked the host and said, "When you rerecord your introduction of us, you will introduce me as Dr. Knox, an expert in x, y, and z, as you did with my colleague." Until I pointed it out, my male colleague had not noticed the difference.

Professionally, I had completed many diversity trainings as a student and practitioner in the federal and local government; however, I was always on the receiving end of the experience. As a faculty member, I was never trained to be a facilitator for diversity or cultural competency dialogues. As I started incorporating these dialogues in my courses and had varying degrees of success, I often walked away feeling frustrated or discouraged from trying it again. The discussions would often fall flat or one voice would dominate the discussion, which ended up alienating part of the class. After years of placing this endeavor aside, Brie arrived and the opportunity to learn from each other arose. The result was the multiple-semester implementation of a diversity case study (Knox & Haupt, 2015), which led to opportunities to present and facilitate similar case studies to faculty and practitioners. Through this partnership, I have learned a great deal, and we share our "ah-ha" moments further in Chapter 4.

Although not every facilitation session ends on a high note with students thanking me for the experience, most of them do. In fact, I have students a semester or year later stop me on campus or at a store and thank me for the opportunity to learn what is in their backpack. The 60-minute facilitation session stays with them, and they continue to process it on levels I never anticipated. The following is one example of a reflection students complete in an online graduate-level course. Used with her permission, the student responds to a piece of information from the case study: 20 first responders are refusing to assist two population groups (burners and hailers). While we do not provide demographic information on these groups, most students assign qualities such as homeless and poor to them during the group discussions. Again, this is something they bring to the case study and an element of the scenario we, the facilitators, try to help them process. She stated:

> With this case study, one perspective that was new to me was the adversity faced when information was released that 20 responders refuse to assist those considered Hailers or Burners. Without my emergency management hat on, my initial response was to be upset and concerned that the individuals who have accepted this field of work as their career could blatantly refuse to help a certain group of people. I wanted to assign them the worst of tasks to show them that their beliefs were not ok. But after reflecting, my thoughts were showing that I didn't respect their beliefs either. This case study showed me the importance and the real-life situations that may occur in emergencies, and how

it is important to be able to have the skill set to be somewhat flexible, open minded, and focused on the goal at hand. Prioritization is essential when managing crisis, and the focus should always be to help alleviate crisis.

When I prompted her to expand upon this initial gut reaction, she explained:

> Professionally, I work with the homeless population of Osceola, Orange, and Seminole counties. I talk to all types of people experiencing homelessness daily, and it is my duty to be aware of cultural differences, especially when I interact with them. To be culturally aware of others' beliefs and values enhances my abilities to better serve the population I work with.

By providing her the space to dig into her backpack and explore what triggered the gut reaction, she pulled her work experience and personal interactions with the population group she felt was being disrespected by the first responders in the scenario. This really hit home for her. Her last sentence in her reflection sums up why I think including this experience in a classroom or online setting is invaluable.

Claire Connolly Knox, Ph.D.
Brittany "Brie" Haupt, Ph.D.

Acknowledgments

We acknowledge our students and practitioners who actively participated in the case studies between 2013 and 2019. It was truly an honor to have individuals share their lives with us and provide learning opportunities.

Thank you to the book proposal reviewers, case study contributors as well as previous journal article reviewers and FEMA Higher Education Symposium attendees, who provided invaluable feedback.

We acknowledge the *Disaster Prevention and Management: An International Journal* and the World Health Organization for permission to reprint material for this book.

Note

1. LGBTTQQIAAP is the initialism representing Lesbian, Gay, Bisexual, Transgender, Transexual, Queer, Questioning, Intersex, Asexual, Ally, and Pansexual identities.

1

Introduction

Claire Connolly Knox and Brittany "Brie" Haupt

Disasters are complex and dynamic events that test emergency and crisis managers and leaders – even the most ethical ones (Boin, Stern, & Sundelius, 2016; Comfort, 2007; Kapucu, Van Wart, Sylves, & Yuldashev, 2011; Van Wart, 2013; Van Wart & Kapucu, 2011; Waugh & Streib, 2006). Within response and recovery efforts, disasters highlight social vulnerabilities that require culturally competent practices. With climate change, communities around the world are experiencing more billion-dollar disasters. In the United States between 1980 and 2019, the National Oceanic and Atmospheric Administration reported 250 weather- and climate-related disasters that met or exceeded $1 billion in damages (National Oceanic and Atmospheric Association, 2019). Moreover, the evolving demographics of the United States and other countries around the world are lending added pressure to the need for credible, empathetic, relatable, trustworthy, and culturally competent practitioners. With each emergency and crisis, the lack of culturally respectable responses to diverse populations highlights the critical need for cultural competency education and training in higher education and practice.

Yet, as we continue to witness, marginalized and socially vulnerable populations are adversely affected during the response and recovery phases of emergency management (Knox, Emrich, & Haupt, 2019). Specifically, they face more economic, political, physical, and sociocultural obstacles during a disaster (Edwards, 2012; Nguyen & Salvesen, 2014; Seidenberg, 2005). Examples include:

- Nursing home and assisted-living residents in hurricanes Katrina, Harvey, and Irma
- The water crisis in Flint, Michigan
- Xenophobia and sheltering
- Migration crisis in Syria
- Non-governmental response in Haiti
- Homeless individuals in the Carr Wildfires in California
- Undocumented workers in Hurricane Harvey

Hurricane Katrina in 2005 impacted the United States in numerous ways, especially rising to the surface social inequities in New Orleans, and resulted in unethical decision-making among first responders, business owners, and political officials. The unethical actions (or inactions in some cases) was not limited to local individuals. When representatives of multiple organizations (e.g., Federal Emergency Management Agency [FEMA], American Red Cross, etc.) arrived in New Orleans after Hurricane Katrina, they faced the following demographics, which were most likely different from those within their organization and/or community:

- 23% lived in poverty (twice the national average)
- 55% did not own a car or have means to evacuate
- 57% had a household income of less than $20,000
- 67% were employed part or full time before landfall
- 68% did not have a useable credit card or money in the bank
- 76% had children under the age of 18 with them at the shelter
- 77% had a high school education or less
- 93% were African American (Heldmann, 2011)

The disaster struck at the end of August. For some individuals, that time of the month may not mean anything. However, for the 78% of Americans living paycheck to paycheck (Friedman, 2019) or who receive public assistance, this is a financially difficult time.

Additionally, the start of the school year meant that many parents had spent remaining funds on school supplies. Therefore, individuals living at or below the poverty line (in which New Orleans was already one of the highest in the nation) were going into the storm disadvantaged.

Coverage of unethical decision-making during the response efforts to Hurricane Katrina by scholars from multiple disciplines shed light on why ethical leadership is vital during a crisis (Jurkiewicz, 2007, 2009; Nguyen & Salvesen, 2014; Seidenberg, 2005; Urby & McEntire, 2014). Inaction by government officials has led to substantial changes. Federal agencies responding to a disaster were required to incorporate vulnerable populations in preparedness, response, and recovery plans, including FEMA, the Environmental Protection Agency, Housing and Urban Development (HUD), and the Department of Agriculture (Knox et al., 2019). Additionally, federal policies focused on increasing the capacity of local governments to prepare for, respond to, recover from, and mitigate all hazards through all phases of emergency management for the whole community (Hu, Knox, & Kapucu, 2014).

U.S. Society's Changing Demographic Trends

Each year, the Pew Research Center reports on changing demographic trends in the U.S. and throughout the world as discussed at the annual Population Association of America Conference. The top six changes discussed in 2019 by Cilluffo and Cohn (2019) include:

1. "Millennials are the largest adult generation in the United States, but they are starting to share the spotlight with Generation Z" (para. 2). In fact, the workforce is a mix of five generations: Baby Boomers, Generation X, Generation Y, Millennials, and Generation Z.
2. "Hispanics are projected to be the largest racial or ethnic minority group in the U.S. electorate when voters cast their ballots next year" (para. 4).

3. "The American family continues to change," with 25% of children living in a single-parent household (para. 6). Unique is the growing trend of unmarried parents cohabiting (35%).
4. "The immigrant share of the U.S. population is approaching a record high but remains below that of many other countries" (para. 10).
5. "The U.S. unauthorized immigrant population is at its lowest level in more than a decade" (para. 13).
6. "Incomes are rising in the U.S., but the increase is not being felt equally by all Americans" (para. 17).

Notice the various differences included in the foregoing information. They are not limited to socioeconomic or citizenship status. They include identities related to generational status, race, location, education level, and physical and mental well-being. We will see many of these differences play out in one or more of the case studies in this book. What is emphasized in the case studies are differences that are not only debatably visible but those invisible differences as well. Similar to the iceberg analogy, the majority of our diversity lies beneath the surface of the water.

International Demographic Shifts

In terms of international demographic shifts, the world is facing a heightened complexity of migration patterns, birth rates, life expectancy, and political constraints (United Nations Population Fund [UNPF], 2019). These intersections ultimately impact population growth, with projections ranging from 7.3 to 16.5 billion by the end of the century. According to UNPF research, the world is undergoing population momentum – an intersection of improved survival rates and past fertility levels – resulting in an increased number of women of reproductive age. Despite political barriers, migration is an increased activity from rural to urban areas and from third-world to first-world countries.

"These megatrends have far-reaching implications. They affect economic development, employment, income distribution, poverty and social protections. They also affect efforts to ensure universal access to health care, education, housing, sanitation, water, food and energy" (UNPF, 2019, para. 5). Most notable is the impact of climate change around the world. However, island nations and third world countries are experiencing the worst effects, which is leading to climate refugees and increased migration pressures (Missirian & Schlenker, 2017).

Case Study Format and Utilization

In preparing participants to assume positions of leadership, case studies can develop higher levels of critical thinking and decision-making skills (Boyne, 2012; Comfort & Wukich, 2013; Corbin, 2018; McCreight, 2009; Richardson & Ice, 2010; Silvia, 2012; Waugh & Sadiq, 2011). These skills are essential at the tactical, operational, and strategic levels in emergency management (Carey, 2018; Kapucu & Knox, 2013; Kiltz, 2009). Moreover, the skills support the emergency management's professional ethical obligation of providing for the general welfare of the public (Dilling, 2009), which is discussed further in Chapter 3. Studies have concluded that participants gain cultural competency knowledge, skills, and abilities through case studies, reflection exercises, and cross-cultural dialogues (Carrizales, 2010; Ensari, Christian, Kuriyama, & Miller, 2012; Gaynor, 2014; Knox & Haupt, 2015; Moore-Thomas, 2010; Norman-Major & Gooden, 2012; Rice, 2004).

As discussed further in Chapters 2 and 3, best pedagogical and andrological practices state that cultural competency knowledge, skills, and abilities should be covered in multiple courses throughout a program (Haupt & Knox, 2018). At a minimum, two case studies should be implemented in a course or training session (whether that is face to face or online). This aligns with recommendations from O'Lawrence (2019) on increasing cultural competency:

♦ "Make a conscious decision to establish friendships with people from other cultures"

- ◆ Place yourself in "situations where you will meet people of other cultures"
- ◆ Examine your "biases about people from other cultures"
- ◆ "Ask questions about their cultures, customs, and views"
- ◆ "Read about other people's cultures and histories"
- ◆ "Listen to people tell their stories"

Actively participating in case studies that are facilitated by an instructor who sets ground rules for a safe environment helps achieve these recommendations.

It should be noted that some of the case studies are purposefully missing demographic information. Based on pedagogy and andragogy literature (Banaji & Greenwald, 2016; Diefenbach, 2009), this enables facilitators to make note of the biases, prejudices, and stereotypes that participants bring into the scenario, which are not directly stated. It is within ambiguity that subconscious prejudices, stereotypes, and biases will surface. If parameters are too clearly defined then self-reflection is limited, and participants are more likely to respond based on what they think will be more socially acceptable. This does not negate the intentional presence of values, beliefs, or norms the case study writer may include. However, the surfacing of these subconscious components leads participants to "a-ha" moments in their reflection statements.

Scenarios created for this book are based on true events experienced firsthand by the author(s), lessons learned in their jurisdiction, or impactful events in recent history. These scenarios highlight complex and dynamic aspects of emergency and crisis management. The decision-making process is never straightforward. As in the real world, these cases are designed not to have a single, simple solution; there is no one correct answer or way of completing the task(s). The purpose is to stimulate discussions, debates, strategic planning, reflections, and theory to practice learning, while enhancing critical thinking skills. It is also meant to help participants unpack their backpack. This may frustrate some participants, especially individuals in the profession, which is what we have experienced repeatedly. Some rely on their training, while others may not want to open their backpack. As a facilitator, recognize/acknowledge this and help them find the root of this gut response. In Chapter 4, we discuss tips for overcoming these challenges.

Structure of Book

Unique to the emergency and crisis management discipline is the challenge of teaching to traditional and non-traditional students (Feldmann-Jensen et al., 2019). Therefore, Chapter 2 reviews the evolution of cultural competence and its inclusion in educational institutions along with its quintessential connection to the emergency and crisis management discipline and profession. Chapter 3 presents pedagogy (teacher-centered approach) and andragogy (student-centered approach) theories that drive the design and implementation of these cultural competency case studies. In Chapter 4, we provide an overview of facilitation guidelines and advice. This essential chapter helps overcome one of the main barriers to implementing cultural competency in academic and practitioner settings: the apprehension of the leader/faculty/trainer to engage in difficult dialogues.

This book features nine U.S.-based (Chapters 5 through 13) and three international scenarios (Chapters 14 through 16), which engage participants in various aspects of cultural competency knowledge, skills, and abilities. The case studies, authored by academics and practitioners, are designed for individual and group implementation within an educational or training setting either face to face or online. The short case study structure allows for more than one to be easily implemented in a course as a group discussion, group assignment, or individual assignment. Each case study includes a goal statement, learning outcomes, definitions, ground rules, facilitator notes, scenario, roles/actors, discussion and supplemental questions, and resources. It then concludes with a pre- and post-test, which allows facilitators to empirically measure the participants' learning outcomes (see Appendix B for additional information about modifying and analyzing these tests for Scholarship of Teaching and Learning research). The appendixes and e-resources (available through Routledge's website) include additional resources and guidance for development for the facilitator, as well as support self and community advocacy regarding cultural competency.

References

Banaji, M. R., & Greenwald, A. G. (2016). *Blindspot: Hidden biases of good people*. New York: Bantam.

Boin, A., Stern, E., & Sundelius, B. (2016). *The politics of crisis management: Public leadership under pressure*. Cambridge: Cambridge University Press.

Boyne, S. M. (2012). Crisis in the classroom: Using simulations to enhance decision-making skills. *Journal of Legal Education, 67*(2), 311–322.

Carey, T. J. (2018). The utilization of client-based service-learning in emergency management graduate curricula for the 21st century. *Journal of Homeland Security Education, 7*, 13–28.

Carrizales, T. (2010). Exploring cultural competency within the public affairs curriculum. *Journal of Public Affairs Education, 16*(4), 593–606.

Cilluffo, A., & Cohn, D. (2019, April 11). 6 demographic trends shaping the U.S. and the world in 2019. *Pew Research*. Retrieved from www.pewresearch.org/fact-tank/2019/04/11/6-demographic-trends-shaping-the-u-s-and-the-world-in-2019/

Comfort, L. K. (2007). Crisis management in hindsight: Cognition, communication, coordination, and control. *Public Administration Review, 67*, 189–197.

Comfort, L. K., & Wukich, C. (2013). Developing decision-making skills for uncertain conditions: The challenge of educating effective emergency managers. *Journal of Public Affairs Education, 19*(1), 53–71.

Corbin, T. B. (2018). Teaching disaster management using a multi-phase simulation. *International Journal of Mass Emergencies & Disasters, 36*, 297–312.

Diefenbach, T. (2009). Are case studies more than sophisticated storytelling? Methodological problems of qualitative empirical research mainly based on semi-structured interviews. *Quality & Quantity, 43*(6), 875.

Dilling, J. (2009). *Locus of an emergent field: Framing emergency management knowledge, values, and priorities within current academic curricula* (Doctoral dissertation). Retrieved from http://search.proquest.com/docview/304878951?accountid=27700

Edwards, F. L. (2012). Cultural competency in disasters. In K. A. Norman-Major & S. T. Gooden (Eds.), *Cultural competency for public administrators* (pp. 197–218). New York, NY: Routledge.

Ensari, N., Christian, J., Kuriyama, D. M., & Miller, N. (2012). The personalization model revisited: An experimental investigation of the role of five personalization-based strategies on prejudice reduction. *Group Processes & Intergroup Relations, 15*(4), 503–522.

Feldmann-Jensen, S., Hackerott, C., Knox, C. C., Ramsay, J., McEntire, D. A., & Jerolleman, A. (2019). The scholarship of teaching and learning in emergency management and homeland security: Trends, gaps, barriers, and opportunities. *Journal of Emergency Management, 17*(1), 27–34.

Friedman, Z. (2019, January 11). 78% of workers living paycheck to paycheck. *Forbes.* Retrieved from www.forbes.com/sites/zackfriedman/2019/01/11/live-paycheck-to-paycheck-government-shutdown/#71f445ee4f10

Gaynor, T. S. (2014). Through the wire: Training culturally competent leaders for a new era. *Journal of Public Affairs Education, 20*(3), 369–392.

Haupt, B., & Knox, C. C. (2018). Measuring cultural competence in emergency management and homeland security higher education programs. *Journal of Public Affairs Education, 24*(4), 538–556.

Heldmann, C. (2011). *Hurricane Katrina and the demographics of death.* Retrieved from https://thesocietypages.org/socimages/2011/08/29/hurricane-katrina-and-the-demographics-of-death/

Hu, Q., Knox, C. C., & Kapucu, N. (2014). What have we learned since September 11, 2001? A network study of the Boston Marathon Bombings response. *Public Administration Review, 74*(6), 698–712.

Jurkiewicz, C. L. (2007). Louisiana's ethical culture and its effect on the administrative failures following Katrina. *Public Administration Review, 67,* 57–63.

Jurkiewicz, C. L. (2009). Political leadership, cultural ethics and recovery: Louisiana post-Katrina. *Public Organization Review, 9*(4), 353.

Kapucu, N., & Knox, C. C. (2013). Utilization of service learning in emergency management programs in the United States. *Journal of Public Affairs Education, 19*(1), 31–51.

Kapucu, N., Van Wart, M., Sylves, R., & Yuldashev, F. (2011). US Presidents and their roles in emergency management and disaster policy 1950–2009. *Risk, Hazards & Crisis in Public Policy, 2*(3), 1–34.

Kiltz, L. (2009). Developing critical thinking skills in homeland security and emergency management courses. *Journal of Homeland Security and Emergency Management, 6*(1).

Knox, C. C., Emrich, C., & Haupt, B. (2019). Advancing emergency management higher education: Importance of cultural competence scholarship. *Journal of Emergency Management, 17*(2), 111–117.

Knox, C. C., & Haupt, B. (2015). Incorporating cultural competency skills in emergency management education. *Disaster Prevention and Management, 24*(5), 619–634.

McCreight, R. (2009). Educational challenges in homeland security and emergency management. *Journal of Homeland Security and Emergency Management, 6*(1).

Missirian, A., & Schlenker, W. (2017). Asylum applications respond to temperature fluctuations. *Science, 358*(6370), 1610–1614.

Moore-Thomas, C. (2010). Cultural identity development. In D. G. Hays & B. T. Erford (Eds.), *Developing multicultural counseling competence: A systems approach* (pp. 32–52). Upper Saddle River, NJ: Pearson Merrill Prentice Hall.

Nguyen, M. T., & Salvesen, D. (2014). Disaster recovery among multi-ethnic immigrants: A case study of southeast Asians in Bayou La Batre (AL) after Hurricane Katrina. *Journal of the American Planning Association, 80*(4), 385–396.

NOAA National Centers for Environmental Information (NCEI). (2019). *U.S. billion-dollar weather and climate disasters.* Retrieved from www.ncdc.noaa.gov/billions/

Norman-Major, K. A., & Gooden, S. A. (2012). *Cultural competency for public administrators.* New York, NY: Routledge.

O'Lawrence, H. (2019). *The benefits and challenges of living, teaching, and working in today's diverse world.* Proceedings of the Informing Science + Information Technology Education Conference. Retrieved from http://proceedings.informingscience.org/InSITE2019/InSITE19p495-499OLawrence5489.pdf

Rice, M. F. (2004). Organizational culture, social equity, and diversity: Teaching public administration education in the postmodern era. *Journal of Public Affairs Education, 10*(2), 143–154.

Richardson, J. C., & Ice, P. (2010). Investigating students' level of critical thinking across instructional strategies in online discussions. *The Internet and Higher Education, 13*(1–2), 52–59.

Silvia, C. (2012). The impact of simulations on higher-level learning. *Journal of Public Affairs Education*, *18*(2), 397–422.

Seidenberg, J. (2005). *Cultural competency in disaster recovery: Lessons learned from the Hurricane Katrina experience for better serving marginalized communities*. Retrieved from www.e-education.psu.edu/drupal6/files/sgam/HT_Seidenberg.pdf

United Nations Population Fund. (2019). *World population trends*. Retrieved from www.unfpa.org/world-population-trends

Urby, H., & McEntire, D. A. (2014). Applying public administration in emergency management: The importance of integrating management into disaster education. *Journal of Homeland Security and Emergency Management*, *11*(1), 39–60.

Van Wart, M. (2013). Lessons from leadership theory and the contemporary challenges of leaders. *Public Administration Review*, *73*(4), 553–565.

Van Wart, M., & Kapucu, N. (2011). Crisis management competencies: The case of emergency managers in the USA. *Public Management Review*, *13*(4), 489–511.

Waugh, W. L., Jr., & Sadiq, A. A. (2011). Professional education for emergency managers. *Journal of Homeland Security and Emergency Management*, *2*(9).

Waugh, W. L., Jr., & Streib, G. (2006). Collaboration and leadership for effective emergency management. *Public Administration Review*, *66*, 131–140.

Additional Resources

Federal Emergency Management Agency. (2018). *Office of disability integration and coordination*. Retrieved from www.fema.gov/office-disability-integration-and-coordination

National Council on Disability. (2009). *Effective emergency management: Making improvements for communities and people with disabilities*. Retrieved from https://files.eric.ed.gov/fulltext/ED507740.pdf

National Council on Disability. (2014). *Effective communications for people with disabilities: Before, during, and after emergencies*. Retrieved from https://ncd.gov/publications/2014/05272014

U.S. Department of Health and Human Services. (2017). *Cultural and linguistic competence in disaster preparedness planning and crisis response*. Retrieved from www.phe.gov/Preparedness/planning/abc/Pages/linguistic.aspx

2

Cultural Competency Historical Presence and Development

Brittany "Brie" Haupt

Cultural competency is the process of developing knowledge, skills, and abilities (KSAs) with a focus on the interaction of cultural backgrounds and the reflective outputs from an individual and/or organization to better serve their diverse demographic (Carrizales, 2010; Cheetham & Chivers, 1998; Cross, 1988; Cross, Bazron, Dennis, & Isaacs, 1989; Garcia, 1995; Gaynor, 2014). Cultural competence expands the dimensionality of diversity by allowing practitioners to gain valuable insight into language and communication patterns, self- and group identities, and relationship interactions (Commission on Peer Review and Accreditation, 2014; Moore-Thomas, 2010; Riccucci, 2012). Continuously changing demographics point to the need for educational institutions and organizations to promote inclusivity (Carrizales, 2010) and provide spaces for administrators and practitioners to become more knowledgeable of diverse cultures and perspectives in society.

Research indicates this extension and inclusiveness leads to more empathetic, credible, trustworthy, and relatable practitioners (Ahmed, Wilson, Henriksen, & Jones, 2011; Guimond et al., 2013; Primo, 2013; Raffel, Maser, & Calarusse, 2011; Rice, 2004). The skill of communicating with diverse cultures assists in multiple outcomes, including conflict resolution, mediation, political sensitivity, and understanding the roles of councils and managers (Lazenby, 2010). Moreover, developing these competencies leads to more equitable distribution of resources, assurance of each individual's rights, and inclusive communities (Brintnall, 2008). A school of thought exists in which education is the avenue to correct societal issues (Brintnall, 2008; Stein, 2004) as "education [is] a tool for both political inclusion and political exclusion" (Brown, 2011, p. 192). Therefore, attention to educational policies is critical (Kraft & Furlong, 2020; Stein, 2004).

Applying cultural competence to educational programs includes (1) acknowledging the importance of culture, (2) having the ability to assess its cross-cultural knowledge, and (3) assessing and adapting services to meet any needs that surface. The application is integral for educational programs because the related KSAs are known to increase practitioners' awareness of their own cultural identity and its effect on their practice. Therefore, this chapter reviews the historical inclusion of cultural competence into educational programs along with the concept of cultural competence. In addition, the chapter discusses theories and models related to developing cultural competence and implications for educational programs and practitioners.

Historical Overview

The impetus for cultural competency begins with a historical investigation of public service and decision-making. Extensive debates and dialogues regarding diversity-related policies of equity and access for the U.S. educational system initiated from two landmark Supreme Court cases: the 1954 *Brown v. Board of Education* case concerning integration (Diem & Frankenberg, 2013; Stein, 2004) and the 1978 case *Regents of the University of California v. Bakke* concerning the need for a diverse student body. In addition, history saw the 2003 case *Gratz v. Bollinger*, which focused on the enrollment process and affirmative action. Although not all dialogues took place in courtrooms, the overarching dialogue of diversity and education has always been highly controversial (Gurin, Dey, Hurtado, & Gurin, 2002; Louis & van Velzen, 2012).

With the consequences of social inequality reaching its breaking point, a movement began in the 1980s within public administration called the New Public Service. This period challenged administrators and educators to integrate cultural identity into conversations on a grander scale. Within this movement, researchers such as Denhardt and Denhardt (2007) proclaimed the importance of acknowledging each individual for their unique differences. Moreover, a call to action resounded throughout the nation in the hopes that administrators would take responsibility for their actions, challenge their preconceptions, and evaluate their roles in society.

The 1960s were a tumultuous time for the United States because of the Civil Rights Movement and other efforts related to cultural identity. For example, the Watts riots of 1964 ripped the veil from America's eyes by exposing the reality for many citizens. "In the minds of most Americans at the time, poverty, and certainly hunger and starvation, did not exist in America – nor did brutality in prisons, environmental pollution, sexism, family dysfunction, child abuse, and so on. Even the obvious racism had not yet configured active opposition" (McSwite, 1997, p. 200). Progress in the area of social equity and cultural competency began, but its pace was slow.

The impact of the 1960s into the 1970s saw the beginning of a multicultural education movement that dominated the 1980s. Banks (1981), a pioneer of multicultural education, advocated for an examination of educational institutions in all of their essence: policies, educators, subject matter, styles, and more. The work of Banks and other advocates, such as Gay, Grant, Nieto, and Sleeter, led to development of assessment methods and brought evaluation into the forefront of educational institutions (Gorski, 1999). From the 1990s into the current period, multicultural education became connected to other branches of movements, such as diversity, cross-cultural, inter-cultural, social justice, social equity, and more. Yet, at the heart of it all, is an emphasis on creating educational forums focused on transformative experiences leading to impactful practice.

Cultural Competence Development

There are limited models and frameworks when it comes to developing cultural competence as emergency and crisis managers. The disciplines of anthropology, sociology, education, healthcare, social work, and the like connect to cultural competence through a variety of definitions and concepts (Akombo, 2013; Gurin et al., 2002; Rice, 2004). In some areas, culture is in conjunction with social justice, multiculturalism, diversity, race, nations, ethnicities, citizenship, and communities (Brubaker & Cooper, 2000). For our purposes, culture is defined as "shared knowledge and schemes created by a set of people for perceiving, interpreting, expressing, and responding to social realities around them" (Farrell & Littlefield, 2012, p. 2). Cultural competence then represents the process of developing KSAs focused on the interaction of cultural backgrounds and the reflective outputs from an individual and/or organization to better serve their diverse demographic (Carrizales, 2010; Cheetham & Chivers, 1998; Cross, 1988; Cross et al., 1989; Garcia, 1995; Gaynor, 2014).

Within the social work discipline, Terry Cross (1988) developed a cultural competence continuum focused on a developmental process throughout an individual or organization's lifetime. This process relates to individual and organizational cultural development and the development of culturally competent practice. Transitioning over to healthcare, multiple models and frameworks have been developed for enhancing culturally sensitive practices, including Larry Purnell's (2002) model that conceptualized theories and research from organizational development, communication, family development, psychology, and more. Purnell's (2002) model incorporated a schematic design with primary and secondary cultural characteristics covering domains of heritage, communication, family roles and organization, workforce issues, biocultural ecology, high-risk behaviors, nutrition, pregnancy and childbearing practices, death rituals, spirituality, and healthcare practice. Although Purnell's model has an impressive breadth and depth to its framework, its complexity does not translate easily into emergency and crisis management or public administration. Therefore, Cross's Cultural Competence Continuum is selected because of its applicability to public organizations along with its focus on the individual, which is essential for management development.

Cross's Cultural Competence Continuum

Cross's Cultural Competence Continuum (1988, Cross et al., 1989) consists of seven stages in a developmental timeline. The first stage is *cultural destructiveness*, which is evident in practitioners or programs that actively try to harm others due to the perception they are superior. A general understanding is a program with formal or informal policies, practices, and structures that are destructive to a cultural group – for example, a higher education institution that seeks to only recruit students who promote certain images to the public or funding avenues. Another example is institutions that accept students to fulfill a quota requirement. These examples highlight exclusionary practices, policies, and infrastructures.

The second stage, *cultural incapacity*, is exemplified in individuals who or programs that perpetuate cultural stereotypes and are unable to push past those biases and preconceived notions. It is the inability of a program to respond effectively to the needs, preferences, and interests of culturally and linguistically diverse groups. Incapacity exists in programs that discriminate within their hiring practices or exude messages of one cultural group being superior or inferior to another, or make comments and policies that further stereotypes (Cross, 1988; Cross et al., 1989).

Cultural blindness, the third stage, exists in programs and individuals experiencing a different culture for the first time. Because of lack of experience, there are limited opportunities to assess their knowledge base and limited or no opportunities to learn more about any culture they are newly exposed to. Moreover, there is a common statement or belief that all cultures or cultural groups are the same. Culturally blind policies only promote assimilation with staff and support services failing to view other cultures as equal (Cross, 1988; Cross et al., 1989). In addition, little value is placed on training and development. Cultural blindness is shown in exchange programs in which incoming students are assumed to understand all the nuances of the host country, and little is done to support the transition in and out of the program.

The fourth stage, *cultural pre-competence*, values diversity. The individuals and programs understand the importance of culture and may even recognize some of their biases, preconceived notions, and stereotypes; however, they are stuck in their development and unsure of how to grow. A commitment to social equity and justice exists, yet the concept of "token" individuals as the voice of an entire culture also still exists (Cross, 1988; Cross et al., 1989). The act of seeking out information displays an awareness of cultural differences, but there still remains a "they are all the same" mentality.

Cultural competence, the fifth stage, demonstrates respect and acceptance, with the impact highlighted in programmatic mission statements, structural and strategic development, policies and procedures, and resource support. There is a focus on increasing the capacity of the program and the individuals within. There will be a plethora of forums and dialogues acknowledging cultural differences and policies to support educational endeavors.

The sixth stage, *cultural proficiency*, consists of programs known for positive contributions to their fields and disciplines. They are active participants in research, conferences, trainings, and workshops related to diverse cultures. There is a general understanding that education is essential to competency development. The final stage, *advanced cultural competence and proficiency*, speaks to the experts. They are sought out to assist in educational sessions and conduct evidence-based research to improve practice. They are innovative and can transfer knowledge within all educational interactions. Moreover, they have the knowledge base and constantly add to the body of knowledge, theoretical foundations, models, and frameworks to study the concept (Cross, 1988; Cross et al., 1989).

Integration Into Education

Individual Level

A dominant method to developing cultural competency is the process of self-reflection. It is important for current and future administrators and practitioners to examine their lives and the times when they have been an "other." Othering is when an individual recognizes difference between themselves and other individuals (Canales, 2000; Dharamsi, 2011). Within this acknowledgment, a phenomenon of meaning-making takes place. Meaning-making is how an individual makes sense of life events, individuals, and places they encounter and how it impacts their identity (Carlsen, 1988). It is considered a humanistic philosophy promoting the importance of relationships and is quintessential to public service. Through relationships, one can gain more understanding as to the importance of an activity or experience by how it can affect their relationships (Garcia, 1995; Goleman, Boyatzi, & McKee, 2013).

The process of self-reflection can cause several situations to occur. The first opportunity is for administrators and practitioners to acknowledge and take pride in the cultural groups with which they identify. Moreover, providing workshops and spaces for learning allows facilitators to develop "perceptual flexibility, valuing diversity, cultivating awareness, and gauging readiness" (Norman-Major & Gooden, 2012, p. 248). It can be argued that emergency and crisis managers and public administrators enter the field of public service as a result of having experienced significant events themselves that subsequently created a need to help others. A second situation, during the self-reflection experience, is the realization of individual biases and prejudices that will ultimately affect their work and how they interact with others. Though this situation can cause internal conflict, many see this struggle as an essential step to growth and development. "One cannot see experience without being a part of it, for life never stops long enough to be tested, and one cannot get outside life to view it" (Fry & Raadschelders, 2008, p. 116).

In tandem with self-reflection, discomfort is anticipated, and there is a chance of resistance within the faculty and administrators. Resistance materializes as a lack of preparation, lack of desire to participate in activities, and lack of commitment to cross-cultural interactions and research (Norman-Major & Gooden, 2012). Educators have an important responsibility to their students. Through their instruction, educators are guiding and transferring imperative knowledge, which will affect their students' decision-making and affect societal contributions. If faculty does not take the time to prepare themselves for their increasingly diverse student population, then there is a risk of complacency, increased liability, and hindered student development.

Within the Classroom

Faculty and staff must be intentional in empowering themselves and students to engage in culture-related dialogue (Rice, 2004) and promote linking concepts of cultural competency as being central to practice vs. peripheral (Villegas & Lucas, 2002). For example, discussions need to include definitions, demographics, equity, and access issues, as well as the policy and legal implications of cultural competency (Carrizales, 2010). Not only will intentional dialogues facilitate learning, but they also cultivate indirect benefits, such as critical rhetoric skills (Carrizales, 2010; Guimond et al., 2013):

> It is essential to develop the ability to adapt to the changing environment and appreciate the value of living as responsible students in complex democratic societies. A meaningful education should allow students to develop the ability to reason thoroughly about critical questions and issues, and consider facts in a broader context and question them effectively, and also allow students to nurture a habit of lifelong learning behaviors outside the formal academic setting.
>
> (Kayaoglu, 2006, pp. 114–115)

In tandem with self-reflection and the meaning-making process, experiential learning theory (ELT) is widely used in management learning research and practice and offers a learning cycle–based theory (Cunningham, 1997; Kolb & Kolb, 2012). ELT defines learning as "the process whereby knowledge is created through the transformation of experience. Knowledge results from the combination of grasping and transforming experience" (Kolb, 1984, p. 41). ELT focuses on a holistic, multi-level learning space between individuals and the environment in commensurate ways at the individual, group, and organizational levels (Kolb & Kolb, 2012). The primary focus is on engaging students in a process that best enhances their learning. Similar to self-reflection and meaning-making, ELT requires the resolution of conflicts. Conflict is a driver of the learning process, as one must oscillate among opposing modes of reflection, action, feeling, and thinking.

In traditional education models, the conflict between academic and practitioner learning styles is exaggerated because the subject matter is usually filtered through the learning style of the educator in their lectures or presentation and analysis of cases. Within ELT, this filtering process is reduced since the facilitator and student both interpret information according to their own learning style. The academician's role is self-directed and more facilitative in nature; it assists students in reflecting the phenomena of their field of specialization and are ready with alternative theories and concepts as students process through their individual conception of reality (Kolb & Kolb, 2012). This supports cultural competence development through Cross's Cultural Competence Continuum (1988).

Program Level

Emphasis for degree programs to instill KSAs focused on the importance of culture, context, and representation for society in response to ever-changing demographics is growing within public administration and emergency and crisis management programs (Ahmed et al., 2011; Akombo, 2013; Bailey, 2004; Carrizales, 2010; Clark, Ochs, & Frazier, 2013; Diem & Frankenberg, 2013; Gooden & Koliba, 2013; Haupt & Knox, 2018; Knox, Emrich, & Haupt, 2019; Knox & Haupt, 2015; Riccucci, 2012; Stein, 2004; Villegas & Lucas, 2002). A product of this evolution is the creation and utilization of best practices focused on "definitions and terms, local and national demographics, discussions of societal disparities and social equity, and an understanding of the legal and policy implications of cultural competency" (Carrizales, 2010, p. 597).

An accreditation body does not exist for emergency and crisis management programs, so we turn to the Network of Schools of Public Policy, Affairs, and Administration's (NASPAA) guidance because public administrators are emergency and crisis managers and vice versa (Comfort, Waugh, & Cigler, 2012; Haupt, 2018; Haupt, Kapucu, & Hu, 2017; Kapucu, 2011; Knox et al., 2019; Urby & McEntire, 2013; Petak, 1985). (FEMA's Next Generations Core Competencies are discussed in Chapter 3.)

NASPAA assists in this call to action through a set of standards for curriculum-based competencies to help bring the goal of cultural competency to the forefront. The challenge surfaces with promoting diversity initiatives in public administration education, yet the push for cultural competency appears to be more of an abstract ideology versus being practically implemented. To achieve any measurable success, administrators must acknowledge the elements of NASPAA's diversity initiatives while also expanding these efforts toward those of cultural competency (Ryan, 2012). Over the years, educators have intentionally guided the development of future public administrators and want to establish programs that legitimize the field and achieve a common foundation fostering KSAs for future public administrators and emergency and crisis managers (Haupt & Knox, 2018; Knox & Haupt, 2015; Raffel et al., 2011; Rice, 2004; Villegas & Lucas, 2002).

An essential element for any program's success is the quality of the educators. Matching operations with the mission means faculty performance becomes a priority. Faculty from a variety of backgrounds must give students a chance to experience diverse perspectives and life events. Through diverse opinions and stylistic teaching methods, faculty need to continuously engage in research relating to the field as it helps in the development of relevant, current instructors who are knowledgeable in cutting-edge methods and applications.

One challenging aspect of developing cultural competence within an education program is distinguishing the transformational aspect of the curriculum. Will the program provoke intentional, critical dialogue relating to society's dynamics and issues? Will students be able to engage in uncomfortable conversations to challenge their perceptions of the world and their role within it? When an individual abandons accepted rules of conduct, then the mind opens (Stivers, 2008). Through this abandon, deep and critical thinking can occur. Stivers (2008) emphasized the importance of deep thought, but, more importantly, the meaning behind the deep thought.

Summary

In essence, knowledge is power, and the majority of public administrators and emergency and crisis managers receive their knowledge from certification or accredited programs. If avenues for developing cultural competency are not provided, then graduates of the programs are less capable of positively impacting society (Brintnall, 2008; Rice, 2004). The classroom provides an ideal setting for individuals to be exposed to new perspectives and participate in critical discourse (Akombo, 2013; Gooden & Koliba, 2013) in preparation for being active representatives in diverse communities (Brintnall, 2008; Bryer & Sahin, 2012). A journey of self-reflection and understanding is the pathway from which cultural competence and related knowledge, skills, and abilities are derived.

References

Ahmed, S., Wilson, K., Henriksen, R., & Jones, J. (2011). What does it mean to be a culturally-competent counselor? *Journal for Social Action in Counseling and Psychology, 3*(1), 17–28.

Akombo, D. O. (2013). Scholarship and diversity in higher education. *Journal of Cultural Diversity, 20*(1).

Bailey, M. (2004). Representative bureaucracy: Understanding its past to address its future. *Public Administration Review, 64*(2), 246–249.

Banks, J. (1981). *Education in the 80s: Multiethnic education.* Washington, DC: National Education Association.

Brintnall, M. (2008). Preparing the public service for working in the multiethnic democracies: An assessment and ideas for action. *Journal of Public Affairs Education, 14*(1), 39–50.

Brown, G. K. (2011). The influence of education on violent conflict and peace: Inequality, opportunity and the management of diversity. *Prospects, 41*(2), 191–204.

Brubaker, R., & Cooper, F. (2000). Beyond "identity". *Theory and Society, 29,* 1–47.

Bryer, T. A., & Sahin, I. (2012). Administrators as deliberative representatives: A revised public service role. *International Journal of Public Administration, 35*(14), 925–933.

Canales, M. K. (2000). Othering: Toward an understanding of difference. *Advances in Nursing Science, 22*(4), 16–31.

Carlsen, M. B. (1988). *Meaning-making: Therapeutic processes in adult development.* New York, NY: W.W. Norton & Co.

Carrizales, T. (2010). Exploring cultural competency within the public affairs curriculum. *Journal of Public Affairs Education, 16*(4), 593–606.

Cheetham, G., & Chivers, G. (1998). The reflective (and competent) practitioner: A model of professional competence which seeks to harmonise the reflective practitioner and competence-based approaches. *Journal of European Industrial Training, 22*(7), 267–276.

Clark, R. C., Ochs, H. L., & Frazier, M. (2013). Representative bureaucracy: The politics of access to policy-making positions in the federal executive service. *Public Personnel Management, 42*(1), 75–89.

Comfort, L. K., Waugh, W. L., & Cigler, B. A. (2012). Emergency management research and practice in public administration: Emergence, evolution, expansion, and future directions. *Public Administration Review, 72*(4), 539–547.

Commission on Peer Review and Accreditation. (2014). *Detailed summary of changes in the 2014 NASPAA self-study instructions.* Retrieved from https://naspaaaccreditation.files.wordpress.com/2014/05/2014sum maryofchanges.pdf

Cross, T. L. (1988). Cultural competence continuum. In *Research and training center on family support and children's mental health.* Portland, OR: Portland State University.

Cross, T. L., Bazron, B., Dennis, K., & Isaacs, M. R. (1989). Towards a culturally competent system of care. *National Institute of Mental Health.* Retrieved from http://files.eric.ed.gov/fulltext/ED330171.pdf

Cunningham, B. (1997). Experiential learning in public administration education. *Journal of Public Administration Education,* 219–227.

Denhardt, J. V., & Denhardt, R. B. (2007). *The new public service: Serving, not steering.* Armonk, NY: M.E. Sharpe.

Dharamsi, S. (2011). Moving beyond the limits of cultural competency training. *Medical Education, 45*(8), 764–766.

Diem, S., & Frankenberg, E. (2013). The politics of diversity: Integration in an era of political and legal uncertainty. *Teachers College Record, 115*(11).

Farrell, L., & Littlefield, R. (2012). Identifying communication strategies in cases of domestic terrorism: Applying cultural context to the Fort Hood shooting. *Journal of Homeland Security and Emergency Management, 9*(1).

Fry, B. R., & Raadschelders, J. C. N. (2008). *Mastering public administration: From Max Weber to Dwight Waldo* (2nd ed.). Washington, DC: CQ Press.

Garcia, M. H. (1995). An anthropological approach to multicultural diversity training. *The Journal of Applied Behavioral Science, 31*(4), 490–504.

Gaynor, T. S. (2014). Through the wire: Training culturally competent leaders for a new era. *Journal of Public Affairs Education, 20*(3), 369–392.

Goleman, D., Boyatzi, R., & McKee, A. (2013). *Primal leadership: Unleashing the power of emotional intelligence.* Boston, MA: Harvard Business Review Press.

Gooden, S. T., & Koliba, C. (2013). Review of cultural competency for public administrators. *Journal of Public Affairs Education, 19*(2), 377.

Gorski, P. C. (1999). *A brief history of multicultural education.* Retrieved from www.edchange.org/multicultural/papers/edchange_history.html

Guimond, S., Crisp, R. J., De Oliveira, P., Kamiejski, R., Kteily, N., Kuepper, B., ... Zick, A. (2013). Diversity policy, social dominance, and intergroup relations: Predicting prejudice in changing social and political contexts. *Journal of Personality and Social Psychology, 104*(6), 941.

Gurin, P., Dey, E. L., Hurtado, S., & Gurin, G. (2002). Diversity and higher education: Theory and impact on educational outcomes. *Harvard Educational Review, 72*(3), 330–367.

Haupt, B. (2018). *The use of crisis communication strategies to build community resilience: Evidence from emergency managers* (Doctoral dissertation). Orlando, FL: University of Central Florida.

Haupt, B., Kapucu, N., & Hu, Q. (2017). Core competencies in master of public administration programs: Perspectives from local government managers. *Journal of Public Affairs Education, 23*(1), 611–624.

Haupt, B., & Knox, C. C. (2018). Measuring cultural competence in emergency management and homeland security higher education programs. *Journal of Public Affairs Education.* doi:10.1080/15236803.2018.1455124

Kapucu, N. (2011). Developing competency-based emergency management degree programs in public affairs and administration. *Journal of Public Affairs Education, 17*(4), 501–521.

Kayaoglu, M. N. (2006). Pathways to catching up with the twenty-first century in higher education. In K. J. McGinley (Ed.), *New bearings in higher education: Papers from the first international congress on higher education.* Istanbul: Fatih University.

Knox, C. C., Emrich, C. T., & Haupt, B. (2019). Advancing emergency management higher education: Importance of cultural competence and pedagogy scholarship. *Journal of Emergency Management, 17*(2), 111–117.

Knox, C. C., & Haupt, B. (2015). Incorporating cultural competency skills in emergency management education. *Disaster Prevention and Management, 24*(5), 619–634.

Kolb, A. Y., & Kolb, D. A. (2012). Experiential learning theory. In *Encyclopedia of the sciences of learning* (pp. 1215–1219). New York, NY: Springer US.

Kolb, D. A. (1984). *Experience as the source of learning and development.* Upper Saddle River: Prentice Hall.

Kraft, M. E., & Furlong, S. R. (2020). *Public policy: Politics, analysis, and alternatives.* New York, NY: CQ Press.

Lazenby, S. (2010). The adequacy of MPA course content in preparing local government managers. *Journal of Public Affairs Education, 16*(3), 337–360.

Louis, K. S., & van Velzen, B. (Eds.). (2012). *Educational policy in an international context: Political culture and its effects.* New York, NY: Palgrave Macmillan.

McSwite, O. C. (1997). *Legitimacy in public administration: A discourse analysis.* Thousand Oaks, CA: Sage Publications.

Moore-Thomas, C. (2010). *Developing multicultural counseling competence: A systems approach.* New York, NY: Pearson Education.

Norman-Major, K. A., & Gooden, S. T. (2012). *Cultural competency for public administrators.* Abingdon, UK: Routledge.

Petak, W. J. (1985). Emergency management: A challenge for public administration. *Public Administration Review, 45,* 3–7.

Primo, N. (2013). *NASPAA diversity report 2013: Over a decade in review.* Retrieved from http://naspaaaccreditation.files.wordpress.com/2014/06/diversityreport_2013.pdf

Purnell, L. (2002). The Purnell model for cultural competence. *Journal of Transcultural Nursing, 13*(3), 193–196.

Raffel, J. A., Maser, S. M., & Calarusse, C. (2011). Accreditation and competencies in education for leadership in public service. *The State of Public Administration: Issues, Challenges, and Opportunities,* 70–88.

Riccucci, N. M. (2012). *Public personnel management: Current concerns, future challenges* (5th ed.). Glenview, IL: Pearson Education, Inc.

Rice, M. F. (2004). Organizational culture, social equity, and diversity: Teaching public administration education in the postmodern era. *Journal of Public Affairs Education,* 143–154.

Ryan, S. E. (2012). Assessing diversity in public affairs curricula: A multi-methodological model for student-led programmatic self-study. *Journal of Public Affairs Education, 18*(4), 757.

Stein, S. J. (2004). *The culture of education policy.* New York, NY: Teachers College Press.

Stivers, C. (2008). *Governance in dark times: Practical philosophy for public service.* Washington, DC: Georgetown University Press.

Urby, H., & McEntire, D. A. (2013). Applying public administration in emergency management: The importance of integrating management into disaster education. *Journal of Homeland Security and Emergency Management, 11*(1), 39–60.

Villegas, A. M., & Lucas, T. (2002). Preparing culturally responsive teachers rethinking the curriculum. *Journal of Teacher Education, 53*(1), 20–32.

3

Cultural Competency in Emergency and Crisis Management

Claire Connolly Knox and Brittany "Brie" Haupt

Cultural Competency in the Emergency and Crisis Management Discipline

Since the terrorist attacks of September 11, 2001, that profoundly impacted the United States, emergency and crisis management academic programs have drastically increased from 75 to approximately 330. Degrees range from the two-year associate level through to the doctoral level (Federal Emergency Management Agency [FEMA], 2019a). Comfort, Waugh, and Cigler (2012) contribute this increase to the size, frequency, and scope of disasters in the United States and around the world. As mentioned in Chapter 1, billion-dollar disasters are increasing. In fact, $250 billion weather and climate disasters spanning 39 years totaled an estimated $2.7 trillion in the United States alone (National Oceanic and Atmospheric Association [NOAA], 2019). Additionally, technological advancements, rapid globalization, and increased expectations for communities to prepare for, respond to, recover from, and mitigation these disasters have contributed to the rise in academic programs (Kapucu, 2011).

Unlike more established disciplines in the social sciences, emergency and crisis management faculty continue to discuss core competencies and accreditation standards within their programs, across universities, and at FEMA's annual Higher Education Symposium. Part of the complexity is the interdisciplinary nature of this discipline. A search of emergency management academic programs leads to results in which a program is organizationally placed within public administration/management, business, criminal justice, public health, political science, public safety, or emergency services departments (Kapucu & Knox, 2013; Haupt & Knox, 2018). As a discipline, it draws foundational knowledge from each of these other disciplines, adding to confusion and a potential identity crisis. In many ways, this discipline is unique since it crosses all levels of government and each sector; spans over all phases of emergency and crisis management; and requires quantitative and qualitative methods to answer questions.

Because it is a relatively new discipline, it lacks substantial, empirical scholarship of teaching and learning studies, especially for cultural competence (Feldmann-Jensen et al., 2019; Knox & Haupt, 2015; Knox, Emrich, & Haupt, 2019; Wukich, Frew, & Steinberg, 2016). Recent empirical and descriptive articles called for academicians and practitioners to recognize and implement cultural competence in all phases of emergency and crisis management (Edwards, 2012); identify the lack of women and minorities in the profession and discipline (Bennett, 2019); and measure the implementation of cultural competence in emergency management academic programs (Haupt & Knox, 2018); and reported a positive, statistically significant increase in cultural competence learning through case studies (Knox & Haupt, 2015).

As discussed in Chapter 2, competencies are the essential knowledge, skills, and abilities (KSAs) a student needs to acquire before graduation. These competencies are important because they provide guidance for educators and are understandable for potential students and their future employers (Raffel, Maser, & Calarusse, 2011). Development of these KSAs also gives students necessary insights when interacting with individuals of cross-cultural and multicultural backgrounds (Gaynor, 2014) and consists of the reflective outputs from an organization to better serve their diverse demographic (Carrizales, 2010; Cheetham & Chivers, 1998). Providing emergency services to a multicultural environment requires students of emergency management to understand a wide range of personal and cultural differences that are associated with the profession (Darlington, 2008). This enables them to become an effective risk communicator for diverse populations upon accepting the role of an emergency manager.

With the emergency and crisis management profession increasing in complexity and dynamics, so have the required competencies and skillsets for practitioners. Scholars and practitioners published lists of core competencies along with technical and interpersonal skills an emergency manager should possess and be incorporated in emergency and crisis management academic programs (Alexander, 2012; Blanchard, 2003; Clement, 2011; Cwiak, 2011; Drabek, 1987; Donahue, Cunnion, Balaban, & Sochats, 2010; Kapucu, 2011; Kiltz, 2009; Knox & Haupt, 2015; Marks, 2005; McCreight, 2009; Thomas & Mileti, 2003; Urby & McEntire, 2014; Van Wart & Kapucu, 2011; Waugh & Sadiq, 2011). Tyler and Sadiq (2019) recently analyzed many of these studies and categorized the results into nine themes:

1. Technical/substantial knowledge
2. Professionalism
3. Interpersonal relations
4. Management
5. Leadership
6. Legal/ethical behavior
7. Problem solving
8. Communication
9. Cultural/environmental awareness

Cultural awareness ranked last, with only two studies (i.e., Thomas & Mileti, 2003; Kapucu, 2011) including it as a core for emergency managers in Tyler and Sadiq's (2019) analysis. Some have argued cultural competency is an underlying component of each KSA; however, this recent analysis, as well as recommendations from other scholars (i.e., Bennett, 2019; Edwards, 2012; Knox & Haupt, 2015; Knox et al., 2019), underscores the need to make it explicit. One of the most significant contributions to the evolution of the discipline is FEMA's Next Generation Core Competencies.

TABLE 3.1 FEMA's Next Generation 13 Core Competencies (2017)*

Category	Core Competencies
Competencies that build relationships	♦ Disaster risk management ♦ **Community engagement** ♦ Governance and civics ♦ **Leadership**
Competencies that build the practitioner	♦ Scientific literacy ♦ Geographic literacy ♦ **Sociocultural literacy** ♦ Technological literacy ♦ Systems literacy
Competencies that build the individual	♦ Operate within the EM framework, principles, and body of knowledge ♦ Possess critical thinking ♦ **Abide by professional ethics** ♦ Value continual learning

* Bolding denotes competencies that are aligned with this case study book.

Source: Feldmann-Jensen, Jensen, & Smith, 2017

FEMA's *Next Generation Core Competencies for Emergency Management Professionals: Handbook of Behavioral Anchors and Key Actions for Measurement* (2017) is the latest guiding document for emergency and crisis management academic programs in the United States and abroad. These 13 competencies are organized into three categories (Table 3.1).

Of these 13 competencies, community engagement, leadership, sociocultural literacy, and abide by professional ethics include elements of cultural competence. Specifically, abide by professional ethics is essential to building the individual and states:

> The emergency management professional both abides by and champions professional ethics. Professional ethics delineate expected and appropriate conduct, principles, and moral and ethical values that guide practice in the midst of both known and uncertain environments. Ethics must be approached as a totality of principles, not as individual guidelines; together, the sum of principles provides an important foundation for action.
>
> (p. 8)

TABLE 3.2 Seven Behavioral Anchors for Abiding by Professional Ethics Core Competency

Behavioral Anchor	Description
Respect	Actualizes honoring of individuals and groups of people by promoting dignity, diversity, and the rights of others; recognizes and respects the weight of their own actions as they work in communities
Veracity	Demonstrates truthfulness and accuracy of facts and abstains from misrepresentation in all situations
Justice	Embodies a sense of obligation to the common good and treats others equitably and fairly; honors the rights of all species (present and future) when making decisions regarding the distribution of resources
Integrity	Displays consistency between belief and action in all arenas of life
Service	Acts to help others; is altruistically motivated; puts others first, operating beyond the ego
Duty to protect	Considers the moral obligation to avert harm (both present and future) and works toward a common good; facilitates community building, cognizant that all actions have consequences affecting people and performance
Integrates ethical principles within stakeholder discourse	Guides ethical decision-making across multiple stakeholders, who have varying interests, to derive public value

Source: Feldmann-Jensen, Jensen, & Smith, 2017, pp. 28–35.

Summarized in Table 3.2, this competency is divided into seven behavioral anchors with recommended key actions at the under-graduate, master/executive level, and doctoral level.

Research shows many emergency and crisis management academic programs are incorporating cultural competency into the curriculum (Haupt & Knox, 2018). While the information is self-reported, these results and the *Next Generation* guidelines support a growing awareness. The discipline is also experiencing a surge of culturally competent literature from rising scholars (e.g., Bennett, 2019; Jerolleman, 2019; Remington, 2019; Rivera & Miller, 2010). However, response to a national survey of emergency management academic program directors highlighted the need for cultural competence resources (e.g., case studies, scenarios, exercises) for face-to-face and online courses, as well as more facilitator training to better engage participants in hard discussions (Haupt & Knox, 2018).

Cultural Competency in the Emergency and Crisis Management Profession

Historically and up until the late 1990s, the emergency and crisis management field employed individuals who were older, predominantly male, and Caucasian (Alexander, 2012; Brown, 2015; Farris & McCreight, 2014). This was primarily because emergency management evolved from the civil defense era, which was dominated by similar individuals; retired military, fire, and police officers were the first emergency managers and were underfunded and generally ignored by political officials (Tyler & Sadiq, 2019). The terrorist attacks on September 11, 2001, made the position more important at each level of government; this led to more funding and political support, especially with the creation of the U.S. Department of Homeland Security. Yet, in rural counties in the United States, the emergency management position remains part time and located in the police or fire departments – therefore, staying with the status quo (Brown, 2015).

In more urban communities, the profession is shifting to one more representative of all genders, age groups, races, and ethnicities (Alexander, 2012; Knox & Haupt, 2015). However, it is a slow shift. As Bennett (2019, p. 148) states, "The lack of women and racial/ethnic minorities in the profession and their perceived absence in research or scholarly study may have impacts on the effectiveness of response and recovery efforts as well as the broader scientific knowledge within the field." The profession needs to continue working to be representative of the communities they are serving, which ties into the whole community approach.

Before the profession moves forward, it must reflect on its mistakes. As mentioned in Chapter 1, Hurricane Katrina in 2005 was an alarm for the profession to increase cultural competency KSAs. Craig Fugate, FEMA director during this disaster, stated:

> We (FEMA) have a duty to the taxpayers, and if we cannot hold ourselves to that standard, how can we expect the public to trust us in very complex disaster responses where we're making decisions and our ethical motives are called into question?
>
> (as cited in Lavarias, 2013, para. 4)

It is not enough to make ethical decisions, but for the public to perceive it being timely and legitimate. Decision-making under stress with varying levels of uncertainty and time constraints will test all leaders, even the most ethical ones (Boin, Stern, & Sundelius, 2016; Comfort, 2007; Kapucu, Van Wart, Sylves, & Yuldashev, 2011; Van Wart, 2013; Van Wart & Kapucu, 2011; Waugh & Streib, 2006). Real-time decisions are made without space for self-reflection, extra time for complete information, or discussion with multiple stakeholders. Therefore, if the public did not know the ethical standing of its leader(s), then a disaster or crisis will make it evident for all to see. These unethical decisions will not only "reflect the values inherent in the community or organizations existent at the time of the crisis" but also could result in the mistreatment of socially vulnerable populations (Jurkiewicz, 2016, p. 110). Stivers (2007, p. 49), who researched the racial aspects of the hurricane's response efforts, noted, "racism may have shaped policy and bureaucratic decision-making and magnified the death, destruction, and misery that storm produced." While Hurricane Katrina is a well-documented example of unethical decision-making, it is not the first nor the last. More recent examples include the 2010 Haitian earthquake, 2017 Hurricane Harvey in Texas, and 2017 Hurricane Maria in Puerto Rico.

Initiatives at the federal level of government included culturally competent practices, which are rooted in the development and implementation of engagement strategies tailored to specific populations, while also keeping in mind the whole community, so as to build trust and sustain long-term partnerships (FEMA, 2010). The whole community approach was introduced in Presidential Policy Directive 8 and is defined as:

> A means by which residents, emergency management practitioners, organizational and community leaders, and government officials can collectively understand and assess the needs of their respective communities and determine the best ways to organize and strengthen their assets, capacities, and interests. By doing so, a more effective path to societal security and resilience is built. In a sense, Whole Community is a philosophical approach on how to think about conducting emergency management.
>
> (FEMA, 2018, p. 3)

This approach depends upon having strong relationships with a range of cultural communities through all phases of emergency management (FEMA, 2018), as well as continuous training of practitioners who oversee the protection of life and property. Consequently, it is critical for emergency and crisis managers to understand the relationship between cultural competence and the ability to effectively protect and serve vulnerable populations. As Knox et al. (2019, p. 115) stated:

> Practitioners who reflect on their cultural identities and continue their efforts to reduce marginalization and increase equity across emergency management functions lead to more fruitful results. Moreover, the sustenance of these efforts is attributed toward positive intercultural relationships and encourages empathetic skills and abilities. As practitioners validate and value "unique perceptions, interpretations, and responses shared by different sets of people involved in a situation," they support a shared, national identity.

The Whole Community approach also supports the efforts of the national preparedness goal. A 2019 FEMA *Building Cultures of Preparedness* initiative states "no one's socioeconomic status, age,

ability, race, culture, gender, religion, or any other form of difference should prevent access to the same Federal, State or local
support in the face of disaster" (2019b, p. 9). The report provides
four guiding principles to build cultures of preparedness, increase
cultural competence, and sustain these efforts:

- ◆ Trust – developed through getting an understanding of
  history, culture and context
- ◆ Inclusion – accomplished by bringing the perspectives of all
  stakeholders to the table
- ◆ Cross-cultural communication – recognizing that efforts at
  communications are also cross-cultural encounters
- ◆ Supporting local practices and successes – to build upon
  existing strengths within the community

Organizations have a hard time implementing these principles. As
Barnes (2002) warned, gaining public trust can be difficult since
many citizens perceive that there is inequity in exposure to harm.
To incorporate the recommended principles, an understanding of
each unique culture's perspective of the world is required. Every
individual comes to a situation with a certain lens in which they
see the world, and this lens has been constructed from the individual's views, experiences, and beliefs. Quoting George Mason,
"to make representation real and actual, the number of Representatives ought to be adequate; they out to mix with the people, think
as they think, feel as they feel, ought to be perfectly amenable to
them, and thoroughly acquainted with their interest and condition"
(Rohr, 1986, p. 40).

Greater administrative comfort is needed given that individuals infer and ingest meaning within themselves and their world,
and the meaning will influence the world around them. At some
point in an administrator's lifetime, they will become an "other" in
society. The term "other" began in literature to denote certain marginalized groups. The "other" was a group deemed inferior and,
mostly, did not have the same political freedoms as other citizens.
For public servants, the call to action consists of developing cultural competency and understanding the importance thereof. "Cultures are dramatic conversations about things that matter to their

TABLE 3.3 IAEM Principles and Code of Ethics

Principles		
	◆	Respect
	◆	Commitment
	◆	Professionalism
Code of Ethics	◆	Quality
	◆	Professional independence
	◆	Legal requirements
	◆	Objectivity
	◆	Competence
	◆	Abuse of membership
	◆	Conflict of interest
	◆	Confidentiality
	◆	Professional responsibility
	◆	Upholding aims and objectives
	◆	Professional reputation
	◆	Members relations inter se
	◆	Financial propriety

Source: IAEM, 2019

participants, and American culture is no exception. . . . American culture stays alive so long as the conversation continues and the argument is intense" (Bellah, Madsen, Sullivan, Swidler, & Tipton, 2008, pp. 27–28).

As noted by Knox and Haupt (2015, p. 540):

In the world's increasingly complex society, individuals are denoting differences through categorization based on race, class, age, gender, occupation, religion, and/or sexual orientation and identify. These cultural groupings interact with each other on a daily basis and the acknowledgement of these differences varies based on the individual. As discussed within identity development dialogue by Dharamsi (2011), othering is the process of distancing oneself from those deemed different that can result in detrimental effects on social thoughts and behaviors. The detrimental impact is seen when an individual engages in exclusionary othering, where the experiences and beliefs of an individual result in stark disconnects between cultural groups (Canales, 2000; Dharamsi, 2011). Although seemingly harmless, these disconnects lead to tensions between cultural groups and disparate communities.

An integral aspect with cultural competency is addressed through professional ethics. For public administrators, it is the American Society for Public Administration's (ASPA) Code of Ethics.[1]

For emergency managers, the International Association of Emergency Managers' (IAEM) Code of Ethics[2] generates the necessary principles and codes to assist in the call for credible, empathetic, relatable, trustworthy, and culturally competent practitioners.

Summary

As the emergency and crisis management profession evolved from the civil defense era to a recognized profession with certifications and professional standards, so did the discipline. As the degree programs around the United States and abroad increased, faculty and practitioners engaged in discussions regarding core competency knowledge, skills, and abilities. These conversations occurred among colleagues and universities, and at FEMA's annual Higher Education Symposium. As the discipline moves closer to accreditation standards and more robust scholarship of teaching and learning research, there is a need to explicitly include cultural competency as a core requirement in the standards. Ideally, programs are designed to include cultural competency from the start. However, as discussed, the vast majority of emergency and crisis management programs are integrating it years later. One challenge to fully integrating this competency into existing programs is the lack of training for the faculty. Faculty diversity does not necessitate a culturally competent faculty. The next chapter reviews common challenges and recommends techniques to overcome them.

Notes

1. ASPA's Code of Ethics is available here: www.aspanet.org/ASPA/Code-of-Ethics/Code-of-Ethics.aspx
2. IAEM's Code of Ethics is available here: www.iaem.com/page.cfm?p=about/code-of-ethics

References

Alexander, D. (2012). Approaches to emergency management teaching at the master's level. *Journal of Emergency Management*, *11*(1), 59–72.

Barnes, M. (2002). Bringing difference into deliberation? Disabled people, survivors and local governance. *Policy & politics*, *30*(3), 319–331.

Bellah, R. N., Madsen, R., Sullivan, W. M., Swidler, A., & Tipton, S. M. (2008). *Habits of the heart: Individualism and commitment in American life*. Los Angeles, CA: University of California Press.

Bennett, D. D. (2019). Diversity in emergency management scholarship. *Journal of Emergency Management*, *17*(2), 148–154.

Blanchard, B. W. (2003). *Outlines of competencies to develop successful 21st century hazard or disaster or emergency or hazard risk managers*. Retrieved from https://training.fema.gov/emiweb/down loads/corecompetenciesemhied.doc

Boin, A., Stern, E., & Sundelius, B. (2016). *The politics of crisis management: Public leadership under pressure*. Cambridge: Cambridge University Press.

Brown, J. (2015). *The emergency manager: Changing of the guard*. Retrieved from www.govtech.com/templates/gov_print_article?id=320089701

Canales, M. K. (2000). Othering: Toward an understanding of difference. *Advances in Nursing Science*, *22*(4), 16–31.

Carrizales, T. (2010). Exploring cultural competency within the public affairs curriculum. *Journal of Public Affairs Education*, *16*(4), 593–606.

Cheetham, G., & Chivers, G. (1998). The reflective (and competent) practitioner: A model of professional competence which seeks to harmonise the reflective practitioner and competence-based approaches. *Journal of European Industrial Training*, *22*(7), 267–276.

Clement, K. E. (2011). The essentials of emergency management and homeland security graduate education programs: Design, development, and future. *Journal of Homeland Security and Emergency Management*, *8*(2).

Comfort, L. K. (2007). Crisis management in hindsight: Cognition, communication, coordination, and control. *Public Administration Review*, *67*, 189–197.

Comfort, L. K., Waugh, W. L., & Cigler, B. A. (2012). Emergency management research and practice in public administration: Emergence, evolution, expansion, and future directions. *Public Administration Review, 72*(4), 539–547.

Cwiak, C. L. (2011). Framing the future: What should emergency management graduates know? *Journal of Homeland Security and Emergency Management, 8*(2), 14.

Darlington, J. (2008). *The profession of emergency management: Educational opportunities and gaps.* Macomb, IL: Western Illinois University.

Dharamsi, S. (2011). Moving beyond the limits of cultural competency training. *Medical Education, 45*(8), 764–766.

Donahue, D. A., Cunnion, S. A., Balaban, C. D., & Sochats, K. (2010). Meeting educational challenges in homeland security and emergency management. *Journal of Homeland Security and Emergency Management, 7*(1).

Drabek, T. E. (1987). *The professional emergency manager: Structures and strategies for success, institute of behavioral science* (p. 274). Boulder, CO: University of Colorado.

Edwards, F. L. (2012). Cultural competency in disasters. In K. A. Norman-Major & S. T. Gooden (Eds.), *Cultural competency for public administrators* (pp. 197–218). New York, NY: Routledge.

Farris, D., & McCreight, R. (2014). The professionalization of emergency management in institutions of higher education. *Journal of Homeland Security and Emergency Management, 11*(1), 73–94.

Federal Emergency Management Agency (FEMA). (2010). *Tips for competently engaging culturally diverse communities.* Retrieved from https://emilms.fema.gov/IS0505/assets/FEMA%20Tip%20Sheet%20-%20Cultural%20Competency%20v1.pdf

Federal Emergency Management Agency (FEMA). (2018). *Whole community.* Retrieved from www.fema.gov/whole-community

Federal Emergency Management Agency (FEMA). (2019a). *The college list.* Retrieved from www.training.fema.gov/EMIWeb/edu/collegelist/

Federal Emergency Management Agency (FEMA). (2019b). *Building cultures of preparedness: A report for the emergency management higher education community.* Washington, DC: FEMA.

Feldmann-Jensen, S., Hackerott, C., Knox, C. C., Ramsay, J., McEntire, D. A., & Jerolleman, A. (2019). The scholarship of teaching and learning in emergency management and homeland security: Trends, gaps, barriers, and opportunities. *Journal of Emergency Management, 17*(1), 27–34.

Feldmann-Jensen, S., Jensen, S. J., & Smith, S. M. (2017). *The next generation core competencies for emergency management professionals: Handbook of behavioral anchors and key actions for measurement.* Emmitsburg, MD: Federal Emergency Management Agency. Retrieved from https://training.fema.gov/hiedu/docs/emcompetencies/final_%20ngcc_and_measures_aug2017.pdf

Gaynor, T. S. (2014). Through the wire: Training culturally competent leaders for a new era. *Journal of Public Affairs Education, 20*(3), 369–392.

Haupt, B., & Knox, C. C. (2018). Measuring cultural competence in emergency management and homeland security higher education programs. *Journal of Public Affairs Education, 24*(4), 538–556.

International Association of Emergency Managers. (2019). *IAEM Code of Ethics and Professional Conduct.* Retrieved from https://www.iaem.com/page.cfm?p=about/code-of-ethics

Jerolleman, A. (2019). *Disaster recovery through the lens of justice.* Switzerland: Palgrave Pivot.

Jurkiewicz, C. L. (2016). Hurricane Katrina and the crisis of emergency management. In A. Farazmand (Ed.), *Global cases in best and worst practice in crisis and emergency management.* Boca Raton, FL: CRC Press.

Kapucu, N. (2011). Developing competency-based emergency management degree programs in public affairs and administration. *Journal of Public Affairs Education, 17*(4), 501–521.

Kapucu, N., & Knox, C. C. (2013). Utilization of service learning in emergency management programs in the United States. *Journal of Public Affairs Education, 19*(1), 31–51.

Kapucu, N., Van Wart, M., Sylves, R., & Yuldashev, F. (2011). US Presidents and their roles in emergency management and disaster policy 1950–2009. *Risk, Hazards & Crisis in Public Policy, 2*(3), 1–34.

Kiltz, L. (2009). Developing critical thinking skills in homeland security and emergency management courses. *Journal of Homeland Security and Emergency Management, 6*(1).

Knox, C. C., Emrich, C., & Haupt, B. (2019). Advancing emergency management higher education: Importance of cultural competence scholarship. *Journal of Emergency Management, 17*(2), 111–117.

Knox, C. C., & Haupt, B. (2015). Incorporating cultural competency skills in emergency management education. *Disaster Prevention and Management, 24*(5), 619–634.

Lavarias, R. (2013). The role of ethical behavior in emergency management. *PA Times*. Retrieved from https://patimes.org/role-ethical-behavior-emergency-management/

Marks, C. A. (2005). *Professional competencies for the master's level emergency manager*. Retrieved from https://training.fema.gov/hiedu/downloads/craigmarksprofessionalemgraddoc.doc

McCreight, R. (2009). Educational challenges in homeland security and emergency management. *Journal of Homeland Security and Emergency Management, 6*(1).

NOAA National Centers for Environmental Information (NCEI). (2019). *U.S. billion-dollar weather and climate disasters*. Retrieved from www.ncdc.noaa.gov/billions/

Raffel, J. A., Maser, S. M., & Calarusse, C. (2011). Accreditation and competencies in education for leadership in public service. *The State of Public Administration: Issues, Challenges, and Opportunities*, 70–88.

Remington, C. L. (2019). Cultural competence in long term recovery: Lessons from the 2010 Haitian Earthquake. *Housing Recovery after Disasters, 153*.

Rivera, J. D., & Miller, D. S. (2010). *How ethically marginalized Americans cope with catastrophic disasters: Studies in suffering and resiliency*. Lewiston, NY: Edwin Mellen Press.

Rohr, J. A. (1986). *To run a constitution: The legitimacy of the administrative state* (Vol. 86). Lawrence: University Press of Kansas.

Stivers, C. (2007). So poor and so black: Hurricane Katrina, public administration, and the issue of race. *Public Administration Review, 67*, 48–56.

Thomas, D., & Mileti, D. (2003). *Designing educational opportunities for the hazards manager of the 21st Century*. Retrieved from https://training.fema.gov/hiedu/downloads/thomas%20and%20milleti.pdf

Tyler, J., & Sadiq, A. A. (2019). The essential skill set of a resilient emergency manager. *Journal of Emergency Management, 17*(1), 35–43.

Urby, H., & McEntire, D. A. (2014). Applying public administration in emergency management: The importance of integrating management into disaster education. *Journal of Homeland Security and Emergency Management, 11*(1), 39–60.

Van Wart, M. (2013). Lessons from leadership theory and the contemporary challenges of leaders. *Public Administration Review, 73*(4), 553–565.

Van Wart, M., & Kapucu, N. (2011). Crisis management competencies: The case of emergency managers in the USA. *Public Management Review*, *13*(4), 489–511.

Waugh, W. L., Jr., & Sadiq, A. A. (2011). Professional education for emergency managers. *Journal of Homeland Security and Emergency Management*, *2*(9).

Waugh, W. L., Jr., & Streib, G. (2006). Collaboration and leadership for effective emergency management. *Public Administration Review*, *66*, 131–140.

Wukich, C., Frew, S. L., & Steinberg, A. (2016). Teaching key elements of decision making online for homeland security and emergency management. *Journal of Homeland Security Education*, *5*, 8–24.

Facilitating Difficult Conversations

Brittany "Brie" Haupt and Claire Connolly Knox

Realities of Facilitating Hard Conversations

As a facilitator, your background and experiences shape your facilitation style. We share our stories in the preface of this book. If you have not read it, we ask that you take a few minutes to do so. In this section, we share two "a-ha" moments that shape much of the recommendations included in this chapter.

First, within an undergraduate disaster response and recovery course, Brie created a diversity case study based on situations that occurred in 2015 with homeless populations in urban environments and discrimination by small businesses and wealthier populations. The case study was placed in a futuristic, fictional place to see what students would bring with them in terms of social norms and beliefs. During the first semester of facilitating the case study, the students discussed one of the population groups that stereotypically is connected to the homeless population. Yet, most of the students viewed this population as victims and not helpful in a response situation – a large downtown fire. After some discussion, one female student spoke up and disagreed with the class's assessment of this population. Brie asked her to elaborate more on her disagreement. Brie commented about how the female student's opinion seemed connected to personal experience. After a moment, the female student explained that she and her daughter were homeless for a while and did not view themselves as "helpless" or "victims". She would use the "homeless" population to assist those evacuating the fires to get to safety. You could have heard a pin drop, but Brie's facilitation experience was helpful in engaging in a deeper discussion.

One main technique utilized was Brie's connection to active reflection (discussed further in this chapter). If a student offers an opinion, ask if they could elaborate more on what was behind the opinion and lead students to connect to the experiences that supported their positions. Through these active reflections, the class shared their perceptions of stereotypes related to homeless populations and other connections made in the case study.

The second moment was with emergency managers and the same case study. Shortly after starting the exercise, a female participant stated to the group, "I have an issue with the word 'citizen' in this scenario." We paused the individual group discussions and opened the floor to allow her the space to elaborate upon this strong reaction to this term. The individual was visibly angered by the term "citizen" to the point of shaking and seemed as if she was ready to walk out of the room.

Some new facilitators might have the following initial reaction: "What did we just do to make this participant so upset," which could stem from past negative facilitation experiences or a lack of experiences. Brie noted her reaction and asked, "What is in your background that helps explain this reaction? You seem triggered by this term. Help me to understand." The individual stated how she works directly with non-documented farm workers in Florida and often advocates for them in emergencies and disasters. Through her advocacy work, she was often met with opposition, and most of it was connected to the term "citizen". At one point, the conversation needed to be pulled back to the group discussion as a whole, so Brie asked the woman if she would be willing to speak after the workshop ended to gain more understanding and also be respectful of her reaction along with the remainder of the group's time. She agreed to "put a pin in it," and we were able to revisit "citizen" along with other revelations pulled from the group discussions. This experience resolved well but highlights the challenges facilitators face, which we cover in the following section.

Challenges and Techniques

While many facilitators are comfortable in front of a room (or presenting materials), some of us were never trained to facilitate difficult or controversial conversations. Some common challenges with facilitation include releasing control of the discussion and an inability to fully prepare for what may occur within the room. Brie utilizes the phrase "Become comfortable with being uncomfortable." There is an unpredictability to facilitation, and you can try your hardest to set up a space that encourages dialogue, but you may still face situations such as these:

◆ What happens if no one talks? What if someone talks too much?
◆ What happens if someone gets really angry? Walks out? Cries?
◆ What if only one person shows up? What if 100 people show up?

These questions are natural to consider as they affect the ability to convey concepts and achieve outcomes. To break down the challenges and techniques, this section starts with an acknowledgment of what difficult conversations bring to the surface and the use of case studies to assist in facilitating dialogue. Then, tips are presented, beginning with how to engage and direct the dialogue. The section ends with techniques for the facilitators themselves and how to process the experience.

Facilitating Difficult Dialogues

When it comes to cultural competence–related conversations, many find facilitation intimidating because the topics can be sensitive, uncomfortable, controversial, emotional, and the like (Hughes, Huston, & Stein, 2010; Vogelsang & McGee, 2015; Warren & Center, 2006). The next section highlights tips for facilitating difficult conversations in a classroom or training session and includes sample language.

Tips for Facilitating

The main challenges that surface include managing ourselves in the environment and engaging in opportunities to help participants learn and develop. In terms of facilitation, there are techniques that assist with guiding conversation. Ultimately, some individuals will have difficulty hearing what other participants are saying or even what the facilitator is saying. The goal of these techniques is to promote and exemplify the process of listening, understanding, and validating the voices in the room. These techniques include the following:

♦ **Laying the foundation**. Before engaging in any dialogue, begin with ground rules. This establishes the expectations for the participants. Moreover, have the participants demonstrate that they will adhere to the ground rules. Doing this assists with buy-in. For the case studies in this book, we use Gorski's (2019) ground rules (see the following box) and discuss them further subsequently. Later in the chapter, we modify these ground rules for facilitating the case studies in an online environment.

Ground Rules (Gorski, 2019)

1. Listen actively – respect others when they are talking.
2. Speak from your own experience instead of generalizing ("I" instead of "they," "we," and "you").
3. Do not be afraid to respectfully challenge one another by asking questions but refrain from personal attacks – focus on ideas.
4. Participate to the fullest of your ability – community growth depends on the inclusion of every individual voice.
5. Instead of invalidating somebody else's story with your own spin on their experience, share your own story and experience.
6. The goal is not to agree – it is to gain a deeper understanding.
7. Be conscious of body language and nonverbal responses – they can be as disrespectful as words.

- **Active listening**. This is a component of reflection where you can state what you believe you heard and then ask the participant to elaborate or to clarify what was said. This allows the participant to engage with you and helps others understand the background that has led to specific statements and ideologies.
- **Divert a thread of the conversation to other participants**. This is a technique to utilize if a participant seems uncomfortable with something they stated, and it can be a way to connect to others in the room.
  - For example: "Many people think this way. Why do you think they hold such views?" "What are different views? Why do you think people hold those views?" Or ask if others hold the same view (show of hands). Ask who holds a different view (show of hands). Ask if someone is willing to share the opposite view.

    (Vogelsang & McGee, 2015, p. 6)

- **Reflection time**. Provide time for personal reflection before open dialogue occurs (Vogelsang & McGee, 2015). A pre-test can begin the reflection period by having participants begin to understand the important terms and concepts of the case study. In addition, the post-test can include an area for reflection, such as the prompt "I used to think _____, but now I think _____", allows participants to reflect on the entirety of the case study facilitation and their personal experiences.
- **Foster understanding**. This is a technique to utilize if a debate occurs between participants, and it begins to halt the progression of the case study. In this situation, you can ask why the stances are important to the participants, what has led them to this particular view, and whether they have considered or are willing to consider the opposing stance.
  - For example: Ask students, when things get hot, to step back and reflect upon what they might learn from this moment. This can move the discussion to a level that helps everyone see what issues have been at stake and what the clash itself might mean.

    (Warren & Center, 2006, p. 3)

◆ **Staying on track**
  ○ If you encounter a participant who is especially passionate about their viewpoint, then try acknowledging this passion and providing a space to discuss it further. For example: "I can see you are very passionate about this aspect; let's meet after the facilitation to speak further" and then move on to the next component of the case study.
  ○ Another example is when a participant seems unwilling to actively listen to other participants in the room. You can pose the following: "I'd like to offer another point of view. . . ."
  ○ What about those participants who are silent and may be processing the situation but uncomfortable or are not prone to speak up? You may be able to see nonverbal cues like crossed arms, lack of direct eye contact when looking in their direction, and/or physically distancing themselves by turning in their chair to the area that is farthest away from you. A technique is to call on these individuals and present the opportunity to be heard. For example: "I'm wondering if you have some thoughts or feelings about what you've been hearing?" Or, "You seem like you have a thought on this subject; would you like to share?"
  ○ If they remain silent and not actively participating, then just keep them in your periphery. Some individuals may just be listeners, or they may disconnect. It is natural to have some participants remain silent throughout the activity.
◆ **Do not avoid or ignore remarks.** Avoiding or ignoring remarks has two components to it. The first is that it reflects the facilitator's discomfort or inexperience in addressing the issue. The second is that it reinforces that certain behavior or remarks are OK.
  ○ Allow the remark to be acknowledged. If you are comfortable with respectfully challenging the remark, then ask the participant to elaborate and to help you understand their point of view. A common situation is that the intent of the remark is often different than the impact. Some may make a statement and not realize its impact on others in the room. Respectfully challenging

the remark and asking the participant to elaborate allows them to help you see their thought progression and will unveil more about their own experiences and perceptions.

o For example: When a participant uses the plural pronoun "they" in a statement, ask them, "Who is 'they'?" This can help them break down the preconceived notion about a particular group of individuals. It can also help the participant push past a "talking point" and into a reflective state.

Tips for the Facilitator

This section includes tips for the facilitator; the tips are compiled from a variety of resources (Hughes et al., 2010; Vogelsang & McGee, 2015; Warren & Center, 2006).

- ◆ **Respond rather than react**. Remember, do not personalize any remarks. Many individuals will question the experience of the facilitator. Try to move past initial emotional responses and try to find the root of where the question comes from. In our experiences, many individuals speak from personal events and may lash out because of the negative emotions connected to those events and not being provided a space to process it.
- ◆ **Breathe and take your time**. Take a moment to acknowledge your own feelings and recognize that you have a choice as to whether you will act on them. Many facilitators will rush through the process because of their own discomfort. A tip is to allow for pauses throughout the facilitation; silently counting to ten is a helpful practice. Give the participants, and yourself, some room to breathe as you transition through the case study, process the information presented, and reflect on past experiences.
- ◆ **Remain curious and realize it is how we think about the facilitation**. Keep the mindset that you are there to learn from the participants and to understand their experiences. It may seem like a commonsense idea, but walking into

the facilitation with the mindset of learning and engaging the participants will open up your active listening skillsets and will emulate to others that you want and are willing to validate their experiences. "The first route to making such unanticipated and difficult occurrences productive lies in how we think about the moment – as instructors. If we can get out of our own emotional confusion, we can begin to see the heat as an opportunity to explore different views about the topic."

(Warren & Center, 2006, p. 2)

♦ **Prepare**. Before facilitating a case study, review the material and determine how it may be impacted depending on the number of participants, arrangement of the space, materials needed, time, case study breakdown, etc. Do your best to be as prepared as possible before facilitating the case study as each of them brings with it professional experience, knowledge, and research.

♦ **Invite a practitioner to join in the discussion.** One way to decrease your bias in facilitating a case study is to have a practitioner join the larger group discussion; this is especially helpful in a classroom setting (Silenas, Akins, Parrish, & Edwards, 2008). Additionally, having an emergency or crisis manager present can raise expectations among the participants to take the exercise seriously.

♦ **Bring in a trained facilitator.** Many universities and organizations have a diversity center with staff who are willing to assist you. Besides attending free training sessions, ask them to co-facilitate a case study with you or be an observer. They can help you "connect nuisances in student responses with the rich cultural competency literature, which can lead to meaningful discussions" (Knox & Haupt, 2015, p. 629). Also, they can highlight your strengths and identify weaknesses to improve upon as you develop your facilitation skillset. For online instruction, work with an instructional designer for new ways to engage participants in the case studies.

♦ **Consider completing online evaluations.** Use individual diversity and cultural competency evaluations to assess any potential blind spots and uncover your preconceived notions, stereotypes, and attitudes before facilitating a case study. For example, Project Implicit (2011) at Harvard University is a series of Implicit Association Tests that help participants identify beliefs and attitudes on a variety of topics.

Online Facilitation

If you are facilitating the case studies in an online, asynchronous environment, then take the time to understand how to translate the experience. The following box includes example online ground rules; see Appendix A for an example module to use in an online setting.

Online Ground Rules (Modified From Gorski, 2019)

◆ Respect what others have written.
◆ Speak from your own experience instead of generalizing ("I" instead of "they," "we," and "you").
◆ Do not be afraid to respectfully challenge one another by asking questions but refrain from personal attacks; focus on ideas.
◆ Respect what others have written, and do not write in all caps. When posting a response, you can demonstrate respect by including statements such as: "I see where you are coming from; however, I . . ." or "I respect your opinion. From my perspective, I. . . ."
◆ Participate to the fullest of your ability. Community growth depends on the inclusion of every individual voice.
◆ Re-read your response before posting to make sure you are on topic and answering all questions or requests.
◆ Instead of invalidating somebody else's story with your own spin on their experience, share your own story and experience.
◆ The goal is not to agree; it is to gain a deeper understanding.

For instance, the ground rules can be modified as follows:

- ♦ Acknowledge the unique aspects of an online environment. The online environment may not allow for your tone, voice inflection, and/or gestures. Re-read your messages to make sure you are being professional and respectful. Try not to relax your spelling or grammar either.
- ♦ Be mindful that the goal is not for everyone to agree but to discuss their opinions and perspectives that acknowledge the experiences and viewpoints of each participant.
- ♦ Respect what others have written and do not write in all caps. When posting a response, you can demonstrate respect by including statements such as: "I see where you are coming from; however, I . . ." or "I respect your opinion. From my perspective, I. . . ."
- ♦ Speak from your own experience instead of generalizing ("I" instead of "they," "we," and "you").
- ♦ Do not be afraid to respectfully challenge one another by asking questions but refrain from personal attacks; focus on ideas and stay on topic. Instead of saying, "You're wrong," you can respectfully challenge by stating "Personally, I disagree because . . ." or "I can see your point, but my experience teaches me. . . ."
- ♦ Participate to the fullest of your ability. Community growth depends on the inclusion of every individual voice.
- ♦ Re-read your response before posting to make sure you are on topic and answering all questions or requests.
- ♦ Instead of invalidating somebody else's story with your own spin on their experience, share your own story and experience.
- ♦ Remember: The goal is not to agree; it is to gain a deeper understanding.

In addition to the modified ground rules, you may want to tape some videos describing the exercise and what the process is or generate a module that progresses participants through the case study according to the suggested time breakdowns.

References

Gorski, P. C. (2019). *Guide for setting ground rules*. Retrieved from www. edchange.org/multicultural/activities/groundrules.html

Hughes, B., Huston, T., & Stein, J. (2010). Using case studies to help faculty navigate difficult classroom moments. *College Teaching*, *59*(1), 7–12.

Knox, C. C., & Haupt, B. (2015). Incorporating cultural competency skills in emergency management education. *Disaster Prevention and Management*, *24*(5), 619–634.

Project Implicit. (2011). *Harvard university*. Retrieved from https://implicit. harvard.edu/implicit/takeatest.html

Silenas, R., Akins, R., Parrish, A. R., & Edwards, J. C. (2008). Developing disaster preparedness competence: An experiential learning exercise for multiprofessional education. *Teaching and Learning in Medicine*, *20*(1), 62–68.

Vogelsang, J. D., & McGee, S. (2015). *Handbook for facilitating difficult conversations in the classroom*. City University of New York. Retrieved from https://www.qc.cuny.edu/Academics/Centers/Democratic/ Documents/Handbook%20for%20Facilitating%20Difficult%20 Conversations2.pdf

Warren, L., & Center, D. B. (2006). *Managing hot moments in the classroom*. Cambridge, MA: Derek Bok Center for Teaching and Learning. Retrieved from http://isites.harvard.edu/fs/htms/icb.topic58474/ hotmoments.html

Additional Resources

Block, P. (2018). *Community: The structure of belonging*. San Francisco: Berrett-Koehler Publishers.

Community Toolbox. (2018a). *Cultural competence in a multicultural world*. Retrieved from https://ctb.ku.edu/en/table-of-contents/culture/ cultural-competence

Community Toolbox. (2018b). *Enhancing cultural competence*. Retrieved from https://ctb.ku.edu/en/enhancing-cultural-competence

Community Toolbox. (2018c). *Tools to change our world: How do you build relationships with people from other cultures*. Retrieved from https:// ctb.ku.edu/en/table-of-contents/culture/cultural-competence/ building-relationships/main

Dweck, C. S. (2019). *Mindset: The new psychology of success*. New York: Random House.

Gracious Space. (2011). *Center for ethical leadership*. Retrieved from www.ethicalleadership.org/gracious-space-toolkit.html

Sue, D. W. (2016). *Race talk and the conspiracy of silence: Understanding and facilitating difficult dialogues on race*. Hoboken, NJ: John Wiley & Sons.

5

Case Study

Preparing Schools for Active Threats

Mark Landahl and Stephen Stuart Carter

Overview of the Context

Preparedness for active shooting events has been a priority issue for school systems, law enforcement, emergency medical professionals, and emergency management since the 1999 mass shooting at Columbine High School. The Federal Bureau of Investigation (FBI) (2019) defines an active shooting event as "one or more individuals actively engaged in killing or attempting to kill people in a populated area" (p. 2). While statistics do not support the supposition of a recent rise in school shooting incidents (Carlton, 2017), the events of 2018 led to legislative intervention in many states related to school safety (National Conference on State Legislatures, 2018). The U.S. Department of Education (2013) provides national guidance on the construction of school-based emergency plans, but a uniform definition of a prepared school does not exist. Additionally, research findings have not produced a standardized measure or set of components that indicate school preparedness. Studies often construct metrics for general preparedness, or for a particular hazard that consists of checklists for plans, activities, equipment, training, and exercises.

As the components of general preparedness lack consensus, the integration of the access and functional needs of persons with disabilities and other cultural aspects that impact preparedness and response have also lagged (Meyers, 2006). The U.S. Census Bureau (2017) estimates show 11.5 million Americans with a hearing disability. Specific to services for deaf and hard-of-hearing (deaf/HH) populations in disasters, Ivey and colleagues (2014) found that states have improved since a 2006 review, but continue to show deficiencies in communication access and understanding of needs. Engelman and colleagues (2013) found that emergency management agencies and community-based organizations lack training related to deaf/HH populations, resulting in an underserved and vulnerable community. While some improvement exists in the integration of access and functional needs into emergency management planning and practice, additional work is necessary for full inclusion.

From a disability policy perspective in emergency management, several resources are available to support the development of inclusive plans and procedures. The National Council on Disability (NCD) (2009) report, *Effective emergency management: Making improvements for communities and people with disabilities*, is a core document for emergency management practitioners. In 2014, the NCD developed a guidance document specific to communication titled *Effective communications for people with disabilities: Before, during, and after emergencies*. The Federal Emergency Management Agency (FEMA) (2018) maintains an Office of Disability Integration and Coordination focused on meeting the needs of people with disabilities throughout the phases of emergency management. FEMA (2014) also provides training through the Emergency Management Institute for inclusive emergency management.

Facilitator Information

This case study uses interest in active shooting events as an avenue to explore issues of access and functional needs for preparedness and response with emergency management practitioners. Participants should have a baseline understanding of emergency planning as background to engage in the activity. This case is an introductory activity and gateway to connect curriculum to inclusive emergency management planning, access and functional needs for emergency preparedness and response, or targeted specifically to the hazard warning function. The activity centers on sensory disabilities such as those experienced by deaf/HH persons but can be extended to other disabilities, such as mobility. One of the core takeaways from the case is the "hidden" nature of some disabilities (Mackenzie & Smith, 2009).

The case reinforces FEMA's (2011) "whole community" orientation of emergency management policy in the post-Katrina environment. The case is titled so as not to reveal the true intention of the activity. While the initial activity focuses on K–12 school emergency planning, the intent is to expose and discuss potential biases and assumptions regarding the construction of preparedness plans and initial response actions, including hazard warnings. The case will be more effective if the intent of the activity is masked until engagement of the update in the second handout. The second section of the case provides for revision of initial planning recommendations based on new information and reflection on the assumptions made in the initial portion of the case.

The facilitator may choose to share this background information and the references and additional resources provided later with participants at the conclusion of the activity for further research or extension activities.

Case Study: Preparing Schools for Active Threats

Goals of the Case Study

The goal of this exercise is to engage participants with content knowledge in aspects of emergency planning in the recognition of unique aspects of preparedness for schools with high populations of students with access and functional needs.

Learning Outcomes

◆ Given a case activity, participants will apply knowledge of emergency management planning to a multi-stage scenario involving emergency preparedness at a school.

◆ When provided with additional information, participants will recognize the need for inclusion of access and functional needs of students into emergency planning activities for whole community school-based emergency planning.

◆ Participants will reflect on their thoughts and recommendations at each stage of the scenario and recognize assumptions that informed decisions.

Definitions

◆ Active Shooter: One or more individuals actively engaged in killing or attempting to kill people in a populated area (FBI, 2018).

◆ Access and Functional Needs: Individual circumstances requiring assistance, accommodation, or modification for mobility, communication, transportation, safety, health maintenance, etc., as a result of any temporary or permanent situation that limits an individual's ability to take action in an emergency (FEMA, 2017).

◆ Hidden Disabilities: Disabilities that are not readily apparent through observation (Federal Partners in Transition Workgroup, 2015).

◆ Whole Community: A focus on enabling the participation in incident management activities of a wide range of players from the private and nonprofit sectors, including non-governmental organizations and the general public, in conjunction with the participation of all levels of government, to foster better coordination and working relationships (FEMA, 2017).

Breakdown

- Divide participants into manageable groups of four to six people.
- Provide the initial scenario in Participant Handout #1 or display in a group setting (the initial scenario will not reveal key details and the purpose of the activity).
- Allow participants time to work and discuss as a group (at least 15–20 minutes depending on course format).
- Discuss ideas and content of solutions developed to this point in the scenario (10–15 minutes).
- Provide the scenario update in Participant Handout #2 or display in a group setting.
- Allow participants additional time to work and discuss the update in groups (at least ten minutes).
- Consider referring to the picture in Handout #1 and discussion the issue of *hidden disabilities* for emergency planning.
- Facilitate group discussion about the update and individual and group initial planning assumptions.
- Utilize supplemental questions as a resource if needed.

Ground Rules (Gorski, 2019)

1. Listen actively – respect others when they are talking
2. Speak from your own experience instead of generalizing ("I" instead of "they," "we," and "you").
3. Do not be afraid to respectfully challenge one another by asking questions but refrain from personal attacks – focus on ideas.
4. Participate to the fullest of your ability – community growth depends on the inclusion of every individual voice.
5. Instead of invalidating somebody else's story with your own spin on their experience, share your own story and experience.
6. The goal is not to agree – it is to gain a deeper understanding.

7. Be conscious of body language and nonverbal responses – they can be as disrespectful as words.

Supplemental Questions

1. Describe your initial thoughts after the second scenario update. Did your recommendations require modification?
2. In your initial work, did you consider students with disabilities that result in access and functional needs in the solutions?
3. How would you apply these issues for other hazards that a school may face? Do different hazards bring different challenges for those with access and functional needs?
4. Do you see the issues raised in this exercise as relative to emergency management practice? How do these issues apply at the community level?
5. What does the term *hidden disability* mean to you?
6. What do you see as the key takeaway from this exercise?

School Preparedness for Active Assailant Events

Handout #1

The Situation

Your group has been contacted by a local school to consult on the development of plans and procedures for an active shooting event on campus. Recent national events have raised the concern of parents and the community about plans and procedures at the school for these types of hazards. The school has some basic plans and instructions for teachers for locking down classrooms.

The school campus (Figure 5.1) consists of several buildings in which students attend class. The superintendent is particularly concerned about early identification of an emergency event on campus to initiate emergency procedures, including rapid notification of the campus population. The superintendent expressed concern for notification of students who would potentially be transitioning between buildings. Resources are not available for structural changes to the campus. The

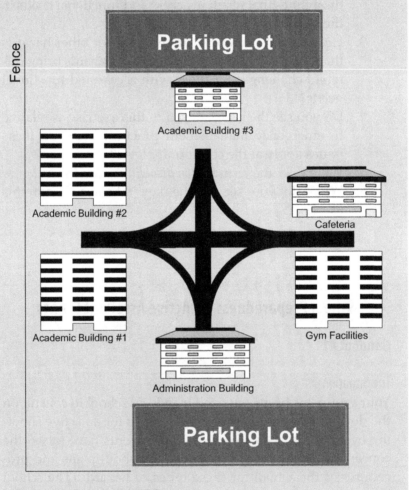

FIGURE 5.1 Map of the School Campus

Source: Landahl & Carter

superintendent is using limited resources to hire your expertise on emergency planning to focus on the early identification of the event, notification of the campus population, and initial actions of the event within the current facilities.

The Facility
The school campus is a combined middle and high school setting consisting of multiple academic and support buildings located on the outer edge of an urban area. The front of the campus faces a busy city street and is protected by a wrought iron fence that covers the front of the school property. The fence does not cover driveways or the other areas to access the school campus nor does it protect the rear of the campus, which is open to a less busy portion of the city. The campus consists of open areas, including the central "quad" where benches are found for students and is in use throughout the day for academic, recreational, and social activities (see Figure 5.1).

Things to Know
+ The school is public and has a daily student population of approximately 1,000, with nearly 100 school staff (administrators, teachers, and support staff).
+ The surrounding community has a crime rate below the national average for similar-sized cities.
+ Most of the students ride buses to and from school.
+ The school is a state educational facility for deaf students.
+ The majority of the student population is deaf.
+ 60% of the teachers and staff are deaf.

Your Role
Your task is to develop recommendations for these aspects to present to the superintendent. Be prepared to present your recommendations related to event recognition, campus notification, and initial staff actions.

Questions for Discussion
1. What are your recommendations for recognition of active assailant events?
2. What are your recommendations for campus notification?
3. What are your recommendations for staff training?
4. What should the staff procedures be in the initial moments of the event?
5. Although resources are limited, what are your recommendations for campus improvements related to recognition and campus notifications?

School Preparedness for Active Assailant Events

Handout #2

Additional Information
◆ The most frequently used method is a combination of speech reading (lip-reading) and residual hearing, which is often amplified by hearing aids.
◆ A small percentage of the students have other disabilities, such as limited vision or mental health issues.

Your Role
Be prepared to present your revised recommendations related to event recognition, campus notification, and initial staff actions.

Questions for Discussion
1. In your initial work, how did your understanding of access and functional needs assist the planning process? How did it hinder?

2. How do these additional facts change your recommendations for:
   a. Recognition of active assailant events?
   b. Campus notification?
   c. Staff procedures in the initial moments of the event?
3. How would you apply these issues for other hazards that a school may face? Do different hazards bring different challenges for those with access and functional needs?
4. What are your thoughts on *hidden disabilities* and disaster preparedness?

Pre-Test Assessment

PURPOSE OF THE SURVEY

This assessment survey is designed to demonstrate understanding of cultural competence–related aspects and establish a baseline of participant attitudes before the exercise.

DEFINITIONS

Directions: Please match the terminologies with their definitions.

_____ Active Shooter

A. A focus on enabling the participation in incident management activities of a wide range of players from the public, private, and nonprofit sectors.

_____ Whole Community

B. One or more individuals actively engaged in killing or attempting to kill people in a populated area.

_____ Access and Functional Needs

C. Individual circumstances requiring assistance, accommodation, or modification as a result of any temporary or permanent situation that limits an individual's ability to take action in an emergency.

ATTITUDINAL SCALE

Directions: Please use the following scale to represent your reaction to the questions.

1	2	3	4	5
Strongly Agree	Agree	Neither Agree nor Disagree	Disagree	Strongly Disagree

1. I believe personal culture influences my role(s).

2. I believe cultural groups influence my role(s).

3. I believe stereotypes influence my role(s).

4. I believe I have adequate knowledge of how my own cultural identities influence my role(s).

5. I believe I have adequate knowledge of other cultures and their influence on my role(s).

6. I believe I have adequate knowledge of stereotypes and their influence on my role(s).

7. I believe I have adequate knowledge of my cultural identities and their influence on emergency and crisis management.

8. I believe I have adequate knowledge of other cultural identities and how they influence emergency and crisis management.

9. I believe I have adequate knowledge of stereotypes and how they influence emergency and crisis management.

Post-Test Assessment

PURPOSE OF THE SURVEY

This assessment survey is designed to demonstrate understanding of culturally related impacts and establish a baseline of participant attitudes after the exercise.

DEFINITIONS

Directions: Please match the terminologies with their definitions.

_____ Active Shooter

A. A focus on enabling the participation in incident management activities of a wide range of players from the public, private, and nonprofit sectors.

_____ Whole Community

B. One or more individuals actively engaged in killing or attempting to kill people in a populated area.

_____ Access and Functional Needs

C. Individual circumstances requiring assistance, accommodation, or modification as a result of any temporary or permanent situation that limits an individual's ability to take action in an emergency.

ATTITUDINAL SCALE.

Directions: Please use the following scale to represent your reaction to the questions.

1	2	3	4	5
Strongly Agree	Agree	Neither Agree nor Disagree	Disagree	Strongly Disagree

1. I believe personal culture influences my role(s).

2. I believe cultural groups influence my role(s).

3. I believe stereotypes influence my role(s).

4. I believe I have adequate knowledge of how my own cultural identities influence my role(s).

5. I believe I have adequate knowledge of other cultures and their influence on my role(s).

6. I believe I have adequate knowledge of stereotypes and their influence on my role(s).

7. I believe I have adequate knowledge of my cultural identities and their influence on emergency and crisis management.

8. I believe I have adequate knowledge of other cultural identities and how they influence emergency and crisis management.

9. I believe I have adequate knowledge of stereotypes and how they influence emergency and crisis management.

OPEN RESPONSE

Please answer the following question: "I used to think_____, but now I think_____."

(Use back of page if needing extra space.)

References

Carlton, M. P. (2017). *National institute of justice report: Summary of school safety statistics*. Retrieved from www.ncjrs.gov/pdffiles1/nij/250610. pdf

Engelman, A., Ivey, S. L., Tseng, W., Dahrouge, D., Brune, J., & Neuhauser, L. (2013). Responding to the deaf in disasters: Establishing the need for systematic training for state-level emergency management agencies and community organizations. *BMC Health Services Research, 13*(84), 1–10.

Federal Bureau of Investigation (FBI). (2018). *Active shooter incidents in the United States in 2016 and 2017*. Retrieved from www.fbi.gov/file-repository/active-shooter-incidents-us-2016-2017.pdf/view

Federal Bureau of Investigation (FBI). (2019). *Active shooter incidents in the United States in 2018*. Washington, DC: GPO.

Federal Emergency Management Agency (FEMA). (2011). *A whole community approach to emergency management: Principles, themes, and pathways for action*. Retrieved from www.fema.gov/media-library-data/20130726-1813-25045-0649/whole_community_ dec2011__2_.pdf

Federal Emergency Management Agency (FEMA). (2014). *IS-368: Including people with disabilities & others with access & functional needs in disaster operations*. Retrieved from https://training.fema.gov/is/ courseoverview.aspx?code=IS-368

Federal Emergency Management Agency (FEMA). (2017). *National incident management system*. Retrieved from www.fema.gov/media-library/ assets/documents/148019

Federal Emergency Management Agency (FEMA). (2018). *Office of disability integration and coordination*. Retrieved from www.fema.gov/ office-disability-integration-and-coordination

Federal Partners in Transition Workgroup. (2015). *The 2020 federal youth transition plan: A federal interagency strategy*. Retrieved from www.dol. gov/odep/pdf/20150302-fpt.pdf

Gorski, P. C. (2019). *Guide for setting ground rules*. Retrieved from www. edchange.org/multicultural/activities/groundrules.html

Ivey, S. L., Tseng, W., Dahrouge, D., Engelman, A., Neuhauser, L., Huang, D., & Gurung, S. (2014). Assessment of state- and territorial-level preparedness capacity for serving deaf and hard-of-hearing populations in disaster. *Public Health Reports*, *129*, 148–155.

Mackenzie, I., & Smith, A. (2009). Deafness-the neglected and hidden disability. *Annals of Tropical Medicine & Parasitology*, *103*(7), 565–571.

Meyers, L. (2006). Katrina trauma lingers long: Disaster experts shared lessons learned from Katrina about diversity and long-term response. *Monitor on Psychology*, *37*(5), 46–47.

National Conference on State Legislatures. (2018). *School safety*. Retrieved from www.ncsl.org/research/education/school-safety.aspx

National Council on Disability. (2009). *Effective emergency management: Making improvements for communities and people with disabilities*. Retrieved from https://files.eric.ed.gov/fulltext/ED507740.pdf

U.S. Census Bureau. (2017). *Disability characteristics American community survey 1-year estimates*. Retrieved from https://factfinder.census.gov/faces/tableservices/jsf/pages/productview.xhtml?pid=ACS_17_1YR_S1810&prodType=table

U.S. Department of Education. (2013). *Guide for developing high-quality school emergency operations plans*. Washington, DC: U.S. Department of Education.

Additional Resource

Neuhauser, L., Ivey, S. L., Huang, D., Engelman, A., Tseng, W., Dahrouge, D., . . . Kealey, M. (2013). Availability and readability of emergency preparedness materials for deaf and hard-of-hearing and older adult populations: Issues and assessments. *PloS One*, *8*(2), 1–11.

6

Evacuation of an At-Risk Population

Cultural Competency and Ensuring Safety

Alessandra Jerolleman and Jerry V. Graves

Overview of the Context

Emergency managers seeking to engage with all local populations
and identify those communities that may be particularly at risk
must consider the unique needs of minority populations. In terms
of being engaged in emergency management processes and ben-
efitting from the full range of associated public services, minority
populations may face a number of unique challenges, including:
(1) linguistic barriers; (2) diverging cultural needs, worldviews,
and preferred means of communication; and (3) a lack of familiarity with and/or willingness to navigate bureaucratic processes
(Carter-Pokras, Zambrana, Mora, & Aaby, 2007; Peguero, 2006; Tiefenbacher & Wilson, 2012).

The term *undocumented* immigrant refers to "foreign nationals
residing in the US without legal immigration status" (U.S. Legal, n.d.).
Conversely, *documented* immigrants have a legal right to be or remain
in the United States, including individuals ranging from those who
have been issued temporary visas to those who were foreign-born

but have since become U.S. citizens. It is certainly worth noting that many immigrants who are otherwise undocumented may have the right to remain in the United States "based upon a claim of asylum, Temporary Protected Status, or another form of immigration relief" (NOLO, 2019).

Latin America is generally defined as those countries located from south of the U.S.-Mexico border to the southernmost extremity of the continent of South America (McKeown, 2017). According to the Public Policy Institute of California (2017), 78% of all undocumented immigrants in the United States are from Latin America. Undocumented Latin American immigrants, who comprise a large segment of the population in many communities across the United States, face additional challenges relative to their legal citizenship status and the real or perceived lack of available emergency management information and resources (Fussell & Diaz, 2015; Tiefenbacher & Wilson, 2012). The cumulative impact of the aforementioned challenges in the undocumented Latin American community is that "they are disadvantaged when preparing for the onset of disaster, for evacuation, when looking for response and recovery resources, and during the post-disaster period (Tiefenbacher & Wilson, 2012, p. 195). It is also important to note that Latin American and other minority communities often have strong social capital and relationships that increase resilience. However, catastrophic risk can strain those relationships beyond what they can support (Jerolleman, 2019).

Several studies have addressed cultural competency and emergency management in Latin American communities across the United States. Peguero (2006) found that in Florida, Spanish-speaking Latin American homeowners preferred to obtain information regarding hurricanes from friends and family rather than government officials. The author ultimately recommends that "emergency managers and community leaders should utilize social, family, and kin networks to disseminate hazard, emergency, and hurricane mitigation information" (Peguero, 2006, p. 18). In Carter-Pokras et al. (2007), the authors found Latin American communities in Washington, D.C., to be particularly at risk because of their location (large, urban, segregated areas) and at a unique disadvantage during emergencies because of their level of isolation and lack of access to information.

Latin American participants in the study made a number of recommendations to the researchers, including that public agencies begin offering emergency management training opportunities and providing additional economic resources in their community (Carter-Pokras et al., 2007, p. 473).

Other studies have focused specifically on undocumented Latin Americans. In their study regarding the undocumented Latin American community in Texas following Hurricane Ike (2008), Tiefenbacher and Wilson (2012) found them to be "ultra-marginalized" during emergencies as a result of a number of factors, most notably because of their lack of legal standing and political influence. The authors highlighted the need for emergency management professionals to improve upon "emergency communication to undocumented immigrant populations, especially in regions of the United States where higher levels of hazard require concerted collective community action" (Tiefenbacher & Wilson, 2012, p. 209).

New Orleans, an extremely vulnerable community on the Gulf Coast, has also been the subject of similar studies. Andrulis, Siddiqui, and Gantner (2007) found that minorities in New Orleans were at greater risk during Hurricane Katrina because of a lack of cultural competency or a risk communication strategy from public officials leading up to the event. Compounding matters in New Orleans, it has been estimated that 77% of undocumented workers living in the city as of 2007 had actually arrived after Hurricane Katrina (Fletcher, Pham, Stover, & Vinck, 2007). This new influx of undocumented residents reflects an even greater need for cultural competence in emergency management around the New Orleans metropolitan area, particularly in managing the City-Assisted Evacuation program.

The Latin American community in the New Orleans metropolitan area grew significantly between 2000 and 2013. According to the U.S. Census Bureau (2013), Latin Americans as a percentage of overall population increased from 4.4% (2000) to 8.3% (2013) and more than 50,000 foreign-born Latin Americans were residing in the area as of 2013. Additionally, the U.S. Census Bureau (2013) found that 64.4% of all foreign-born people residing in the New Orleans metropolitan area speak English "less than very well." Although the growth of the Latin American population in the area between

2000–2013 is significant, it is worth noting the actual number of undocumented Latin Americans who relocated to the New Orleans area following Hurricane Katrina is likely much higher (Fussell & Diaz, 2015).

Evacuation poses many challenges, even for those who have access to vehicles, because it can require a significant time and financial investment. For example, families must pay for gas; account for increased traffic, which increases drive times; and be able to either arrive at a state-operated shelter, stay with relatives/family, or pay for lodging. This is simply not feasible for many families.

Case Study: Meeting the Needs of a Growing Minority Population: The Undocumented Latin American Community in Post-Katrina New Orleans

Goals of the Study

The goal of the exercise is to discuss ways in which to include the undocumented Latin American population in emergency management planning in a major U.S. city through a fictional case study. In attempting to relate the fictional setting to the real world, this extreme situation aids in uncovering biases, stereotypes, and preconceived notions, which will influence the role of an emergency manager.

Learning Outcomes

◆ Participants will demonstrate greater understanding of the unique challenges faced by a community such as the undocumented Latin American community in the city of New Orleans.

◆ Participants will identify strategies for building relationships, trust, and understanding with at-risk communities.

◆ Participants will demonstrate comprehension of how their assumptions about the homogeneity of the community they serve impacts their role as an emergency manager via pre- and post-test assessment tools.

Definitions

♦ City-Assisted Evacuation: An evacuation program led by the city of New Orleans in which individuals are given transportation to state-run shelters.

♦ Culture Brokers: Trusted individuals within a community with local knowledge and relationships.

♦ Undocumented Immigrants: "Foreign nationals residing in the US without legal immigration status" (U.S. Legal, n.d). Some immigrants who are otherwise undocumented may have the right to remain in the U.S. "based upon a claim of asylum, Temporary Protected status, or another form of immigration relief" (NOLO, 2019).

♦ Documented Immigrants: Those foreign nationals who have a legal right to be or remain in the United States including individuals ranging from those who have been issued temporary visas to those who were foreign-born but have since become U.S. citizens.

Break-Down

♦ Divide into groups of four to five people.

♦ Discuss the ground rules to set the tone.

♦ Review the scenario and the group's discussion questions.

♦ Allow ample time for discussion (approximately 45 minutes).

♦ Facilitate group dialogue about responses to questions.

♦ Utilize supplemental questions if needed.

Ground Rules (Gorski, 2019)

1. Listen actively – respect others when they are talking
2. Speak from your own experience instead of generalizing ("I" instead of "they," "we," and "you").
3. Do not be afraid to respectfully challenge one another by asking questions but refrain from personal attacks – focus on ideas.

4. Participate to the fullest of your ability – community growth depends on the inclusion of every individual voice.
5. Instead of invalidating somebody else's story with your own spin on their experience, share your own story and experience.
6. The goal is not to agree – it is to gain a deeper understanding.
7. Be conscious of body language and nonverbal responses – they can be as disrespectful as words.

Supplemental Questions
1. What are your first thoughts about this scenario? Did you have any emotional reactions to this scenario? If yes, why? If no, why?
2. Was there anything thought provoking about how your fellow participants reacted to this exercise? (Please use generalizations and avoid attacking the beliefs of any of your peers).
3. What would your reaction to this exercise be if you had been raised as a Latin American immigrant?

The Undocumented Latin American Community in Post-Katrina New Orleans

The Situation
The city of New Orleans is at risk from hurricanes and flooding, both of which require a range of preparedness actions as well as occasional evacuation.

You are tasked with ensuring that the vehicle-less population of the city, as well as those who cannot afford to evacuate on their own, are able to safely evacuate the city in the event of a hurricane. The city maintains a *city-assisted evacuation* list, but you have struggled to identify all of the families who will require assistance. You are aware that the Latin American population, particularly those who are undocumented, is unwilling to register and will be at risk.

A hurricane has formed in the Gulf of Mexico, and it appears that a mandatory evacuation order may need to be issued within the next 24 hours. The center of the storm is located just north of Cuba and is slowly moving west-northwest toward New Orleans. It is anticipated that the hurricane will make landfall near New Orleans in approximately 96 hours, the time frame at which evacuation planning must begin given the need to also evacuate many persons closer to the coast.

The Responders

- ◆ Evacuteer, a local nonprofit organization, is under contract with the city of New Orleans to support the creation of an evacuation registry as well as to manage the city-assisted evacuation and related volunteers.
- ◆ Local churches, community organizations, and advocacy groups have a long history of working with the local Latin American population.
- ◆ The New Orleans Office of Homeland Security and Emergency Preparedness has a volunteer coordinator tasked with working with local nonprofits.
- ◆ The mayor will issue a mandatory evacuation order within the next day.

Things to Know

- ◆ The estimated population in the New Orleans metropolitan area was 1,270,399 in 2018. There were 115,396 Latin Americans in the metro area as of 2017, representing 9% of the total population. As previously discussed, this figure likely does not account for all Latin Americans residing the in the metro area, including undocumented residents. The two largest known populations are from Honduras (33%) and Mexico

(21%) (The Data Center, 2019). The exact percentage that is undocumented is unknown but estimated to be significant.

◆ Families can register with the city-assisted evacuation and/or special needs registry by calling 311 or visiting ready.nola.gov, a service managed by the city's Office of Homeland Security and Emergency Preparedness.

◆ Announcements regarding mandatory evacuations are made over local media and are primarily disseminated in English.

◆ Evacuating the city can require a significant time and financial investment. Families must pay for gas; account for increased traffic, which increases drive times; and be able to either arrive at a state-operated shelter, stay with relatives/family, or pay for lodging.

◆ The state operates mega-shelters in central and north Louisiana, the closest about two hours from New Orleans, and the farthest in Shreveport, about six hours away.

◆ Employers do not always allow their employees to leave ahead of a hurricane, because they wish to remain operational until the last minute. Hourly employees lose wages, and some may lose their jobs.

◆ Those who chose to use the city-assisted evacuation program must register before getting on the buses and will not know where they are being sent.

◆ Undocumented families, and those with undocu-mented relatives, are afraid that registering with the city will put them at risk of deportation.

◆ Much of the immediate disaster recovery work will begin before the time frame in which those who have evacuated can readily return.

Your Role

You are the emergency manager for the city of New Orleans and are responsible for ensuring the safety of all residents, regardless of legal status. You have convened local partners to identify the best path forward to ensure a safe and complete evacuation.

Questions for Discussion

1. How can you best engage with the Latin American population?
2. What steps could have been taken before the evacuation order that might have made working with this community easier?
3. Who might you partner with?
4. What unique needs does the Latin American population have?
5. What are the key tasks that you need to accomplish?
6. What resources do you have available?

Pre-Test Assessment

PURPOSE OF THE SURVEY

This assessment survey is designed to demonstrate understanding of cultural competence–related aspects and establish a baseline of participant attitudes before the exercise.

DEMOGRAPHICS

What is your age? _____

What is your gender? _____

DEFINITIONS

Directions: Please match the terminologies with their definitions.

_____ City-Assisted Evacuation   A.   An evacuation program led by the city of New Orleans in which individuals are given transportation to state-run shelters.

_____ Culture Brokers   B.   Trusted individuals within a community with local knowledge and relationships.

_____ Undocumented Immigrants   C.   "Foreign nationals residing in the US without legal immigration status" (U.S. Legal, n.d).

_____ Documented Immigrants   D.   Those foreign nationals who have a legal right to be or remain in the United States, including individuals ranging from those who have been issued temporary visas to those who were foreign-born but have since become U.S. citizens.

ATTITUDINAL SCALE

Directions: Please use the following scale to represent your reaction to the questions.

1	2	3	4	5
Strongly Agree	Agree	Neither Agree nor Disagree	Disagree	Strongly Disagree

1. I believe personal culture influences my role(s).

2. I believe cultural groups influence my role(s).

3. I believe stereotypes influence my role(s).

4. I believe I have adequate knowledge of how my own cultural identities influence my role(s).

5. I believe I have adequate knowledge of other cultures and their influence on my role(s).

6. I believe I have adequate knowledge of stereotypes and their influence on my role(s).

7. I believe I have adequate knowledge of my cultural identities and their influence on emergency and crisis management.

8. I believe I have adequate knowledge of other cultural identities and how they influence emergency and crisis management.

9. I believe I have adequate knowledge of stereotypes and how they influence emergency and crisis management.

Post-Test Assessment

PURPOSE OF THE SURVEY

This assessment survey is designed to demonstrate understanding of culturally related impacts and establish a baseline of participant attitudes after the exercise.

DEFINITIONS

Directions: Please match the terminologies with their definitions.

_____ City-Assisted Evacuation A. An evacuation program led by the city of New Orleans in which individuals are given transportation to state-run shelters.

_____ Culture Brokers B. Trusted individuals within a community with local knowledge and relationships.

_____ Undocumented Immigrants C. "Foreign nationals residing in the US without legal immigration status" (U.S. Legal, n.d).

_____ Documented Immigrants D. Those foreign nationals who have a legal right to be or remain in the United States, including individuals ranging from those who have been issued temporary visas to those who were foreign-born but have since become U.S. citizens.

ATTITUDINAL SCALE

Directions: Please use the following scale to represent your reaction to the questions.

1	2	3	4	5
Strongly Agree	Agree	Neither Agree nor Disagree	Disagree	Strongly Disagree

1. I believe personal culture influences my role(s).

2. I believe cultural groups influence my role(s).

3. I believe stereotypes influence my role(s).

4. I believe I have adequate knowledge of how my own cultural identities influence my role(s).

5. I believe I have adequate knowledge of other cultures and their influence on my role(s).

6. I believe I have adequate knowledge of stereotypes and their influence on my role(s).

7. I believe I have adequate knowledge of my cultural identities and their influence on emergency and crisis management.

8. I believe I have adequate knowledge of other cultural identities and how they influence emergency and crisis management.

9. I believe I have adequate knowledge of stereotypes and how they influence emergency and crisis management.

OPEN RESPONSE

Please answer the following question: "I used to think_____, but now I think _____."

(Use back of page if needing extra space.)

References

Andrulis, D. P., Siddiqui, N. J., & Gantner, J. L. (2007). Preparing racially and ethnically diverse communities for public health emergencies. *Health Affairs, 26,* 1269–1279.

Carter-Pokras, O., Zambrana, R. E., Mora, S. E., & Aaby, K. A. (2007). Emergency preparedness: Knowledge and perceptions of Latin American immigrants. *Journal of Health Care for the Poor and Underserved, 18*(2), 465–481.

The Data Center. (2019). *Who lives in New Orleans and metro parishes now?* Retrieved from www.datacenterresearch.org/data-resources/who-lives-in-new-orleans-now/

Fletcher, L. E., Pham, P., Stover, E., & Vinck, P. (2007). *Latino workers and human rights in the aftermath of Hurricane Katrina.* Retrieved from https://scholarship.law.berkeley.edu/facpubs/639/

Fussell, E., & Diaz, L. (2015). *Latinos in Metro New Orleans: Progress, problems, and potential.* Retrieved from https://s3.amazonaws.com/gnocdc/reports/The+Data+Center_NOI10_Latinos+in+New+Orleans.pdf

Gorski, P. C. (2019). *Guide for setting ground rules.* Retrieved from www.edchange.org/multicultural/activities/groundrules.html

Jerolleman, A. (2019). *Disaster recovery through the lens of justice.* Switzerland: Palgrave Pivot.

McKeown, M. (2017). *What is Latin America? Geography, language, and culture explained.* Retrieved from https://owlcation.com/social-sciences/What-is-Latin-America

NOLO. (2019). *Who is an undocumented Immigrant?* Retrieved from www.nolo.com/legal-encyclopedia/who-is-undocumented-immigrant.html

Peguero, A. (2006). Latino disaster vulnerability: The dissemination of hurricane mitigation information Among Florida's Homeowners. *Hispanic Journal of Behavioral Science, 28*(1), 5–22.

Public Policy Institute of California. (2017). *Undocumented immigrants in California.* Retrieved from www.ppic.org/publication/undocumented-immigrants-in-california/

Tiefenbacher, J., & Wilson, S. (2012). The barriers impeding precautionary behaviors by undocumented immigrants in emergencies: The Hurricane Ike experience in Houston, Texas. *Environmental Hazards: Human and Policy Dimensions, 11*(3), 194–212.

U.S. Census Bureau. (2013). *American community survey, 2005–2013.* Retrieved from www.census.gov/programs-surveys/acs/

U.S. Legal. (n.d.). *Undocumented immigrant law and legal definition.* Retrieved from https://definitions.uslegal.com/u/undocumented-immigrant/

7

Wildfires and Homelessness in the United States

Brittany "Brie" Haupt

Overview

Wildfires can be caused by lightning, human agents (e.g., arson, campfires, bonfires, discarded cigarettes, etc.), and prescribed events gone awry, such as controlled burns (Federal Emergency Management Agency [FEMA], 2018a). These devastating natural disasters leave death, destruction, and devastation in their wake. The intimidating aspect of these disasters is their uncontrollable nature, as even "controlled" burns can surpass their boundary and negatively affect their environment (FEMA, 2018a; National Disaster Education Coalition, 1999).

Certain conditions heighten the risk of wildfires: fuel, air, and heat sources. Fuel consists of flammable materials that surround a strong flame, such as brush, grass, trees, debris, chemicals, and even buildings. Within the United States, California is considered the most wildfire-prone state because of their fuel load risk (Wolters, 2019). Air not only consists of the oxygen that feeds the fire and increases its severity, but also produces wind currents that can carry sparks for miles. Heat sources assist in sparking the fire and raising temperatures to ignite. The heat sources connect to natural elements, like lightning and sun exposure, and human agents. These elements create a fire triangle, leading to fires anywhere and at any time. In terms of geographical "hot spots," Western states have a higher risk because of the conditions of heat, drought, and frequent thunderstorms (FEMA, 2018a; Wolters, 2019). However, only 10% to 15% of wildfires begin in nature. The startling fact is that 85% to 90% of wildfires are a result of human agents (Wolters, 2019).

Along with the fire triangle, there are three different types of wildfires to be aware of. The first, and most common, is a "surface fire," which wreaks havoc along forest floors in slow progressions, resulting in damaging and killing trees. Second is a "ground fire" that is typically ignited by lightning and burns deeper into the forest floor to the mineral soil. The last type is a "crown fire" and is rapidly spread by the wind, allowing it to jump through the trees (National Disaster Education Coalition, 1999).

Taking into consideration death tolls, acres burned, and financial impact, the National Interagency Coordination Center at the National Interagency Fire Center has compiled wildland fire statistics since 1983, along with researchers that investigate historical reports to discern impact starting with the 1871 Great Michigan Fire (Hultquist, 2019; National Interagency Fire Center, 2019). Table 7.1 lists some of the most devastating wildfires in U.S. history. The statistics in the table indicate more than one billion acres burned as a result of approximately 11 million fires across the United States.

An aspect of wildfire impact is on the human element and the intersection of risk and vulnerability. Experts discuss ways to reduce or prevent wildfire impact through implementation of fire prevention such as these:

◆ Use of non-combustible or fire-resistant materials in property construction
◆ Removal of excess debris (leaves, brush, branches, etc.)
◆ Regular tree maintenance
◆ Proper storage of flammable materials and chemicals
◆ Knowledge of evacuation routes and exit strategies (National Interagency Fire Center, 2019)

TABLE 7.1 Major U.S. Fires and Impact

Fire	Date	Acres Burned	Lives Lost	Property Damage
The Great Peshtigo Fire of Wisconsin/Michigan	October 1871	3.7 million	As many as 2,700	3,000 buildings destroyed
Hinckley Fire of Minnesota	September 1894	160,000	418, with potential of hundreds of Native Americans	Unknown
The Big Burn of the Northern Rockies	August 1910	3 million	87	Estimated $1 billion in timber
Cloquet Fire of Minnesota	October 1918	1.2 million	More than 450	$73 million
The Great Fires of Maine 1947	October – November 1947	More than 200,000	At least 15	854 homes; $50–$100 million in damages
Mann Gulch Fire in Helena National Forest, Montana	August 1949	4,500 (3,000 consumed within 10 minutes)	13 firefighters (including 12 smokejumpers)	Unknown
The Coyote Fire of Santa Barbara, California	September- October 1964	67,000	1 dead, 227 injured	157 structures; $5.7 million in damages
Esperanza Fire of Cbazon, California	October 2006	40,200	5 firefighters	54 structures; $9 million
Trigo Fire of New Mexico	April–May 2008	Nearly 14,000	Unknown	59 homes; $11 million containment cost
California Fire Siege	Summer 2008	1.2 million by autumn	13 firefighters	Unknown
2011 Texas Wildfire Season	November 2010 – October 2011	4,011,709	Unknown	Unknown
Yarnell Hill Fire of Arizona	June 2013	More than 8,000	19 firefighters	Unknown
Tubbs Fire of Santa Rosa, California	October 2017	More than 36,800	22 individuals	Thousands of homes
Oakland Hills Fire of Oakland, California	October 1991	1,520 acres	25 people	$1.5 billion in damages
Camp Fire of Butte County, California	November 2018	153,336 acres	85 people	$7.5–$10 billion in damages

Source: Mitrokostas, 2019; National Disaster Education Coalition, 1999; National Interagency Fire Center, 2019; Public Broadcasting Station, 2019.

Although these are invaluable recommendations, there are other aspects to risk and vulnerabilities that are broader societal issues, such as socioeconomic status and environmental hazards (Cutter, 1996; Eriksen & Simon, 2017; Gaither et al., 2011; Paton & Tedim, 2012; Rauh, Landrigan, & Claudio, 2008). Within this intersection exists a specific population vulnerable to all of the components: the homeless. The term "vulnerability" refers to the demographic and socioeconomic factors that affect community resilience (Cutter, Boruff, & Shirley, 2003; Flanagan, Gregory, Hallisey, Heitgerd, & Lewis, 2011). The homeless population is considered at risk because they lack stable sheltering, finances, and transportation.

Homeless individuals also experience issues when it comes to recovering from a disaster, as they are ineligible for most aid organizations. In terms of FEMA, disaster aid is not provided to individuals who were considered homeless before a disaster (Drury, Olson, & Van Belle, 2005; Ehrlich, 2019; Phillips, 1996; Sar, 1995). The ineligibility links to policies that dictate aid distribution. The Stafford Act, enacted in 1988, specifically outlines how federal aid can be spent and does not include aid to homeless individuals who were not generated as a result of the disaster itself. The Emergency Food and Shelter National Board Program, a product of the McKinney-Vento Homeless Assistance Act of 1987, attempted to address this need but focuses on organizations that aid the homeless vs. the individuals themselves (FEMA, 2018b).

Policy Director for the National Low Income Housing Coalition, Sarah Mickelson stated:

> FEMA programs were designed with white, middle-class families in mind, and the agency fails to address the needs of people who don't fall into that category. For instance, FEMA's transitional shelter program provides motels to people after a disaster. But sometimes there are too few participating hotels, or they're far from where people work, or disaster victims don't have a credit card for the hotel's daily fees.
>
> (Ehrlich, 2019, para. 19)

In addition to these issues, wildfires lead to an increase in numbers because of the loss of homes and businesses. Ehrlich (2019) indicated a 20% increase in homelessness after the 2018 Carr Fire in California.

California has attempted to generate more policies focused on warning and preparation specific to homeless populations. In Los Angeles, a bill was proposed to adjust warning processes from just posting notifications during peak risk periods to more engaged attempts of verbally warning homeless individuals at the start of wildfire season and being more proactive at finding the remote areas where individuals live (Oreskes, 2019).

The unfortunate reality is researchers and practitioners have advocated for more proactive measures for decades, and the battle rages on. Homelessness is an extreme state of poverty, and the harsh reality of wildfire impact is not a negligible connection (Center for Watershed and Community Health & Hatfield, 2001). It is imperative for emergency and crisis managers to understand this connection and integrate understanding, knowledge, and innovative solutions into practice.

Case Study: Wildfire in Whitewater County

Brittany "Brie" Haupt, Ph.D.

Overview of the Context

This case study is futuristic in its setting and is located in a fictional place so as to assess what information the participants will bring in to help them understand the situation. Many participants will assume a governance structure similar to their local or national identity along with social norms and beliefs. Although the case study is intended to see what participants add, the author was influenced by wildfires along the U.S. West Coast, along with challenges faced by homeless populations in urban environments.

Goals of the Case Study

The goal of the exercise is to discuss diversity-related issues through a fictional case study. In attempting to relate the fictional setting to the real world, this extreme situation aids in uncovering biases, stereotypes, and preconceived notions, which will influence the role of an emergency manager.

Learning Outcomes
- ◆ Participants will demonstrate greater understanding of the terms "bias", "stereotypes", and "preconceived notions" via pre- and post-test assessment tools.
- ◆ Participants will demonstrate comprehension of how the aforementioned terms influence their role as an emergency manager via pre- and post-test assessment tools.

Definitions
- ◆ Fuel: Consists of flammable materials that surround a strong flame, such as brush, grass, trees, debris, chemicals, and even buildings.
- ◆ Air: Consists of the oxygen to feed the fire, increases its severity, and produces wind currents that can carry sparks for miles.
- ◆ Heat Sources: Assist in sparking the fire and raising temperatures to ignite. The heat sources connect to natural elements, like lightning and sun exposure, and human agents.
- ◆ Fire Triangle: The combination of fuel, air, and heat sources leading to conditions for wildfires.
- ◆ Surface Fire: The most common fire; wreaks havoc along forest floors in slow progressions, resulting in damaging and killing trees.
- ◆ Ground Fire: Typically ignited by lightning; burns deeper into the forest floor to the mineral soil.
- ◆ Crown Fire: Rapidly spread by the wind, allowing it to jump through the trees.
- ◆ Homeless Population: At risk because of lack of stable sheltering, finances, and transportation.

◆ Social Vulnerability: The demographic and socioeconomic factors that impact community resilience.

Breakdown
◆ Divide into groups of four to five people.
◆ Discuss the ground rules to set the tone.
◆ Review the scenario and the group's discussion questions.
◆ Allow ample time for discussion (approximately 45 minutes).
◆ Facilitate group dialogue about responses to questions
◆ Utilize supplemental questions if needed.

Ground Rules (Gorski, 2019)
◆ Listen actively – respect others when they are talking.
◆ Speak from your own experience instead of generalizing ("I" instead of "they," "we," and "you").
◆ Do not be afraid to respectfully challenge one another by asking questions but refrain from personal attacks – focus on ideas.
◆ Participate to the fullest of your ability – community growth depends on the inclusion of every individual voice.
◆ Instead of invalidating somebody else's story with your own spin on their experience, share your own story and experience.
◆ The goal is not to agree – it is to gain a deeper understanding.
◆ Be conscious of body language and nonverbal responses – they can be as disrespectful as words.

Facilitator Notes
Participant responses will vary as some participants will divulge private information about their identity while others will refrain from self-reflection. This activity presents an opportunity for critical dialogue; facilitators must be aware and guide the exercise with sensitivity.

Supplemental Questions

1. What are your first thoughts about this scenario? Did you have any emotional reactions to this scenario? If yes, why? If no, why?
2. Was there anything thought provoking about how your fellow participants reacted to this exercise? (Please use generalizations and do not target others.)
3. What would your reaction to this exercise be if you had been raised as a member in one of the groups?
4. How do you think this scenario relates to emergency management? Why was this exercise created?

Breaking News: Disaster in Whitewater

The Situation

At 10:30 a.m. on December 2, 2021, the head responder contacts you concerning a tragedy that is occurring within Whitewater County. Despite a ban on outdoor burning, campers in the Snowmont mountain campground started a bonfire that has begun making its way closer to the downtown area. Approximately 15 individuals have been marked as casualties as responders hurry to contain the flame. With the wind direction, the fire is predicted to hit the downtown area in an hour.

The city alarm systems sounded, calling for evacuation of the nearby buildings and inhabitants of downtown.

The Responders

◆ Firefighters are working to put out the fire and help evacuate.
◆ Security personnel are attempting to evacuate all buildings and shut down the power grid.

◆ Leaders are traveling back from a nearby state, but they are unable to assist in decision-making and procedures.

◆ Transients are crowding the area, trying to help.

Things to Know

◆ Whitewater has approximately 100,000 inhabitants living downtown.

◆ The alarm systems do not extend throughout all the downtown area.

◆ The Crisis Response Team is gridlocked trying to get to the hot zone.

◆ A large population of homeless individuals reside within the downtown area and in a tent city between the fire and downtown.

◆ Residents have been steadily making their way out of the area; however, there are numerous reports of car crashes blocking the roads.

◆ The Crisis Response Team only has access to shelters sufficient to house up to 8,000 citizens.

◆ Riots have begun.

◆ The Crisis Response Team has access to approximately 100 emergency responders, 45 of whom are battling the fire and 35 who are trying to quell the riots and resolve the gridlock.

Your Role

You are a member of the Crisis Response Team and have gathered with the rest of the group to discuss the next steps.

Questions for Discussion

1. Who do you assist first? Who do you assist next?
2. How do you divide your resources?
3. What are tasks you need to accomplish?
4. Who are your stakeholders?

Pre-Test Assessment

PURPOSE OF THE SURVEY

This assessment survey is designed to demonstrate understanding of cultural competence–related aspects and establish a baseline of participant attitudes before the exercise.

DEFINITIONS

Directions: Please match the terminologies with their definitions.

_____	Homeless Population	A.	An at-risk population because of a lack of stable sheltering, finances, and transportation.
_____	Fire Triangle	B.	The combination of fuel, air, and heat sources leading to conditions for wildfires.
_____	Social Vulnerability	C.	The demographic and socioeconomic factors that impact community resilience.

ATTITUDINAL SCALE

Directions: Please use the following scale to represent your reaction to the questions.

1	2	3	4	5
Strongly Agree	Agree	Neither Agree nor Disagree	Disagree	Strongly Disagree

1. I believe personal culture influences my role(s).

2. I believe cultural groups influence my role(s).

3. I believe stereotypes influence my role(s).

4. I believe I have adequate knowledge of how my own cultural identities influence my role(s).

5. I believe I have adequate knowledge of other cultures and their influence on my role(s).

6. I believe I have adequate knowledge of stereotypes and their influence on my role(s).

7. I believe I have adequate knowledge of my cultural identities and their influence on emergency and crisis management.

8. I believe I have adequate knowledge of other cultural identities and how they influence emergency and crisis management.

9. I believe I have adequate knowledge of stereotypes and how they influence emergency and crisis management.

Post-Test Assessment

PURPOSE OF THE SURVEY

This assessment survey is designed to demonstrate understanding of culturally related impacts and establish baseline of participant attitudes after the exercise.

DEFINITIONS

Directions: Please match the terminologies with their definitions.

_____	Homeless Population	A.	An at-risk population because of a lack of stable sheltering, finances, and transportation.
_____	Fire Triangle	B.	The combination of fuel, air, and heat sources leading to conditions for wildfires.
_____	Social Vulnerability	C.	The demographic and socioeconomic factors that impact community resilience.

ATTITUDINAL SCALE

Directions: Please use the following scale to represent your reaction to the questions.

1	2	3	4	5
Strongly Agree	Agree	Neither Agree nor Disagree	Disagree	Strongly Disagree

1. I believe personal culture influences my role(s).

2. I believe cultural groups influence my role(s).

3. I believe stereotypes influence my role(s).

4. I believe I have adequate knowledge of how my own cultural identities influence my role(s).

5. I believe I have adequate knowledge of other cultures and their influence on my role(s).

6. I believe I have adequate knowledge of stereotypes and their influence on my role(s).

7. I believe I have adequate knowledge of my cultural identities and their influence on emergency and crisis management.

8. I believe I have adequate knowledge of other cultural identities and how they influence emergency and crisis management.

9. I believe I have adequate knowledge of stereotypes and how they influence emergency and crisis management.

OPEN RESPONSE

Please answer the following question: "I used to think_____, but now I think_____."

(Use back of page if needing extra space.)

References

Center for Watershed and Community Health, & Hatfield, M. (2001). *Wildfires and poverty: An overview of the interactions among wildfires, fire-related programs, and poverty in the western states*. Retrieved from https://scholarsbank.uoregon.edu/xmlui/bitstream/handle/1794/2334/wild_pov.pdf?sequence=1

Cutter, S. L. (1996). Vulnerability to environmental hazards. *Progress in Human Geography*, *20*(4), 529–539.

Cutter, S. L., Boruff, B. J., & Shirley, W. L. (2003). Social vulnerability to environmental hazards. *Social Science Quarterly*, *84*(2), 242–261.

Drury, A. C., Olson, R. S., & Van Belle, D. A. (2005). The politics of humanitarian aid: US foreign disaster assistance, 1964–1995. *The Journal of Politics*, *67*(2), 454–473.

Ehrlich, A. (2019). *After wildfires, homeless people left out of federal disaster aid programs*. Retrieved from www.opb.org/news/article/fema-disaster-aid-wildfires-homeless-people/

Eriksen, C., & Simon, G. (2017). The affluence-vulnerability interface: Intersecting scales of risk, privilege and disaster. *Environment and Planning A: Economy and Space*, *49*(2), 293–313.

Federal Emergency Management Agency (FEMA). (2018a). *Wildfire information sheet: Be prepared for a wildfire*. Retrieved from www.fema.gov/media-library/assets/documents/162063

Federal Emergency Management Agency (FEMA). (2018b). *Emergency food and shelter national board program*. Retrieved from www.fema.gov/media-library/assets/documents/24422

Flanagan, B. E., Gregory, E. W., Hallisey, E. J., Heitgerd, J. L., & Lewis, B. (2011). A social vulnerability index for disaster management. *Journal of Homeland Security and Emergency Management*, *8*(1).

Gaither, C. J., Poudyal, N. C., Goodrick, S., Bowker, J. M., Malone, S., & Gan, J. (2011). Wildland fire risk and social vulnerability in the Southeastern United States: An exploratory spatial data analysis approach. *Forest Policy and Economics*, *13*(1), 24–36.

Gorski, P. C. (2019). *Guide for setting ground rules*. Retrieved from www.edchange.org/multicultural/activities/groundrules.html

Hultquist, T. (2019). *National Weather Service: The great Midwest wildfires of 1871*. Retrieved from www.weather.gov/grb/peshtigofire2

Mitrokostas, S. (2019). *The 10 deadliest wildfires in US history.* Retrieved from www.businessinsider.com/the-deadliest-wildfires-in-us-history-2019-2

National Disaster Education Coalition. (1999). *Talking about disaster: Guide for standard messages.* Retrieved from www.disastercenter.com/guide/wildfire.html

National Interagency Fire Center. (2019). *Total wildland fires and acres (1926–2018).* Retrieved from www.nifc.gov/fireInfo/fireInfo_stats_totalFires.html

Oreskes, B. (2019). *To prevent wildfires, L.A. wants to make it easier to clear homeless encampments.* Retrieved from www.latimes.com/california/story/2019-08-21/homeless-encampment-wildfire-city-council-high-risk-fire

Paton, D., & Tedim, F. (2012). *Wildfire and community: Facilitating preparedness and resilience.* Springfield, IL: Charles C Thomas Publisher.

Phillips, B. D. (1996). Creating, sustaining, and losing place: Homelessness in the context of disaster. *Humanity & Society, 20*(1), 94–101.

Public Broadcasting Station. (2019). *The big burn: America's most devastating wildfires.* Retrieved from www.pbs.org/wgbh/americanexperience/features/burn-worst-fires/

Rauh, V. A., Landrigan, P. J., & Claudio, L. (2008). Housing and health: Intersection of poverty and environmental exposures. *Annals of the New York Academy of Sciences, 1136*(1), 276–288.

Sar, D. W. (1995). Helping hands: Aid for natural disaster homeless vs. aid for ordinary homeless. *Stanford Law & Policy Review, 7*, 129.

Wolters, A. (2019). *National geographic: Wildfires, explained.* Retrieved from www.nationalgeographic.com/environment/natural-disasters/wildfires/

8

Disaster Shelter Planning for Special Needs Populations

Susan Spice

Overview

In a natural disaster, having a disability can be deadly (Hatch, 2018). According to the Centers for Disease Control (CDC) (2015), medical disabilities may include physical, cognitive, or sensory impairment that limits a person's major life activities. These conditions may limit the person's ability to "hear, understand, or respond to a warning" (CDC, 2015, p. 3). In the United States, 10.6% of the population between the ages of 16 and 64 and 35.2% of the population aged 65 and older has a disability that impairs their ability to perform major life activities (Institute on Disability, 2017). As of 2016, one in four U.S. adults reported a medical disability related to mobility (13.7%), cognition (10.8%), independent living (6.8%), hearing (5.9%), vision (4.6%), and self-care (3.7%) (CDC, 2018). The possibility that an individual will experience either a temporary or permanent disability in their lifetime increases with age (CDC, 2015). It is important to remember that not all disabilities require medical intervention, nor does everyone with a disability qualify for special needs sheltering.

Regardless of the type of natural disaster, survival presents additional challenges to those with disabilities. Hemingway and

Priestly (2014) suggest that the barriers for those with disabilities face during disasters mirror the barriers they face in everyday life in terms of access to facilities or information. For example, without sign language interpreters and/or closed-captioned televisions, deaf and hard-of-hearing individuals have difficulty accessing information regarding evacuation and/or sheltering (White, 2014). Issues with mobility, vision, hearing, communication, and cognitive challenges, among others, may make it difficult for an individual to understand and respond to the need to evacuate and the ability to maintain independence while sheltering.

Visible disabilities, such as using a wheelchair or a cane, are commonly what come to mind with the term "disability". Emergency management planners need to be aware of invisible disabilities such as "heart disease, emotional or psychiatric conditions, arthritis, significant allergies, asthma, multiple chemical sensitivities, respiratory conditions, and some visual, hearing, and cognitive disabilities" (Kailes, 2005, p. 7). These conditions may be chronic and inhibit a person's ability to move without assistance, cause fatigue, and reduce stamina. Some conditions may inhibit a person's ability to understand and follow directions and commands, while others may affect a person's ability to communicate. Some conditions may be temporary as the result of an accident or operation (Kailes, 2005). People with disabilities are all ages, races, and genders, and they may have one or a combination of conditions. Some individuals aged 65 and over are physically fit, and some are medically frail. Shelter planners need to be aware of the types of disabilities that manifest in their communities.

Sheltering

Before we proceed, it is also important to understand that there are three levels of disaster sheltering: evacuation shelters, short-term shelters, and long-term shelters. Evacuation shelters are meant to be used for up to 72 hours and include minimal services and amenities. Shelters are considered short term if they are in use after 72 hours and up to two weeks (Federal Emergency Management Agency [FEMA], 2017a). Longer than two weeks is considered a long-term shelter. "[T]he primary distinction between Short- and Long-Term Shelters are per-person considerations, range of services provided, and the sustainment of those services over a long period of time" (FEMA, 2017b, p. 2).

There are also different categories for evacuees. Evacuees are individuals who need to move from danger or a disaster area to somewhere safe. The term "general population evacuee" applies to individuals who are self-evacuees – this means they have the ability and resources to evacuate in the event it is necessary. If they require some form of transportation assistance to evacuate, they would be considered critical transportation needs evacuees. Patient evacuees would apply to individuals in the care of "Emergency Medical Services (e.g., prehospital emergency care, community para-medicine/mobile integrated healthcare), inpatient healthcare facilities (e.g., hospital, skilled nursing facility/nursing home, psychiatric facility), and outpatient healthcare services (e.g., home healthcare, dialysis, ambulatory surgery) prior to, during, or after a disaster" (FEMA, 2018, p. 9). Many patient evacuees can shelter with general populations. Service animal evacuees are service animals that evacuate with their owners to either a general population or special needs population.[1]

General population shelters provide minimal services and amenities. According to one County Emergency Manager, "The shelter is a lifeboat; it's not a cruise ship" (Spice, 2017, p. 78). These temporary shelters provide potable water, food, and a place to sleep. According to FEMA (2017c), planners should estimate 20 square feet per evacuee in general population shelters. More space may be needed to reasonably accommodate Americans with Disabilities Act (ADA)–related requirements and/or functional needs, assistance animals, and access (FEMA, 2017c). Evacuees can expect to have little privacy and be bored; these shelters are crowded, noisy, and often short-staffed (Florida Division of Emergency Management, 2018). Staff at these shelters should be able to provide general first-aid.

Special needs population shelters (SpNS) differ from general population shelters based on the individuals they serve and the services and amenities they provide. There are several unique aspects to planning for SpNS. For example, SpNS clients may seek shelter up to 12 hours before hurricane-force winds arrive and may remain in the shelter for up to, if not more than, 72 hours during and after a major storm. There must be at least two modes of access to the shelter by emergency vehicles. When planning for capacity, occupancy should be calculated based on 60 square feet per occupant (Florida Division of Emergency Management, 2014). A SpNS should plan to have "a minimum of five (5) gallons of potable water per person per day" (Florida Division of Emergency Management, 2014, Appendix F, p. 2). In addition to accessible sanitation facilities, each SpNS needs to have adequate back-up emergency power systems to run medical equipment and air conditioning systems.

Functional Needs Support Services

Since 2010, FEMA (2010) has required support planning for children and adults with functional needs that do not necessitate ongoing medical care that qualifies them for a special needs shelter. Past practices have called for redirecting these individuals to medical special needs facilities rather than sheltering them with the general population. This additional burden can quickly overwhelm medical special needs facilities. In addition, not including this population in shelter planning inhibits their access to equal treatment and denial of services. Functional needs support services (FNSS), as defined by FEMA (2010), make it possible for these individuals to maintain independence in a general population. These services include the following:

> Reasonable modification to policies, practices, and procedures; durable medical equipment (DME); consumable medical supplies (CMS); personal assistance services (PAS); [and] other goods and services as needed. Children and adults requiring FNSS may have physical, sensory, mental health, and cognitive and/or intellectual disabilities affecting their ability to function independently without assistance. Others that may benefit from FNSS include women in the late stages of pregnancy, elders, and people needing bariatric equipment.
> (FEMA, 2017d, para. 2)

Conclusion

Each state is responsible for its own emergency shelter plan. Each state has its own legislation or emergency response plans that determine the structure of how special needs and general population disaster shelters are identified, stocked, and staffed. They may also have specific plans in place to identify individuals who may require special needs sheltering such as pre-registration opportunities. These plans are all prepared based on state-specific circumstances and anticipated disaster situations. Possible disaster situations requiring disaster sheltering might include hurricanes, tornadoes, flooding, wildfires, blizzards, earthquakes, or hazardous materials releases. Responsibility for shelter selection and staffing rests with the local level. Communities, in cooperation with their county emergency officials and public health officials, define the scope of the population to access special needs shelters and the types of services those shelters might provide. Some communities may determine that they do not have sufficient need for, or resources available, to provide special needs shelters and may choose to coordinate with a neighboring community with greater resources.

Case Study: Special Needs Sheltering

About the Activity
The goal of this exercise is to discuss special needs population sheltering in a way that encourages participants to expand their approach to disaster shelter planning and preparedness by participating in a fictional case study. This case study presents realistic events that might occur during a sheltering episode in which emergency managers must make difficult decisions in a high-stress situation. Participants will have any opportunity to adapt the scenario to sheltering needs in their own communities. Anticipating "what if" situations is beneficial because options and plans can be developed in advance

and adjusted to existing conditions as needed. This reduces the response time and enhances staff ability to make appropriate decisions under pressure.

Learning Objectives

♦ Participants will demonstrate understanding of different categories of evacuees, levels of shelters, types of shelters (general population vs. special needs population shelters), disabled, medical special needs shelter, vulnerable elderly, and functional needs support systems via pre- and post-test assessment tools.

♦ Participants will demonstrate comprehension of what special needs sheltering requirements are and considerations in planning for disaster sheltering.

Definitions

♦ Evacuees: Individuals who need to move from danger or a disaster area to somewhere safe.

♦ General Population Evacuees: Individuals who have the ability and resources to evacuate themselves (self-evacuees) or those who may require assistance with transportation (critical transportation needs evacuees).

♦ Patient Evacuees: Individuals in the care of "Emergency Medical Services (e.g., prehospital emergency care, community para-medicine/mobile integrated healthcare), inpatient healthcare facilities (e.g., hospital, skilled nursing facility/nursing home, psychiatric facility), and outpatient healthcare services (e.g., home healthcare, dialysis, ambulatory surgery) prior to, during, or after a disaster" (FEMA, 2018, p. 11).

♦ Service Animal Evacuees: Applies to service animals that evacuate with their owners to either a general population or special needs population.

- ◆ Special Needs Population: Umbrella term in emergency management used to identify groups that require greater levels of support and/or services during a disaster. May include people with disabilities, the elderly, pregnant women, non-English speakers, prisoners, people without transportation, single parents, children, and others (Kailes & Enders, 2007).
- ◆ Disabled: Umbrella term used widely to identify persons with "reduced or inability to see, walk, speak, hear, learn, remember, manipulate, or reach controls, and/or respond quickly." Temporary disabilities may be the result of surgery, accidents and injuries (sprains, broken bones), or pregnancy (Kailes, 2005, p. 7).
- ◆ Medical Special Needs: A more precise term used to identify why some people may require enhanced services during sheltering (Kailes, 2005).
- ◆ Vulnerable Elderly: Those elderly with disabilities, cognitive impairment or dementia, or who are nursing home residents (Rothman & Brown, 2007).
- ◆ Functional Needs Support Services (FNSS): Include "reasonable modification to policies, practices, and procedures; durable medical equipment (DME); consumable medical supplies (CMS); personal assistance services (PAS); [and] other goods and services as needed. Children and adults requiring FNSS may have physical, sensory, mental health, and cognitive and/or intellectual disabilities affecting their ability to function independently without assistance. Others that may benefit from FNSS include women in the late stages of pregnancy, elders, and people needing bariatric equipment" (FEMA, 2017d).

Breakdown

- ◆ Divide into groups of four to five people.
- ◆ Discuss the ground rules to set the tone.
- ◆ Review the scenario and the group's discussion questions

- Allow ample time for discussion (approximately 45 minutes).
- Facilitate group dialogue about responses to questions.
- Utilize supplemental questions if needed.

Ground Rules (Gorski, 2019)

1. Listen actively – respect others when they are talking.
2. Speak from your own experience instead of generalizing ("I" instead of "they," "we," and "you").
3. Do not be afraid to respectfully challenge one another by asking questions but refrain from personal attacks – focus on ideas.
4. Participate to the fullest of your ability – community growth depends on the inclusion of every individual voice.
5. Instead of invalidating somebody else's story with your own spin on their experience, share your own story and experience.
6. The goal is not to agree – it is to gain a deeper understanding.
7. Be conscious of body language and nonverbal responses – they can be as disrespectful as words.

Supplemental Questions

1. How does your community determine who qualifies for special needs sheltering?
2. What kind of process will you use to determine how many individuals will require special needs sheltering and what their needs will be?
3. What criteria will you use to determine when special needs populations should shelter in place and when they should evacuate?
4. How will you ensure availability of sufficient appropriate transportation (ambulances? buses? private vehicles?) in the event evacuation is necessary?
5. Who do you include in your planning for special needs sheltering?

Breaking News: Special Needs Shelter Copes With Unregistered Population

The Situation

Despite press releases encouraging people to register in advance for space in special needs shelters, more than a dozen people and their caregivers reported to the Fifth Street Special Needs Shelter in Hometown today. Since they have not pre-registered, the facility is not clear about which services they will need. The facility may not have enough medications (e.g., pain medications, blood pressure medicine, insulin, asthma inhalers, etc.) or supplies (e.g., bed pans, hospital beds, wheelchairs, nebulizers, syringes, wound care items, etc.) in stock. The disaster situation is deteriorating, and it may not be possible to obtain additional supplies for several days. In fact, there is concern that the community may need to be evacuated altogether.

The Responders

◆ Fifth Street Special Needs Shelter staff
◆ Home County Department of Health
◆ Home County Emergency Operations Center
◆ Sweet Home Hospital staff
◆ American Red Cross

Things to Know

◆ Home County Department of Health is responsible for identifying, staffing, and stocking special needs disaster shelters within Home County. Home County has a memo of understanding with neighboring Bridge County to accept special needs shelterees with specific health conditions (requiring dialysis, requiring ongoing chemotherapy monitoring).
◆ Home County Emergency Management is responsible for identifying, staffing, and stocking general population shelters (including Functional Needs Support

Services) as well as maintaining a list of potential special needs shelterees.

♦ The Fifth Street Special Needs Shelter in Hometown has space for 100 patients and one caregiver per patient (total space available = 200). There are presently 95 patients already registered and present at the shelter along with their caregivers (190 persons present).

♦ Four of the individuals seeking shelter recently moved to Home County from another county. In their old county, they qualified for special needs sheltering. However, Home County has different requirements, and the individuals do not qualify for special needs sheltering here.

♦ Two individuals have conditions that make them eligible to shelter at the neighboring county's Sweet Home Hospital with which Home County has an agreement.

Role

Your role is to generate a needs assessment of the shelterees and put into effect a contingency plan. In addition, your staff must create a plan to adapt sheltering processes for future events.

Discussion Questions

Needs Assessment

1. What supplies/services do the new shelterees need?
2. What supplies do we have on site? What services/providers do we have on site?
3. What do we need to get? Where can we get it? How can we get it to the site? Can we get it there in time?
4. What are our options if we cannot get what we need?

Future Planning

1. How should the community communicate to avoid this issue in the future?
2. What role do families play during special needs sheltering? (Note: Most special needs shelters limit the number of family members that can accompany the shelteree.)

Cultural Competency

1. How did your past experience influence your decision-making?
2. How did your expectations influence your decision-making?
3. How did the activity change how you perceive sheltering?
4. What was the most eye-opening aspect of this case for you?

Pre-Test Assessment

This assessment survey is designed to demonstrate understanding of cultural competence–related aspects and establish a baseline of participant attitudes before the exercise.

DEFINITIONS

Directions: Please match the terminologies with their definitions.

_____	Patient Evacuees	A.	Individuals in medical services care, inpatient healthcare facilities, and outpatient healthcare services before, during, or after a disaster.
_____	General Population Evacuees	B.	Term used to identify groups that require greater levels of support and/or services during a disaster, including but not limited to those who have disabilities, are older adults, or are children.
_____	Special Needs Populations	C.	Individuals who have the ability and resources to evacuate themselves or those who may require assistance with transportation.

ATTITUDINAL SCALE

Directions: Please use the following scale to represent your reaction to the questions.

1	2	3	4	5
Strongly Agree	Agree	Neither Agree nor Disagree	Disagree	Strongly Disagree

1. I believe personal culture influences my role(s).

2. I believe cultural groups influence my role(s).

3. I believe stereotypes influence my role(s).

4. I believe I have adequate knowledge of how my own cultural identities influence my role(s).

5. I believe I have adequate knowledge of other cultures and their influence on my role(s).

6. I believe I have adequate knowledge of stereotypes and their influence on my role(s).

7. I believe I have adequate knowledge of my cultural identities and their influence on emergency and crisis management.

8. I believe I have adequate knowledge of other cultural identities and how they influence emergency and crisis management.

9. I believe I have adequate knowledge of stereotypes and how they influence emergency and crisis management.

Post-Test Assessment

PURPOSE OF THE SURVEY

This assessment survey is designed to demonstrate understanding of culturally related impacts and establish a baseline of participant attitudes after the exercise.

DEFINITIONS

Directions: Please match the terminologies with their definitions.

_____ Patient Evacuees   A. Individuals in medical services care, inpatient healthcare facilities, and outpatient healthcare services before, during, or after a disaster.

_____ General Population Evacuees   B. Term used to identify groups that require greater levels of support and/or services during a disaster, including but not limited to those who have disabilities, are older adults, or are children.

_____ Special Needs Populations   C. Individuals who have the ability and resources to evacuate themselves or those who may require assistance with transportation.

ATTITUDINAL SCALE

Directions: Please use the following scale to represent your reaction to the questions.

1	2	3	4	5
Strongly Agree	Agree	Neither Agree nor Disagree	Disagree	Strongly Disagree

1. I believe personal culture influences my role(s).

2. I believe cultural groups influence my role(s).

3. I believe stereotypes influence my role(s).

4. I believe I have adequate knowledge of how my own cultural identities influence my role(s).

5. I believe I have adequate knowledge of other cultures and their influence on my role(s).

6. I believe I have adequate knowledge of stereotypes and their influence on my role(s).

7. I believe I have adequate knowledge of my cultural identities and their influence on emergency and crisis management.

8. I believe I have adequate knowledge of other cultural identities and how they influence emergency and crisis management.

9. I believe I have adequate knowledge of stereotypes and how they influence emergency and crisis management.

OPEN RESPONSE

Please answer the following question: "I used to think_____, but now I think_____."

(Use back of page if needing extra space.)

Note

1. Household pet evacuees are beyond the scope of this case study.

References

Centers for Disease Control and Prevention (CDC). (2015). Planning for an emergency: Strategies for identifying and engaging at-risk groups. In *A guidance document for emergency managers* (1st ed.). Atlanta, GA: CDC. Retrieved from www.cdc.gov/nceh/hsb/disaster/atriskguidance.pdf

Centers for Disease Control and Prevention (CDC). (2018). Prevalence of disabilities and health care access by disability status and type among adults: United States, 2016. *Morbidity and Mortality Weekly Report (MMWR)*, *67*(32), 882–887.

Federal Emergency Management Agency (FEMA). (2010). *Guidance on planning for integration of functional needs support services in general population shelters*. Retrieved from www.fema.gov/pdf/about/odic/fnss_guidance.pdf

Federal Emergency Management Agency (FEMA). (2017a). *Resource typing definition for mass care services: Short-term shelter*. Retrieved from www.fema.gov/media-library-data/1494265881789-41aa5309742d3fbc91faa5b06dd05064/NIMS_508_Long_Term_Shelter_MAR202017.pdf

Federal Emergency Management Agency (FEMA). (2017b). *Resource typing definition for mass care services: Long-term shelter*. Retrieved from www.fema.gov/media-library-data/1494265881789-41aa5309742d3fbc91faa5b06dd05064/NIMS_508_Long_Term_Shelter_MAR202017.pdf

Federal Emergency Management Agency (FEMA). (2017c). *Resource typing definition for mass care services*. Retrieved from www.fema.gov/media-library-data/1494266026284-7c1983fda7d14a6fbfc0ec0480faa2db/NIMS_508_Evacuation_Shelter_MAR212017.pdf

Federal Emergency Management Agency (FEMA). (2017d). *FEMA's functional needs support services guidance*. Retrieved from www.phe.gov/Preparedness/planning/abc/Pages/functional-needs.aspx

Federal Emergency Management Agency (FEMA). (2018). National engagement planning considerations: Evacuation and shelter-in-place (Pre-decisional draft). *National Integration Center*. Retrieved from www.fema.gov/media-library-data/1533580334064-72e9356ed35b72

6b1a25f4a8c3372c9d/DRAFT_Planning_Considerations_Evacuation_
and_Shelter-in-Place_201808.pdf

Florida Division of Emergency Management. (2014). *2014 statewide emergency shelter plan*. State of Florida. Retrieved from https://portal.floridadisaster.org/shelters/External/Archives/2014SESPlan/0%20-%20 2014-SESP-Complete%20Document%20FINAL.pdf

Florida Division of Emergency Management. (2018). *What to expect in a shelter*. Retrieved from www.floridadisaster.org/planprepare/disability/evacuations-and-shelters/shelter-information/what-to-expect/

Gorski, P. C. (2019). *Guide for setting ground rules*. Retrieved from www.edchange.org/multicultural/activities/groundrules.html

Hatch, J. (2018). In natural disasters, a disability can be a death sentence. *Huffington Post*. Retrieved from www.huffingtonpost.com/entry/in-natural-disasters-a-disability-can-be-a-death-sentence_us_5c1ba22e e4b0407e9077eb58?fbclid=IwAR0EQ3YrFLpCMd89ZN w8R-5hcCDK2ZYilnJob77Z-Ip5rsQQe1PlHo8JN3M

Hemingway, L., & Priestly, M. (2014). Natural hazards, human vulnerability and disabling societies: A disaster for disabled people? *Review of Disability Studies: An International Journal, 2*(3).

Institute on Disability. (2017). *Disability statistics annual report*. Retrieved from https://disabilitycompendium.org/sites/default/files/user-uploads/2017_AnnualReport_2017_FINAL.pdf

Kailes, J. (2005). Disaster services and "special needs": Term of art or meaningless term? Nobody left behind: Disaster preparedness for persons with mobility impairments. *Research and Training Center on Independent Living, University of Kansas*. Retrieved from www2.ku.edu/~rrtcpbs/findings/pdfs/SpecialsNeeds.pdf

Kailes, J., & Enders, A. (2007). Moving beyond "special needs": A function-based framework for emergency management and planning. *Journal of Disability Policy Studies, 17*(4), 230–237.

Rothman, M., & Brown, L. (2007). The vulnerable geriatric casualty: Medical needs of frail older adults during disasters. *Generations, 4*(Winter), 16–20.

Spice, S. (2017). *Disaster shelter planning: Using a social domain heuristic to examine organizational behaviors of policy implementation during the 2004 hurricane season in Florida*. Tallahassee, FL: Florida State University.

White, B. (2014). Disaster relief for deaf persons: Lessons from Hurricanes Katrina and Rita. *Review of Disability Studies: An International Journal, 2*(3).

Additional Resources

American Red Cross. (2002). *Standards for hurricane evacuation shelter selection (ARC 4496)*. Retrieved from www.floridadisaster.org/globalassets/dem/response/sesp/2018/appendices/2018-sesp-appendix-c_arc-4496_final_1-29-18.pdf

Central Florida Regional Planning Council. (n.d.). *Statewide regional evacuation study program: Central Florida region technical data report Vol. 1–7*. Retrieved from www.cfrpc.org/download/sres/Chapter5_Shelter_Analysis.pdf?x64703

Federal Emergency Management Agency (FEMA). (2014). *National engagement-planning considerations: Evacuation and shelter-in-place* (draft). Retrieved from www.fema.gov/media-library-data/1533580334064-72e9356ed35b726b1a25f4a8c3372c9d/DRAFT_Planning_Considerations_Evacuation_and_Shelter-in-Place_201808.pdf

Florida Division of Emergency Management. (2018). *2018 statewide emergency shelter plan*. State of Florida. Retrieved from https://www.floridadisaster.org/globalassets/dem/response/sesp/2018/2018-sesp-a1-main-plan-text_final_1-30-18.pdf

Orange County Florida Government. (2010). *Emergency preparedness for people with special needs*. Retrieved from www.orangecountyfl.net/Portals/0/Library/Emergency-Safety/docs/EmergencyPreparednessSpecialNeedsEnglish.pdf

9

Consequence Management and HAZMAT Incidents

Thomas Carey

Overview of Context

Emergency managers are often tasked with making timely decisions that impact various complex social, political, and cultural issues. Stringer (2014) notes that there is an expectation in social life that trained professionals, applying scientifically derived expertise, will provide answers to the complex problems that confront people in their personal and public lives. Emergency managers are no different, as they must simultaneously struggle to balance the increasing demands made by politicians, local laws, and the communities they serve while addressing the technical aspect of managing the actual disaster at hand. Informed decision-making through the utilization of critical thinking coupled with effective crisis communication can provide favorable outcomes for the good of a community in a crisis.

Today's emergency manager must also have a knowledge base of dealing with technological scenarios such as grid infrastructure malfunctions, hazardous material (HAZMAT) accidents, and non-wildland fires. Hazardous materials include chemical, biological, and radioactive materials that are essential for industry, agriculture, and product manufacturing (Martin, 2016). Transportation routes, such as highways, rail, water, and air, should be identified by local emergency managers, especially through which hazardous materials are transported. Identification can be completed utilizing the collaborative efforts of Local Emergency Planning Committees (LEPCs) and State Emergency Response Commissions (SERCs) (Lindell, Perry, & Prater, 2007; Pine, 2015). The Superfund Amendments and Reauthorization Act (known as SARA Title III) mandates that these agencies protect public health, safety, and the environment from chemical hazards (U.S. Environmental Protection Agency, 2018a).[1]

Consequence management comprises those measures taken to protect public health and safety, restore essential government services, and provide emergency relief to governments, businesses, and individuals affected by the consequences of a chemical, biological, nuclear, radiological, and high-yield explosive situation. For domestic consequence management, the primary authority rests with the states to respond and the federal government to aid as required. In keeping with the Federal Emergency Management Agency's Whole Community Approach (2011), this exercise allows participants to understand the involvement of a full range of first responders, community members, stakeholders, and assets working in coordination to manage an increasingly complex HAZMAT scenario of a derailed train leaking a chemical agent.

Most jurisdictions, except for large municipalities, rely on local county support during a HAZMAT incident. Events that deal with chemical, biological, radiological, nuclear, and explosive (CBRNE) hazards must be addressed in a timely fashion before local first responders become overwhelmed. Emergency managers are a key component in orchestrating the appropriate response of a state National Guard's Weapons of Mass Destruction Civil Support Team (WMD-CST). The implementation of mitigation strategies and risk management initiatives with key stakeholders of the whole community increases a community's capacity to respond and cope with HAZMAT events.

Case Study: Consequence Management and HAZMAT Incidents

Goals of the Study

The goal of the exercise is to enhance one's leadership capacity through the decision-making process while applying technical knowledge to a fictional, HAZMAT-related case study involving consequence management. In attempting to relate the fictional setting to the real world, this extreme situation aids today's emergency manager in identifying the need to grasp technical knowledge, skills, and abilities while serving the needs of a given community. This activity will flesh out each participant's knowledge on dealing with a local, large-scale emergency while addressing risk communication issues and utilizing the decision-making process.

Learning Outcomes

◆ Participants will demonstrate a greater understanding of the terms "consequence management", "risk communication", and "decision-making abilities". Participants will demonstrate the establishment of the three standard contamination control zones and support zone for hazardous material (HAZMAT) or a chemical, biological, radiological, nuclear, or explosive (CBRNE) event as part of this exercise.

◆ Participants will demonstrate comprehension of how the aforementioned terms influence their role as an emergency manager via pre- and post-test assessment tools.

Definitions

◆ Chemical, Biological, Radiological, Nuclear, and Explosive (CBRNE) Materials: These materials are very dangerous and can cause injury or death to humans and animals.

- Decision-Making Abilities: Learned, habitual response patterns exhibited by an individual when confronted with a decision situation. The decision-making process includes the following: (a) realizing that you must decide (make a choice between alternatives), (b) gathering relevant information, (c) identifying the alternatives, (d) weighing the evidence, (e) choosing among the alternatives, (f) taking action, and (g) reviewing the decision and its consequences.
- Risk Communication: The process of informing people about potential hazards to their person, property, or community (U.S. Environmental Protection Agency, 2018b).
- Consequence Management: Measures taken to protect public health and safety, restore essential government services, and provide emergency relief to governments, businesses, and individuals affected by the consequences of a chemical, biological, nuclear, radiological, or high-yield explosive situation.
- HAZMAT: A phrase that encompasses substances in quantities or forms that may pose a reasonable risk to health, property, or the environment. HAZMATs include such substances as toxic chemicals, fuels, nuclear waste products, and biological, chemical, and radiological agents (National Oceanic and Atmospheric Administration, 2019).

Breakdown
- Divide into groups of five to six people and provide participants with key stakeholder positions (mayor, sheriff, fire chief, EMS chief, county emergency manager, etc.).
- Distribute Appendices A and B and scrap paper.
- Discuss the ground rules to set the tone.
- Review the scenario and the group's discussion questions.

- Allow ample time for discussion (approximately 45 minutes).
- Facilitate group dialogue about responses to questions.
- Utilize supplemental questions if needed.

Ground Rules (Gorski, 2019)

1. Listen actively – respect others when they are talking.
2. Speak from your own experience instead of generalizing ("I" instead of "they," "we," and "you").
3. Do not be afraid to respectfully challenge one another by asking questions but refrain from personal attacks – focus on ideas.
4. Participate to the fullest of your ability – community growth depends on the inclusion of every individual voice.
5. Instead of invalidating somebody else's story with your own spin on their experience, share your own story and experience.
6. The goal is not to agree – it is to gain a deeper understanding.
7. Be conscious of body language and nonverbal responses – they can be as disrespectful as words.

Supplemental Questions

1. What are your first thoughts about this scenario? Did you have any emotional reactions to this scenario? If yes, why? If no, why?
2. Was there anything thought provoking about how your fellow participants reacted to this exercise? (Please use generalizations and do not target others.)
3. What would your reaction to this exercise be if you had been raised as a member in one of the groups?
4. How do you think this scenario relates to emergency management? Why was this exercise created?

Facilitator Instructions

- Review the literature and resources on consequence management and incident command (see references and additional resources at the end of the case study).
- Become familiar with the National Guard and military's role in support of civil authorities.
- Provide each group a copy of Appendices A and B, as well as scrap paper.
- Have participants go through the process of establishing the standard control zones for a HAZMAT situation (hot, warm, and cold zones) to contain the contamination.
- Have participants implement a support zone template with noted resources (see Appendix B).
- Advise participants of wind direction and speed (make changes as needed).
- Provide injects based on the experience of class.
- Determine as the facilitator whether pursuing a HAZMAT experience or a WMD incident motivated by terrorism.
- Establish a crime scene for acts of terrorism (suggested for homeland security and criminal justice participants).
- Manage and conduct an After Action Review (AAR) to summarize tasks and analyze performances by participants.

HAZMAT in Valley Cottage

The Situation

At 10:30 a.m. today, the Emergency Operations Center Watch Officer contacts you concerning a train derailment involving hazardous material that occurred within the rural area of Valley Cottage. A fire has erupted along with the spilling of an unknown chemical or chemicals. Approximately 25 citizens have been marked as casualties near the hot zone as the local volunteer fire company attempts to extinguish and contain the chemical spill.

At 10:45 a.m. the Incident Commander (IC) Fire Chief Dozier notifies you that the chemical released from two tanker cars is a non-persistent agent; however, it can cause additional casualties within the next few hours. The IC wants to discuss courses of action with you and your team because local first responders are becoming overwhelmed.

At 12:30 p.m. you receive a weather update from your operations section and learn that the wind direction is changing to the southwest within the next few hours. The wind speed is likely to increase overnight. Based on this new information you determine that the toxic smoke from the hazardous material will head toward the populated area of the township much later in the day.

Community Members
- **Railroad yard workers** who predominately speak French and make up 45% of the local population. They are employed at the rail yard and live just south of the railroad tracks at the edge of town.
- **Shipping and receiving workers** who speak both French and English and make up 25% of the local population. They work near the railroad yard and live in the heart of the town.
- **Truckers and mechanics** who speak both English and Spanish and make up 20% of the local population. They are a transient population with loose community ties. These individuals live in adjacent towns from their work location at the rail yard.
- **The socialites** make up 10% of the local population and predominantly speak English. They live in a semi-retired community near the riverbank of the Wanaque River that leads into Lake Wanaque. These individuals

contribute to local economic success through owner-
ship and good business practices of properties they
manage within the community.

Things to Know

+ Valley Cottage has approximately 10,000 citizens
  within its borders.
+ A released non-persistent chemical agent dissipates
  and/or loses its ability to cause casualties under 30
  minutes. Other contributing factors such as fire and
  temperature can change this situation.
+ Individuals within a five-mile radius of the train derailment are likely in need of some type of medical attention and require decontamination.
+ The Crisis Response Team only has transportation
  vehicles able to hold less than 2,000 citizens.
+ The mayor of the town has requested livestock near
  the river be evacuated first as they are a valuable economic asset to the community.
+ The reservoir is located 10 miles south from the center
  of Valley Cottage where the Wanaque River ends.
+ A volunteer HAZMAT company is located within
  8 miles of the train derailment outside of your county
  and houses one truck.
+ All available volunteer ambulances from the surrounding towns have been dispatched to the on-scene command post.
+ The town depends on the county sheriff to provide all
  law enforcement activities, but resources are limited.
  Only 25 deputies are available to assist at this time.
+ The state police and National Guard headquarters are
  collocated in the state capitol.
+ The state National Guard has a fully functional Weapons of Mass Destruction Civil Support Team (WMD-
  CST) and a host of military resources located two hours
  from your location.

◆ The sheriff's office has notified the local FBI field office of the incident for investigation.
◆ The area is subject to the Superfund Amendments and Reauthorization Act (SARA III), which directs the management of hazardous materials. Industries share data with government, local, and state entities to receive, evaluate, and act on that data.

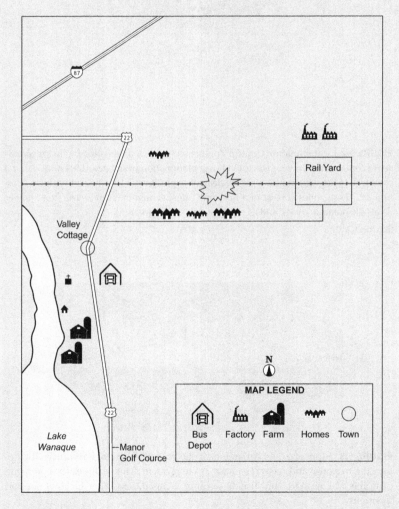

FIGURE 9.1 Map of the Scenario's Area

Source: Carey

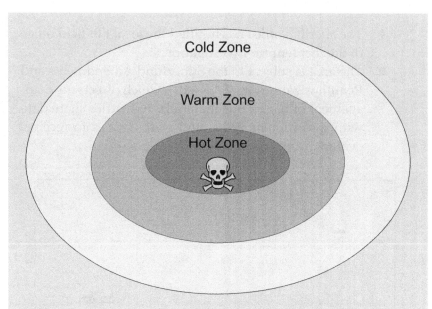

FIGURE 9.2 Contamination Control Zones: Safety zones established by first responders to contain and prevent the spread of contamination from hazardous material or a chemical, biological, radiological, nuclear, or explosive (CBRNE) event within a community. These zones consist of a hot zone (most contamination), warm zone (lower levels of contamination), and a cold zone (no contamination).

Source: Carey

FIGURE 9.3 Support Zone: An area near the cold zone to stage resources to support the response and recovery phase of the incident. This includes the command post, medical support, logistics, base camp, helipad, and other incident support functions.

Source: Carey

Your Role

You are a member of the Crisis Response Team and have gathered with the rest of the group to discuss the next steps.

Questions for Discussion

1. Who do you assist first? Who do you assist next?
2. How do you divide your resources?
3. What are tasks you need to accomplish?
4. Who are your stakeholders?
5. What, if any, were some environmental concerns within this scenario?
6. How can understanding other cultures enhance your role in managing the whole community approach from the standpoint of a local emergency manager?
7. How can you improve risk communication before, during, and after an emergency or disaster to a community?

Pre-Test Assessment

PURPOSE OF THE SURVEY

This assessment survey is designed to demonstrate understanding of cultural competence–related aspects and establish a baseline of participant attitudes before the exercise.

DEFINITIONS

Directions: Please match the terminologies with their definitions.

_____ Consequence Management   A. Encompasses substances in quantities or forms that may pose a reasonable risk to health, property, or the environment.

_____ Risk Communication   B. Measures taken to protect public health and safety, restore essential government services, and provide emergency relief to governments, businesses, and individuals affected by the consequences of a chemical, biological, nuclear, radiological, or high-yield explosive situation.

_____ HAZMAT   C. The process of informing people about potential hazards to their person, property, or community.

ATTITUDINAL SCALE

Directions: Please use the following scale to represent your reaction to the questions.

1	2	3	4	5
Strongly Agree	Agree	Neither Agree nor Disagree	Disagree	Strongly Disagree

1. I believe personal culture influences my role(s).

2. I believe cultural groups influence my role(s).

3. I believe stereotypes influence my role(s).

4. I believe I have adequate knowledge of how my own cultural identities influence my role(s).

5. I believe I have adequate knowledge of other cultures and their influence on my role(s).

6. I believe I have adequate knowledge of stereotypes and their influence on my role(s).

7. I believe I have adequate knowledge of my cultural identities and their influence on emergency and crisis management.

8. I believe I have adequate knowledge of other cultural identities and how they influence emergency and crisis management.

9. I believe I have adequate knowledge of stereotypes and how they influence emergency and crisis management.

Post-Test Assessment

PURPOSE OF THE SURVEY
This assessment survey is designed to demonstrate understanding of culturally related impacts and establish a baseline of participant attitudes after the exercise.

DEFINITIONS

Directions: Please match the terminologies with their definitions.

_____ Consequence Management   A. Encompasses substances in quantities or forms that may pose a reasonable risk to health, property, or the environment.

_____ Risk Communication   B. Measures taken to protect public health and safety, restore essential government services, and provide emergency relief to governments, businesses, and individuals affected by the consequences of a chemical, biological, nuclear, radiological, or high-yield explosive situation.

_____ HAZMAT   C. The process of informing people about potential hazards to their person, property, or community.

ATTITUDINAL SCALE

Directions: Please use the following scale to represent your reaction to the questions.

1	2	3	4	5
Strongly Agree	Agree	Neither Agree nor Disagree	Disagree	Strongly Disagree

1. I believe personal culture influences my role(s).

2. I believe cultural groups influence my role(s).

3. I believe stereotypes influence my role(s).

4. I believe I have adequate knowledge of how my own cultural identities influence my role(s).

5. I believe I have adequate knowledge of other cultures and their influence on my role(s).

6. I believe I have adequate knowledge of stereotypes and their influence on my role(s).

7. I believe I have adequate knowledge of my cultural identities and their influence on emergency and crisis management.

8. I believe I have adequate knowledge of other cultural identities and how they influence emergency and crisis management.

9. I believe I have adequate knowledge of stereotypes and how they influence emergency and crisis management.

OPEN RESPONSE
Please answer the following question: "I used to think_____, but now I think_____."
(Use back of page if needing extra space)

Note

1. The combination of Geographic Information Systems (GIS) technology with the modeling capabilities of the air dispersion modeling software called Areal Locations of Hazardous Atmospheres (ALOHA) has proven to be an invaluable resource for responding to chemical release scenarios (Jakala, 2007). Participants should familiarize themselves with these spatial tools as they affect each phase of the emergency management cycle during a HAZMAT incident.

References

Federal Emergency Management Agency. (2011). *A whole community approach to emergency management: Principles, themes, and pathways for action.* Washington, DC: FEMA.

Gorski, P. C. (2019). *Guide for setting ground rules.* Retrieved from www.edchange.org/multicultural/activities/groundrules.htm

Jakala, S. (2007). *A GIS enabled air dispersion modeling tool for emergency management.* Papers in Resource Analysis, Saint Mary's University of Minnesota Central Services Press, 9. Retrieved from www.gis.smumn.edu

Lindell, M. K., Perry, R. W., & Prater, C. (2007). *Introduction to emergency management.* Hoboken, NJ: Wiley.

Martin. G. (2016). *Understanding homeland security.* Thousand Oaks, CA: Sage Publications.

National Oceanic and Atmospheric Administration. (2019). What is HAZMAT? Retrieved from https://oceanservice.noaa.gov/facts/hazmat.html

Pine, J. C. (2015). *Hazards analysis: Reducing the impact of disasters* (2nd ed.). Boca Raton, FL: CRC Press.

Stringer, E. T. (2014). *Action research* (4th ed.). Thousand Oaks, CA: Sage Publications.

U.S. Environmental Protection Agency. (2018a). *Summary of the emergency planning & community right-to-know act.* Retrieved from www.epa.gov/laws-regulations/summary-emergency-planning-community-right-know-act

U.S. Environmental Protection Agency. (2018b). *Risk communication.* Retrieved from www.epa.gov/risk/risk-communication#self

Additional Resources

Federal Emergency Management Agency [FEMA]. (2011). *Independent study IS-75: Military resources in emergency management.* Retrieved from https://training.fema.gov/is/courseoverview.aspx?code=IS-75

FEMA. (2013). *Independent study IS-5.A: An introduction to hazardous materials.* Retrieved from https://training.fema.gov/is/courseoverview.aspx?code=IS-5.a

FEMA. (2014). *Independent study IS 241B: Decision making and problem solving.* Retrieved from https://training.fema.gov/is/courseoverview.aspx?code=IS-241.b

FEMA. (2018). *Independent study IS-100.C: Introduction to the Incident Command System, ICS 100.* Retrieved from https://training.fema.gov/is/courseoverview.aspx?code=IS-100.c

FEMA. (2019). *HAZUS.* Retrieved from www.fema.gov/plan/prevent/hazus/index.shtm

Hughes, A. L., Palen, L., & Peterson, S. (2014). *Critical issues in disaster science and management: A dialogue between researchers and practitioners.* Federal Emergency Management Agency. Retrieved from https://training.fema.gov/hiedu/docs/critical-issues-in-disaster-science-and-management.pdf

Kapucu, N. (2015). *Emergency management: Whole community approach* (3rd ed.). Orlando, FL: Encyclopedia of Public Administration and Public Policy

Lindell, M. K. (2013). Disaster studies. *Current Sociology, 61*, 797–825.

National Academy of Engineering. (2013). *Fact sheets on terrorist attacks.* Retrieved from www.nae.edu/Activities/Projects/20726/FactSheetsonTerroristAttacks.aspx

National Center for Biomedical Research and Training. (2019). *WMD response guidebook request.* Retrieved from www.ncbrt.lsu.edu/GuidebookRequest

National Guard Bureau. (2011). *National guard regulation 500–3: Weapons of mass destruction civil support team management.* Arlington, VA: NGB.

Phelps, R. (2012). *Emergency management exercises: From response to recovery: Everything you need to know to design a great exercise.* San Francisco: Chandi Media.

U.S. Department of Transportation. (2016). *Emergency response guidebook 2016.* Washington, DC: U.S. Department of Transportation, Pipeline and Hazardous Materials Safety Administration. Retrieved from www.phmsa.dot.gov/hazmat/erg/emergency-response-guidebook-erg

10

Accommodating Special Needs Populations in Disaster Management

The Case of Children With Autism Spectrum Disorder

Keith Douglas Revell

Overview of the Context

Autism spectrum disorder (ASD) is defined broadly as a developmental disability associated with significant deficits in communication, behavior, and social interaction that affect daily functioning and usually last throughout a person's lifetime (Centers for Disease Control, 2019; National Institute of Mental Health, 2019; National Institute of Neurological Disorders and Stroke, 2019). The incidence of ASD has increased dramatically in recent decades and now affects one in every 59 children in the United States (Baio et al., 2018). Because it is a spectrum disorder, children with ASD exhibit a wide range of abilities and variety of symptoms, from mild to severe, although there are a few commonalities:

- ◆ Repetitive behaviors (such as hand-flapping and rocking)
- ◆ Rigidity (restricted or obsessive interests; trouble adapting to changes in routine)
- ◆ Difficulty with social cues and rituals (reading facial expressions; maintaining eye contact; using appropriate social speech; reacting to handshakes and embraces)
- ◆ Hyper- or hyposensitivity to environmental stimuli (reacting either too much or too little to sounds, odors, and lights)

There is no cure for autism and no medication to treat its main symptoms, although some medications have led to improved functioning in some instances. There are a variety of treatments for ASD, including speech therapy, social skills training, dietary changes, and alternative medicine approaches, though these are controversial. Most of these treatments focus on children from birth to three years of age, and all of them have mixed results. Treating ASD is complicated by the fact that children with autism often have other non-ASD diagnoses (e.g., a child may be diagnosed with both ASD and obsessive-compulsive disorder, or ASD and depression), which means they contend with multiple, reinforcing impairments.

Because of the complexity of ASD, children with autism are especially vulnerable in emergency situations, a subject which has just begun to attract the attention of scholars. Peek and Stough (2010) argue that children with disabilities have "clustered" or "layered" vulnerabilities that amplify their risk in disasters. A child's age, place of residence, socioeconomic status, and family structure interact with physical and mental disabilities in times of stress. ASD children therefore require additional assistance with communication, health, and transportation – all common problems for special needs populations generally (Department of Homeland Security, 2019). Children with disabilities are likely to have a harder time taking protective action, escaping danger, or responding to rescuers appropriately. Families of children with disabilities are often excluded from disaster preparedness planning and are less inclined to make their own disaster plans. Disaster also disrupts the social support arrangements that families rely upon to help children with autism, such as schools with special needs teachers and specialized healthcare providers (e.g., speech and behavioral therapists, neurologists, and respite care workers). Helping families restore these support systems promptly in the wake of disaster is a crucial step toward addressing the consequences of disaster-related stress. Because children with autism are sensitive to any change in routine, the disruption and trauma caused by a disaster can lead to increases in aggression, anxiety, and sleep disorders, along with declines in academic performance. Although such reactions to disaster are common among children in general, those with ASD tend to be less resilient, which means that they take longer to "bounce back" after disasters.

Although children with ASD constitute "a nearly wholly neglected group in the field of education for emergency preparedness," according to Edmonds (2017), it is not surprising that existing research indicates that autism magnifies the consequences of disasters. Valenti et al. (2012) studied children with ASD in the aftermath of the 2009 earthquake in L'Aquila, Italy. They found dramatic declines in their ability to communicate, interact with others, and perform daily tasks; however, they emphasize that immediate participation in rehabilitation programs and the restoration of daily routines assisted in the eventual recovery of normal functioning (Berggren & Curiel, 2006). Mehtar and Mukaddes (2011) likewise found that children with autism affected by traumatic incidents showed reduced ability to communicate, interact appropriately with others, and take care of themselves (such as eating and getting dressed). Traumatic incidents also led children with autism to injure themselves more, engage in repetitive behaviors (which are used to self-sooth), and act in an anxious or aggressive manner.

The core characteristics of ASD that limit the ability of children to engage in basic social interactions and contend with daily life will also affect their adaptability during times of disaster. Even in the absence of trauma related to a disaster, children with autism face daily hurdles that often require elevated levels of care (Kalb, Stuart, Freedman, Zablotsky & Vasa, 2012; Van Steensel, Bögels,

Magiati, & Perrin, 2014). Considerable research (Chasson & Jarosie-wicz, 2014; Levine, Conradt, Goodwin, Sheinkopf, & Lester, 2014; Peek & Stough, 2010) indicates that several symptoms of ASD will make it especially difficult for affected children to function in the unpredictable environment of a disaster. Children with ASD may have difficulty doing the following:

- ◆ Recognizing facial expressions
- ◆ Identifying emotions expressed through words, tone of voice, or body language
- ◆ Responding correctly in social situations, which means that they may respond in inappropriate or unpredictable ways
- ◆ Maintaining eye contact and participating in activities that require coordination with others
- ◆ Forming relationships and interacting with people they do not already know
- ◆ Living independently, by making basic life decisions and completing daily tasks (e.g., washing laundry, buying and preparing food, managing money)
- ◆ Recognizing the signs of danger
- ◆ Coping with, and acting appropriately to, new or unpredictable sensory stimuli, such as flashing lights and blaring sirens
- ◆ Communicating their medical condition and needs when asked by a first responder or medical provider

With these deficits, children with autism may either overreact or underreact to situations that are stressful and may not be able to assist adequately in their own care. Although many children with ASD are already undergoing medical treatment, they typically do not do well when their care is improvised or based on incomplete information, as is often the case in emergency situations. For example, they may not know that they are taking medications to address the symptoms of their autism; even if they do know, they may not be able to tell emergency personnel who need information quickly (Johnson & Levine, 2014).

Case Study: Accommodating Special Needs Populations in Disaster Management

Goals of the Case Study

This case study seeks to deepen participants' understanding of special needs populations by employing information about autism spectrum disorder (ASD) in order to decide regarding the use of funding for disaster management. In the process, they will think through the consequences of ASD for disaster managers, who will be confronted with children displaying behaviors that complicate the task of keeping them safe from harm during emergencies.

Learning Outcomes

Upon completion of this exercise, participants will demonstrate increased understanding of the following:

- ◆ The behavioral manifestations of autism spectrum disorder in children
- ◆ The potential consequences of ASD for emergency management
- ◆ The need for increased awareness and resources for cultural competence regarding ASD in emergency management

Definitions

- ◆ Autism Spectrum Disorder: A developmental disability associated with significant deficits in communication, behavior, and social interaction that affect daily functioning and usually last throughout a person's lifetime.
- ◆ Special Needs Populations: Refers to persons who may have additional needs before, during, and after an incident in functional areas, including those who have disabilities; live in institutionalized settings; are older adults; are children; are from diverse cultures; have limited English proficiency or are non-English speaking; or are transportation disadvantaged.

◆ Functional Areas: Maintaining health, independence, communication, transportation, support, services, self-determination, and medical care.

Breakdown

This case study can be conducted in 60 minutes. Facilitators may wish to supplement the case with additional materials listed in the additional resources listed at the end of this chapter.

Step 1. 10 min. Start the exercise with a discussion of the following questions to get a sense of the preconceptions of ASD participants may have:
   ◆ What do you know about "special needs" populations? Who do you think of when you hear the words "special needs" or "autism"?
   ◆ Have you ever heard of autism spectrum disorders? Do you know anyone with ASD or anyone who has a child with ASD?
   ◆ What things (behaviors, characteristics, images) come to mind when you think of ASD?

Step 2. 5 min. Before you proceed with the rest of the exercise, tell the participants that they will be asked to pick one of three disaster funding options and explain the reason for their choice. Emphasize that they can only choose to fund one option: pre-disaster planning and communication; first-responder training; or post-disaster care and recovery (see the Facilitator Notes for the rationale for this aspect of the case).

Step 3. 20 min. Divide the participants into groups of four to five people, distribute the scenario as a handout, and allow the participants to read it and make their decision.

Step 4. 10 min. Have each team present their decision and explain the reasons for their choice.

Step 5. 15 min. Explore the participants' decisions using the discussion questions. If time permits, facilitators can also use the supplemental questions provided.

Facilitator Notes

This decision-forcing case study challenges participants to increase their understanding of autism in children to make informed choices about how to address the needs of this especially vulnerable population before, during, and after a disaster. Cultural competence in this scenario requires a familiarity with the symptoms of autism spectrum disorder (ASD). Participants will decide how to spend their limited resources by thinking through the consequences of ASD for disaster planning, response, and recovery, using their familiarity with autism to consider how its specific behavioral manifestations complicate efforts to protect children in life-threatening situations.

In the case, participants must use their understanding of children with ASD to decide the best way to deploy disaster management funding. Given the behavioral manifestations of ASD, is it better to fund enhanced disaster planning, train first responders, or provide more robust post-disaster support? There are, of course, good arguments to be made for all these choices. The point of the case, therefore, is not to arrive at a single definitive conclusion but to acquire cultural competence sufficient to make informed decisions.

For example, participants might argue that expanded pre-disaster communication would be the best approach. They may suggest that money should be spent to ensure that community support institutions like schools offer better disaster risk reduction programs because lack of information and preparation is a significant problem for families with special needs children (Edmonds, 2017; Ronoh, Gaillard, & Marlowe, 2017; Peek & Fothergill, 2008). On the other hand, they may suggest that programs be developed that would educate families with ASD children about where to go and what to bring during an emergency, thus providing as much normalcy and routine as possible in emergency situations for children who do not react well to changes in routine. Alternatively, participants might focus on shelter management. Because the case provides information that suggests that children with autism may exhibit symptoms of anxiety, engage in repetitive behaviors, and emote in unusual ways, would it be best to spread them among various shelters or handle them all in one place with trained personnel?

Another line of argument might focus on first responders. Would it be better to prepare firefighters, police, and other rescue workers to deal with children who are disoriented by lights and sirens, react inappropriately when touched, display odd or threatening body language, fail to speak or show eye contact, and ignore soothing words and gestures? Yet another line of argument would focus on post-disaster care and recovery. Participants may argue that resources should be spent on quickly restoring and strengthening community support structures (e.g., schools, medical care, counseling) and providing intensive post-disaster therapy (Ducy & Stough, 2011; Valenti et al., 2014). Sorting through these options will engage participants in a detailed exploration of the manifestations of ASD and how they might affect the efforts of disaster managers, which is a goal of cultural competence.

Group discussions should be structured so that participants make a clear decision about which funding choice to pursue. Funding everything should not be an option, since that allows participants to avoid a careful analysis of the behavioral manifestations of ASD and how they affect the efforts of emergency managers to keep children safe during disasters. Groups should explain their perceptions of ASD and articulate the ways in which its manifestations complicate emergency management before, during, and after a disaster. They should also discuss the objectives of emergency management in each phase of a disaster, spelling out the goals to be achieved through preparedness, response, and recovery. Linking specific manifestations of ASD to emergency management objectives will allow the participants to think through the ways that the behaviors of children with ASD would affect the work of first responders, shelter managers, recovery specialists, and other professionals involved in disasters.

Participants should also think about whether it is best to build resiliency and capacity for individuals, families, specific institutions (like schools), or communities. Make sure that the participants remain focused on the issue of ASD and disaster management. ASD is the subject of considerable controversy and on-going study, but it is not the goal of the case to have participants recommend approaches to research or family support that are unrelated to the specific problem of emergency management. In other words, participants should not be allowed to say that funding should be used to find a cure for autism, since that is well beyond the scope of the exercise.

Ground Rules (Gorski, 2019)
1. Listen actively – respect others when they are talking.
2. Speak from your own experience instead of generalizing ("I" instead of "they," "we," and "you").
3. Do not be afraid to respectfully challenge one another by asking questions but refrain from personal attacks – focus on ideas.
4. Participate to the fullest of your ability – community growth depends on the inclusion of every individual voice
5. Instead of invalidating somebody else's story with your own spin on their experience, share your own story and experience.
6. The goal is not to agree – it is to gain a deeper understanding.
7. Be conscious of body language and nonverbal responses – they can be as disrespectful as words.

Supplemental Questions
Facilitators may consider asking the following supplemental questions for the given scenario:
◆ What are your first thoughts about this scenario? Did you have any emotional reactions to this scenario? If yes, why? If no, why?

◆ Was there anything thought provoking about how your fellow participants reacted to this exercise? (Please use generalizations and do not target others.)
◆ What would your reaction to this exercise be if you had been the parent of a child with ASD?
◆ How do you think this scenario relates to emergency management? Why was this exercise created?

The Context: A Regional Disaster Management Office

You are the director of the Metropolitan Disaster Response Office for the Tri-County region. The Federal Emergency Management Agency (FEMA) has offered you additional funding to enhance your disaster preparedness program. In their critique of your disaster management plan, they highlighted the importance of taking more concrete steps toward addressing the needs of children with autism spectrum disorder (ASD). In the past three decades, the incidence of autism has skyrocketed. The Centers for Disease Control estimates that one in every 59 children now has some form of ASD compared with one in 150 in 2002; the reasons for this increase are the subject of considerable debate. Although four times more common in boys than girls, ASD is reported in all racial, ethnic, and socioeconomic groups.

FEMA resources are limited, so they have suggested that you focus your efforts on one of the following areas: pre-disaster planning and communication, first-responder training, or post-disaster care and recovery. Although you may find compelling reasons to fund each of these choices (now or in the future), you must choose only one. You must also explain what aspects of ASD you found most compelling in making your choice.

1. Pre-disaster planning and communication. This option might include the following:
   a. Providing information to families with children with ASD in the form of checklists of items they will need to have available whether they shelter in place or relocate to an official emergency shelter, to help them prepare for disasters.

b. Identifying specific shelters for children with ASD, either to manage as many as possible in a single location or to disperse them to multiple locations.

c. Helping schools with disaster risk reduction programs and training for special needs teachers to prepare children with ASD for disasters.

d. Identifying and enhancing existing community support systems that benefit children with ASD.

2. *First-responder training.* This option might include the following:

a. Providing training to law enforcement, emergency medical services, and search-and-rescue workers who will encounter children with ASD in the field during disasters.

b. Enhancing shelter resources that could be used to manage children with ASD. This might include training doctors, nurses, and counselors, who may not have formal training in ASD. It might also include training dormitory managers and security personal who will manage shelter occupants during disasters.

3. *Post-disaster care and recovery.* This option might include the following:

a. Community restoration, especially in education (including the retention of special needs teachers, facility repair, and measures to quickly resume schooling).

b. Housing restoration expedited for families of children with ASD.

c. Enhanced post-disaster counseling for children with ASD.

FEMA has provided you with an abbreviated list of the signs and symptoms of ASD that have been helpful to other officials making similar decisions.

Autism spectrum disorder (ASD) is a developmental disability that can cause significant social, communication, and behavioral impairments. Because it is a spectrum disorder, people with ASD exhibit a very wide variety of symptoms, ranging from mild to severe. Children or adults with ASD might:

- Not point at objects to show interest (e.g., not point at an airplane flying overhead)
- Not look at objects when another person points at them
- Have trouble relating to others or not have an interest in other people at all
- Avoid eye contact and want to be alone
- Have trouble understanding other people's feelings or talking about their own feelings
- Prefer not to be touched (including embraces, handshakes, pats on the shoulder)
- Appear to be unaware when people talk to them but respond to other sounds
- Be very interested in people, but not know how to talk, play, or relate to them
- Repeat or echo words or phrases said to them or repeat words or phrases in place of normal language
- Be unable to speak
- Take language literally and not understand nuances in the use of speech
- Have trouble expressing their needs using typical words or gestures
- Not play "pretend" games (e.g., not pretend to "feed" a doll)
- Engage in repetitive behaviors (i.e., hand-flapping or rocking), repeating actions over and over again
- Act upset for no apparent reason
- Have trouble adapting to any change in routine
- Have unusual reactions to the way things smell, taste, look, feel, or sound, including appearing insensitive to pain or overly sensitive to a light touch or quiet noise
- Appear anxious and nervous for no apparent reason
- Dart away unexpectedly

- Ask questions repeatedly even though they have been answered
- Lose skills they once had (e.g., stop saying words they had previously used)

Individuals with ASD may respond better if you do the following:
- Speak slowly and use simple language
- Repeat simple questions many times
- Allow extended time for responses (30–60 seconds)
- Give lots of praise
- Do not attempt to physically block repetitive behaviors
- Do not touch them
- Explain what you are about to do several times before proceeding

As you make your funding decision, be sure to explain how these specific features of ASD might affect your efforts to keep such children safe in a disaster scenario.

Roles and Tasks

Participants will play the role of the director of the Metropolitan Disaster Response Office. In that capacity, participants must choose which aspect of disaster management preparation for children with ASD (e.g., pre-disaster communication, first-responder training, or post-disaster care) they will fund and articulate a rationale for their choice based on their understanding of the ways that the specific behavioral manifestations of ASD listed in the case might affect each aspect of disaster management.

Questions for Discussion

1. What was the most surprising feature of ASD that you encountered in this case?
2. What additional knowledge would help you make your decision? In other words, what aspects of ASD most concern you? Where do you feel that gaps in your knowledge might have the most serious repercussions during a disaster?

3. What choice did you make? Will you fund pre-disaster communication with families of ASD children, first-responder training, or post-disaster care?

4. Why did you decide to focus your resources on that aspect of disaster management for children with ASD? That is, what features of ASD identified in the case struck you as the most relevant for disaster management?

5. How do you think your decision was affected by your preconceptions of children with disabilities generally and ASD in particular?

6. What role do you think the families of children with ASD should play in disaster management? That is, what do you expect from the families of children (or people in general) with disabilities? How did your expectations influence your decision-making?

7. What role do you think community institutions, such as schools, should play when it comes to addressing the needs of children with ASD in disaster management? That is, what do you expect from community institutions when it comes to children with ASD? How did your expectations influence your decision-making?

Pre-Test Assessment

PURPOSE OF THE SURVEY

This assessment survey is designed to demonstrate understanding of cultural competence–related aspects and establish a baseline of participant attitudes before the exercise.

DEFINITIONS

Directions: Please match the terminologies with their definitions.

_____ Autism Spectrum Disorder   A.   Maintaining health, independence, communication, transportation, support, services, self-determination, and medical care.

_____ Functional Areas   B.   Refers to persons who may have additional needs before, during, and after an incident in functional areas, including but not limited to those who have disabilities, are older adults, or are children.

_____ Special Needs Populations   C.   A developmental disability associated with significant deficits in communication, behavior, and social interaction that affect daily functioning and usually last throughout a person's lifetime.

ATTITUDINAL SCALE

Directions: Please use the following scale to represent your reaction to the questions.

1	2	3	4	5
Strongly Agree	Agree	Neither Agree nor Disagree	Disagree	Strongly Disagree

1. I believe personal culture influences my role(s).

2. I believe cultural groups influence my role(s).

3. I believe stereotypes influence my role(s).

4. I believe I have adequate knowledge of how my own cultural identities influence my role(s).

5. I believe I have adequate knowledge of other cultures and their influence on my role(s).

6. I believe I have adequate knowledge of stereotypes and their influence on my role(s).

7. I believe I have adequate knowledge of my cultural identities and their influence on emergency and crisis management.

8. I believe I have adequate knowledge of other cultural identities and how they influence emergency and crisis management.

9. I believe I have adequate knowledge of stereotypes and how they influence emergency and crisis management.

Post-Test Assessment

PURPOSE OF THE SURVEY

This assessment survey is designed to demonstrate understanding of culturally related impacts and establish a baseline of participant attitudes after the exercise.

DEFINITIONS

Directions: Please match the terminologies with their definitions.

_____ Autism Spectrum Disorder

A. Maintaining health, independence, communication, transportation, support, services, self-determination, and medical care.

_____ Functional Areas

B. Refers to persons who may have additional needs before, during, and after an incident in functional areas, including but not limited to those who have disabilities, are older adults, or are children.

_____ Special Needs Populations

C. A developmental disability associated with significant deficits in communication, behavior, and social interaction that affects daily functioning and usually last throughout a person's lifetime.

ATTITUDINAL SCALE

Directions: Please use the following scale to represent your reaction to the questions.

1	2	3	4	5
Strongly Agree	Agree	Neither Agree nor Disagree	Disagree	Strongly Disagree

1. I believe personal culture influences my role(s).

2. I believe cultural groups influence my role(s).

3. I believe stereotypes influence my role(s).

4. I believe I have adequate knowledge of how my own cultural identities influence my role(s).

5. I believe I have adequate knowledge of other cultures and their influence on my role(s).

6. I believe I have adequate knowledge of stereotypes and their influence on my role(s).

7. I believe I have adequate knowledge of my cultural identities and their influence on emergency and crisis management.

8. I believe I have adequate knowledge of other cultural identities and how they influence emergency and crisis management.

9. I believe I have adequate knowledge of stereotypes and how they influence emergency and crisis management.

OPEN RESPONSE

Please answer the following question: "I used to think_____, but now I think_____."

(Use back of page if needing extra space.)

References

Baio, J., Wiggins, L., Christensen, D. L., Maenner, M. J., Daniels, J., Warren, Z., . . . Durkin, M. S. (2018). Prevalence of Autism Spectrum Disorder among children aged 8 years: Autism and developmental disabilities monitoring network, 11 sites, United States, 2014. *MMWR Surveillance Summaries, 67*(No. SS-6), 1–23.

Berggren, R. E., & Curiel, T. J. (2006). After the storm: Health care infrastructure in post-Katrina New Orleans. *The New England Journal of Medicine, 354*(15), 1549–1552.

Centers for Disease Control. (2019). *Autism Spectrum Disorder (ASD).* Retrieved from www.cdc.gov/ncbddd/autism/index.html

Chasson, G., & Jarosiewicz, S. R. (2014). Social competence impairments in Autism Spectrum Disorders. In V. Patel, V. Preedy, & C. Martin (Eds.), *Comprehensive guide to Autism* (pp. 1099–1108). New York: Springer.

Department of Homeland Security. (2019). *National response framework* (4th ed.). Retrieved from https://www.fema.gov/media-library-data/1572366339630-0e9278a0ede9ee129025182b4d0f818e/National_Response_Framework_4th_20191028.pdf

Ducy, E. M., & Stough, L. M. (2011). Exploring the support role of special education teachers after Hurricane Ike: Children with significant disabilities. *Journal of Family Issues, 32*(10), 1325–1345.

Edmonds, C. O. (2017). Designing emergency preparedness resources for children with Autism. *International Journal of Disability, Development and Education, 64*(4), 404–419.

Gorski, P. C. (2019). *Guide for setting ground rules.* Retrieved from www.edchange.org/multicultural/activities/groundrules.html

Johnson, H. M., & Levine, T. P. (2014). Health care and services for individuals with ASDs: Disparities and transitions. In V. Patel, V. Preedy, & C. Martin (Eds.), *Comprehensive guide to Autism* (pp. 1195–1217). New York: Springer.

Kalb, L. G., Stuart, E. A., Freedman, B., Zablotsky, B., & Vasa, R. (2012). Psychiatric-related emergency department visits among children with an Autism Spectrum Disorder. *Pediatric Emergency Care, 28*(12), 1269–1276.

Levine, T. P., Conradt, E., Goodwin, M. S., Sheinkopf, S. J., & Lester, B. (2014). Psychophysiological arousal to social stress in Autism Spectrum Disorders. In V. Patel, V. Preedy, & C. Martin (Eds.), *Comprehensive guide to Autism* (pp. 1177–1193). New York: Springer.

Mehtar, M., & Mukaddes, N. M. (2011). Posttraumatic stress disorder in individuals with diagnosis of Autism Spectrum Disorders. *Research in Autism Spectrum Disorders*, *5*(1), 539–546.

National Institute of Mental Health. (2019). *Autism Spectrum Disorder*. Retrieved from www.nimh.nih.gov/health/topics/autism-spectrum-disorders-asd/index.shtml

National Institute of Neurological Disorders and Stroke. (2019). *Autism Spectrum Disorder information page*. Retrieved from www.ninds.nih.gov/Disorders/All-Disorders/Autism-Spectrum-Disorder-Information-Page

Peek, L., & Fothergill, A. (2008). Displacement, gender, and the challenges of parenting after Hurricane Katrina. *National Women's Studies Association Journal*, *20*(3), 69–105.

Peek, L., & Stough, L. M. (2010). Children with disabilities in the context of disaster: A social vulnerability perspective. *Child Development*, *81*(4), 1260–1270.

Ronoh, S., Gaillard, J. C., & Marlowe, J. (2017). Children with disabilities in disability-inclusive disaster risk reduction: Focusing on school settings. *Policy Futures in Education*, *15*(3), 380–388.

Valenti, M., Ciprietti, T., Di Egidio, C., Gabrielli, M., Masedu, F., Tomassini, A. R., & Sorge, G. (2012). Adaptive response of children and adolescents with autism to the 2009 earthquake in L'Aquila, Italy. *Journal of Autism and Developmental Disorders*, *42*(6), 954–960.

Valenti, M., La Malfa, G., Tomassini, A., Masedu, F., Tiberti, S., & Sorge, G. (2014). Burnout among therapists working with persons with autism after the 2009 earthquake in L'Aquila, Italy: A longitudinal comparative study. *Journal of Psychiatric and Mental Health Nursing*, *21*(3), 234–240.

Van Steensel, F. J. A., Bögels, S. M., Magiati, I., & Perrin, S. (2014). Anxiety in individuals with ASD: Prevalence, phenomenology, etiology, assessment, and interventions. In V. Patel, V. Preedy, & C. Martin (Eds.), *Comprehensive guide to Autism* (pp. 601–623). New York: Springer.

Additional Resources

Facilitators may want to use the additional resources below to enhance participants' knowledge of ASD and emergency management responses to it. These resources can be used with the case, to enhance understanding before participants make their decisions, or afterwards as a means of comparing participants' choices with those made by organizations that deal with ASD and emergency care.

- ◆ A four-page pamphlet distributed by the Autism Society with recommendations for paramedics and emergency room staff who may encounter individuals with autism. www.autism-society.org/wp-content/uploads/2014/04/Paramedics_and_Emergency_Room_Staff.pdf
- ◆ A four-page pamphlet distributed by the Autism Society with recommendations for law enforcement and other first responders who may encounter individuals with autism. www.autism-society.org/wp-content/uploads/2014/04/Law_Enforcement_and_Other_First_Responders.pdf
- ◆ Recommendations for law enforcement officials, fire fighters, emergency medical providers, and search and rescue professionals who may encounter individuals with autism. www.autismspeaks.org/information-first-responders

11

Diversity During a Storm

Accommodating Religious Minorities in an Evacuation Shelter

Abdul Samad, Keith Douglas Revell, and N. Emel Ganapati

Overview of the Context

This case study immerses participants in a very common disaster management scenario – managing an evacuation shelter – in which familiarity with religious minority groups will lead to better outcomes. Shelter management can be extremely stressful. Exhausted, frightened residents, fleeing from danger and struggling to care for loved ones, face an uncertain future. Shelter residents typically arrive carrying only a few possessions, unprepared to sustain themselves for long. They are suddenly thrown into close proximity with strangers who will now eat, sleep, and attend to their personal hygiene in the same confined space.

Research also shows that safety is a top concern for some, who associate shelters with violence and sexual crime (Farmer, Zelewicz, Wachtendorf, & DeYoung, 2018). For a short time, occupants will rely on shelter managers to provide them with the necessities of life and to keep them safe in crowded conditions. Shelter managers are trained to provide for the immediate, basic needs of residents (e.g., food and water, sanitation, and medical care), but in so doing they are always compelled to make choices about how resources are deployed and how problems are addressed. In this regard, increased understanding of religious minority groups can assist evacuation shelter managers in making thoughtful choices to ensure that all of the residents under their care have the best possible experience despite difficult circumstances.

There is a small but growing literature on disasters in Muslim countries (e.g., Aldrich, 2011; Chan, Kim, Lin, Cheung, & Lee, 2014; Ganapati, 2012, 2013; Ghafory-Ashtiany, 2009; Gianisa & Le De, 2018; Joakim & White, 2015; Malik, 2011; Paradise, 2005; Schenk, 2013). Studies that focus on the Muslim-American population in the United States are less extensive but nonetheless revealing. They highlight Muslim-American concerns about cleanliness and access to prayer rooms in hurricane shelters (Mando, Peek, Brown, & King-Kallimanis, 2011) and sociocultural factors including, but not limited to, safety and privacy in their day-to-day lives in the post-9/11 era (Peek, 2004, 2011).

As of 2017, there were approximately 3.5 million Muslims in the United States, comprising about 1.1% of the total population; by 2050, the Muslim-American population is estimated to reach 8.1 million (2.1% of the total population) (Mohamed, 2018). American-Muslims (immigrants, children of immigrants, and native-born converts) reflect the diversity of Islam globally (Smith, 2002). With nearly two billion adherents worldwide, Islam is practiced in Europe, North Africa, the Middle East, Central Asia, and across the Asian-Pacific region, which contains the largest number of Muslims in the world. However, although Islam is exceptionally diverse, in the U.S. public attitudes have tended to focus on a very limited range of its expression in the Arab world, resulting in stereotyping that associates Muslims with terrorism. Contemporary bias against Muslims partakes of negative images of Islam based on centuries of misunderstanding, making it particularly difficult to identify and address (Bleich, 2012; Casey, 2018; Said, 1978).

This case takes a positive approach to cultural competence by emphasizing two arenas in which knowledge of Muslim groups could contribute to improved emergency management. First, by familiarizing themselves with a few common features of Muslim life, evacuation shelter managers will be better prepared to make reasonable accommodations for their clients and to negotiate satisfactory compromises in the face of scarce resources. Second, by observing how bias might affect the behavior of non-Muslim staff and residents, disaster managers will be better prepared to resolve conflicts that may arise in the close quarters and tense atmosphere of an evacuation shelter.

Although Islam is as diverse as its many ethnic expressions, there are several common features of Muslim life that may emerge in the context of an evacuation shelter, involving food preparation, religious expression, personal hygiene, clothing, and medical care (Mando et al., 2011).

- ◆ Muslims prefer food that is "halal" (permissible) as opposed to "haram" (impermissible), and there are guidelines for food preparation and service to ensure that it is "halal". Certain types of food (such as pork) or food preparation (with alcohol, gelatin, or meat stock) do not meet this standard. Muslims may also prefer to eat at certain times, such as before sunrise and after sunset, particularly during the month of Ramadan (when daylight fasting is required).
- ◆ Religious observance is also a crucial element of Muslim practice. Muslims prefer a dedicated place for daily prayers ("salat"), with separate facilities for men and women, which can be accessed from three to five times each day, depending on the branch of Islam (Shia or Sunni). First prayers are often done before sunrise, which means that Muslim shelter occupants will likely ask for lights to be turned on before dawn.
- ◆ Muslims wash themselves, including, but not limited to, hands, mouth, arms, and feet, before prayer or the handling of the Quran (known as "abdest" or "wudu") and will thus use bathrooms in preparation for religious expression.
- ◆ Muslims may wear traditional garb, including "hijabs" (headscarves) for women and turbans for men (although not all turbans indicate adherence to Islam).
- ◆ Muslims typically prefer same-gender medical care from doctors and nurses.

These cultural expressions are common throughout the Muslim world and are no more controversial than going to choir practice, cellphone usage, baseball caps, or earrings in contemporary American culture. Emergency managers equipped with an understanding of these basic issues will be in a better position to provide reasonable accommodations to Muslim shelter occupants and to negotiate good-faith compromises when limited resources prevent more satisfactory arrangements (e.g., food choices may be unavailable and medical providers may be scarce).

Shelter residents typically speak their native languages, which means that shelters in areas of diverse populations may be filled with the sounds of multiple languages. Differences in language can reinforce a sense of "otherness" and thus stereotypes. This general problem applies with special force to Muslims in regard to the use of the phrase, "Allahu Akbar," which means "God is Great." "Allahu Akbar" is a common, non-threatening utterance employed in a very wide variety of circumstances: as greeting, prayer, meditation, self-affirmation, exclamation of happiness, and expression of hope, among other things. Unfortunately, terrorists and their supporters have misappropriated "Allahu Akbar" as an expression of violence. News reports have amplified this one aspect of what is otherwise an expression of peace. Evacuation shelter managers with knowledge of this frequently misunderstood element of Muslim culture should be prepared to intervene in situations in which lack of familiarity with its usage might lead to unreasonable suspicion and the perpetuation of bias.

Case Study: Sheltering and Muslim Communities

Goals of the Case Study

The goals of this case study are threefold: (1) to help participants think about diversity-related issues in emergency management; (2) to familiarize participants with cultural competencies that are helpful when dealing with minority religious groups (Muslims, specifically) in the context of a disaster; and

(3) to enable participants to work cooperatively and brainstorm ideas to solve issues that may arise as they assume the roles of emergency managers, staff, and volunteers at a public shelter before and during a major storm.

This case study is intended for participants and focuses on cultural competencies associated with the American-Muslim community in the context of a fictional hurricane scenario. It may also be of value to international aid agency officials deployed to majority-Muslim countries (e.g., Albania, Algeria, Indonesia, Pakistan, and Turkey) or countries with Muslim minorities (e.g., Canada, Denmark, Germany, India, and Singapore) before, during, and in the aftermath of a disaster (e.g., earthquake, flood). By enhancing practitioner awareness of their biases, prejudices, and stereotypes regarding Muslim populations, it may allow them to gain the trust of the affected populations they serve and solve problems in disaster contexts in a more effective and culturally competent manner.

Learning Outcomes

Upon completion of this exercise, participants will demonstrate understanding of the following:

- ◆ Their conscious/visible and unconscious/invisible biases, prejudices, and stereotypes regarding Muslim populations
- ◆ The ways these biases, prejudices, and stereotypes might influence how they think and what they do in their future roles as emergency management practitioners
- ◆ How they can confront and address their biases, prejudices, and stereotypes toward Muslim populations

Pre- and post-tests will assess student learning during the case study, allowing the facilitators to compare what the participants knew before and after the case study.

Definitions

For this case study, the facilitators may want to provide definitions for several terms, including, but not limited to, the following:

- ◆ Evacuation Shelter: A structure that houses populations who are temporarily at risk of an imminent emergency (e.g., up to 72 hours), such as those who reside in trailer parks or in areas that will be subjected to storm surge in the event of a hurricane. Evacuation shelters typically include buildings (e.g., schools, community centers, and convention centers) that are designated to be safe for taking shelter before and in the immediate aftermath of the emergency. Evacuation shelters are intended to address residents' immediate, basic needs (e.g., food and water, sanitation, and medical care).
- ◆ Prayers (salat) and Wudu (ablution/washing ritual): Muslims offer three to five daily prayers (salat) during, or shortly after, specific hours of the day. Muslims remove their footwear before entering the prayer area, and it is expected that floors be cleaned and covered. These daily prayers are prefaced by a gender-segregated ablution ritual (wudu), involving the washing of feet, hands, and face in clean, running water.
- ◆ Ramadan: Ramadan is considered one of the holiest months in the Islamic faith. Muslims observe fasting from dawn to dusk during the entire month of Ramadan. They eat breakfast (sahoor) before dawn and refrain from eating and drinking until dusk when they break their fast by eating dates (fruit of the date palm tree) with water, if available. Because of differences between the Gregorian and Muslim calendars, the specific dates of Ramadan will vary from year to year.
- ◆ Turban: A head covering based on a cloth wrapping worn by some Muslim men, including religious

leaders. Turbans (known as "dastarr" or "pagg") are also worn by Sikh men; Sikhism is a monotheistic offshoot of Hinduism founded in the Punjab region in India.

◆ Hijab: A head covering worn by Muslim women to cover their hair, ears, and neck.

◆ Halal: The word "halal" denotes things that are permitted or allowed in the Islamic faith. Halal, when used concerning food or drink, means permissible or allowable for consumption by a Muslim.

◆ Islamophobia: Islamophobia is defined as "a hostile attitude toward Islam and Muslims based on the image of Islam as the enemy and as a vital, irrefutable and absolute threat whether on the basis of religious or ethnic criteria" (López, 2011, p. 570).

Breakdown

The facilitators may carry out the case study using the following steps. As the suggested time for this exercise is 120 minutes, facilitators may want to allow a break, preferably after Step 4.

Step 1. 10 min. Start the exercise with the pre-/post-tests described herein. After the participants complete Parts I and II of the test, the facilitators may ask the participants to keep their answers and do the following:

◆ Visit the list they put together for Part II

◆ Circle the characteristics that they think they were not conscious of before this exercise

After these preliminary steps, facilitators can explain that the purpose of this exercise was to help participants uncover their conscious/visible and unconscious/invisible biases, prejudices, and stereotypes. They may also add that the participants will have a chance to revisit and reflect on these at the end of the case study.

Step 2. 5 min. Before proceeding with the rest of the exercise, develop and clarify ground rules that articulate a set of expected behaviors for discussions (see the Ground Rules section for further guidance).

Step 3. 15 min. Have an open conversation on the following questions with everyone:

♦ What are some of the biases, prejudices, and stereotypes regarding Muslim populations in our society?

♦ Are these biases, prejudices, and stereotypes gendered? How?

♦ What do you think are some of the biases, prejudices, and stereotypes for populations that speak Arabic?

♦ How do the biases, prejudices, and stereotypes for Muslim populations compare with those for other religious groups (Christians, Jews, Hindus, and Sikhs)?

Step 4. 30 min. Divide the participants into groups of four to five people and distribute the scenario as a handout. Tell them that they are to read the scenario and imagine themselves in the role of the shelter manager. During their discussions, they must make two decisions:

1. How do you respond to the concerns of the group of Muslim men who have asked you for accommodations?

2. How do you respond to the concerns of the group of non-Muslim occupants who demand that you either kick out the Muslims or search their belongings?

Step 5. 30 min. Use the Questions for Discussion herein to explore the participants' decisions made in Step 4.

1. What accommodations do you think you should provide to the Muslim occupants of the shelter?

2. If you do not have the resources to provide everything the Muslims occupants have requested, what reasonable compromises might be possible?

3. If you feel you must deny a request for an accommodation, what would be the best way to phrase your decision?

4. How would you respond to occupants who ask for kosher food? Gluten-free food? Food that does not contain peanuts or peanut oil?

5. How do you think the biases, prejudices, and stereotypes toward Muslims discussed in the first part of this exercise might affect your decisions about what accommodations to provide?

6. How would you address the request to search the belongings of the Muslims occupants?

7. Would you institute a search of occupants' belongings if they had used the phrases, "Praise the Lord," "Hallelujah," or "Shabbat Shalom"?

8. If you feel you must deny the request for a search of belongings, what would be the best way to phrase your decision?

9. How do you think the biases, prejudices, and stereotypes toward Muslims discussed in the first part of this exercise might affect your decisions about whether to conduct a search?

10. Both Muslim and non-Muslim occupants of the shelter have voiced concern over the bathrooms. How would you handle this issue?

11. If you were put in charge of training shelter staff in the county as part of preparedness efforts for next year, what kind of training would you provide?

12. Research indicates that minority populations are often unprepared for disasters and fearful of their safety in shelters. With this in mind, how might disaster pre-planning assist you in avoiding or reducing the conflicts that emerged in this case?

Step 6. 20 min. Use the definitions provided in this case study to facilitate a larger group discussion on the following:
   ◆ How might a shelter manager approach the conflicts presented in this case?
   ◆ If you were the FEMA director and wanted to enhance the cultural competencies of emergency management

professionals toward different religious groups, what would you do?

Step 7. 10 min. Distribute the post-test and ask participants to reflect on what they can do to address their visible/conscious and invisible/unconscious stereotypes, prejudices, and biases.

Ground Rules (Gorski, 2019)

We recommend that, at the beginning of the exercise, the facilitators allow the participants to create the ground rules themselves so that they have more of an incentive to observe the rules they helped design. The facilitators should also explain the purpose of the ground rules (e.g., to make sure that everyone is heard), make them visible to participants once they are decided, and remind them of the ground rules when problems occur. If the participants are having difficulty establishing ground rules for the exercise, then the facilitators might want to ask participants to reflect on the best and the worst group discussions they have had in the past so that this exercise will result in a lively, passionate, and respectful debate.

Should the facilitators choose to introduce their own ground rules, the following are some sample rules for the exercise:

- Respect one another – avoid talking at each other or engaging in private conversations with others while someone is speaking.
- Focus on the ideas rather than on people – value people's right to hold opinions, beliefs, and values that are different from your own.
- Listen carefully to what others are saying even though you may disagree with them.
- Challenge one another, ask questions, and seek clarifications, but do so respectfully.
- Be considerate of others – avoid monopolizing the discussion.

- Avoid generalizing (e.g., *"they* always do this sort of thing") and speak from your personal experience (e.g., "I observed this").
- Be open-minded and willing to learn and change your perspective.
- Display respectful body language.
- Keep what you heard in the discussion strictly confidential to ensure an open and honest exchange – do not share it with those outside the classroom.

Before the exercise, the facilitators should also reflect on the ground rules they should observe to ensure a critical yet respectful discussion. Some suggestions include the following:

- Appreciate differences of opinion.
- Refrain from taking sides.
- Ensure that some people do not dominate the discussion.
- Encourage everyone to take part in the discussion.
- Periodically summarize the discussion and encourage reflection.
- Keep track of time to ensure that all elements of the exercise are adequately explored.
- Conclude the discussion by reviewing topics that were adequately explored and highlighting those that remain open to further debate.

The facilitators should also have a plan for managing emotionally charged situations that may arise as part of the discussion. (See Chapter 4 for advice and strategies to manage these situations.)

Supplemental Questions
For the scenario provided herein, facilitators may consider asking the following supplemental questions:

- What are your first thoughts about this scenario? Did you have any emotional reactions to this scenario? If yes, why? If no, why?

- Was there anything thought provoking about how your fellow participants reacted to this exercise? (Please use generalizations and do not target others.)
- What would your reaction to this exercise be if you had been raised as a Muslim American?
- How do you think this scenario relates to emergency management? Why was this exercise created?

Hurricane Gina and Delta County

Scenario

Hurricane Gina has strengthened into a dangerous Category 4 storm and is tracking toward the Atlantic Coast. The National Hurricane Center has indicated possible landfall near Delta County, when the storm may reach Category 5 status, with sustained winds of more than 160 miles per hour and gusts more than 182 miles per hour. The Mayor of Delta County have ordered the mandatory evacuation of all persons on barrier islands and within ten miles of the coast. Local highways have been jammed with those fleeing the coast. Tourists and residents with no other place to go have moved into designated hurricane shelters, all of which are expected to be full.

You are the manager of a shelter capable of accommodating 800 individuals. You think of yourself as the "Mayor of a Micro City" where people will need to be sheltered, fed, and kept safe. You have a capable, experienced staff of professionals with expertise in public safety, dormitory management, medical care, and psychological counseling, but your resources are limited and you are not able to call for extra staff or supplies until the storm passes, which will be a minimum of 48 hours, perhaps longer. Shelter occupants come from diverse socio-economic, ethnic, racial, and religious backgrounds and include residents from luxury high-rises, middle-class suburbs, and mobile home parks, along with tourists and the homeless. Some mistrust and suspicion already exist among shelter occupants, who are strangers who have had minimal day-to-day interactions with one another before the storm.

You have been approached by a group of men who say that they represent the Muslim occupants of the shelter. They tell you that they are dissatisfied with the way the shelter is run and that their religious rights are not being respected. "We are in the holy month of Ramadan," they tell you, and it is important that they fast during daylight hours. They ask you to provide them with "halal" food before dawn and after sunset. They want you to create two clean, quiet rooms that can be used for prayers during various times of the day. They insist that shelter staff turn on lights before dawn. They also want you to secure the services of a female doctor for female members of their families. They conclude their demands by complaining that the bathrooms are filthy and unfit for use by members of their faith.

Shortly thereafter, another group of shelter occupants complains that women wearing headscarves and men with beards and turbans are washing their feet in the sinks in the bathroom several times a day and making a mess. Those same people are praying aloud, kneeling on the floor, and murmuring suspiciously. They also believe that some of the men in that group may be dangerous because they heard them shouting "Allahu Akbar," which, as everyone has seen on the news, is something that terrorists scream before they attack. "I don't feel safe around these Muslims," one of them says. "What if they have guns? Please ask them to leave the shelter. We have women, children, and elderly Americans here who you are supposed to protect!" You tell them that storm conditions will not allow anyone to leave the building for at least 48 hours. They acknowledge that it may be impossible to kick them out but insist that the next best thing would be to conduct a search of their belongings to ensure that they do not have any weapons.

Pre-Test Assessment

PURPOSE OF THE SURVEY

This assessment survey is designed to demonstrate understanding of cultural competence–related aspects and establish a baseline of participant attitudes before the exercise.

DEFINITIONS

Directions: Please match the terminologies with their definitions.

_____ Halal

    A. A head covering based on a cloth wrapping worn by some Muslim men, including religious leaders.

_____ Hijab

    B. A head covering worn by Muslim women to cover their hair, ears, and neck.

_____ Turban

    C. Denotes things that are permitted or allowed in the Islamic faith.

ATTITUDINAL SCALE

Directions: Please use the following scale to represent your reaction to the questions.

1	2	3	4	5
Strongly Agree	Agree	Neither Agree nor Disagree	Disagree	Strongly Disagree

1. I have biases, prejudices, and stereotypes.

2. I have adequate knowledge of diverse religious groups.

3. I have adequate knowledge regarding Muslim populations.

4. My biases, prejudices, and stereotypes will influence my work should I choose a career in emergency management.

5. Being subjected to crime is likely to be a top concern for those staying in an evacuation shelter.

6. Shelter managers need to accommodate the needs of diverse religious minority groups.

7. Shelter managers need to provide prayer room for diverse faith groups.

8. Shelter managers need to provide food that is acceptable to diverse faith groups.

9. Shelter managers need to address cleanliness and sanitation needs of diverse faith groups.

10. Shelter managers need training in conflict resolution.

FIRST THOUGHTS
Write down the first characteristics (negative or positive) that come to mind regarding the groups listed herein. The rules to follow for this question are these: • Take no more than five seconds for each group • Move on if you cannot think of any negative or positive characteristics for a particular group • Resist your urge to edit or second guess your responses • Keep in mind that your responses will be anonymous and kept confidential • Be honest with yourself to get the most out of this exercise

A tourist:

A homeless person:

A person who lives in a high-rise condominium on the beach:

A trailer park resident:

A woman wearing a hijab:

A male wearing a turban:

A person who speaks Arabic:

A Christian person:

A Jewish person:

A Muslim person:

A Hindu person:

A Sikh person:

Post-Test Assessment

PURPOSE OF THE SURVEY

This assessment survey is designed to demonstrate understanding of culturally related impacts and establish a baseline of participant attitudes after the exercise.

DEFINITIONS

Directions: Please match the terminologies with their definitions.

_____ Halal   A. A head covering based on a cloth wrapping worn by some Muslim men, including religious leaders.

_____ Hijab   B. A head covering worn by Muslim women to cover their hair, ears, and neck.

_____ Turban C. Denotes things that are permitted or allowed in the Islamic faith.

ATTITUDINAL SCALE

Directions: Please use the following scale to represent your reaction to the questions.

1	2	3	4	5
Strongly Agree	Agree	Neither Agree nor Disagree	Disagree	Strongly Disagree

1. I have biases, prejudices, and stereotypes.

2. I have adequate knowledge of diverse religious groups.

3. I have adequate knowledge regarding Muslim populations.

4. My biases, prejudices, and stereotypes will influence my work should I choose a career in emergency management.

5. Being subjected to crime is likely to be a top concern for those staying in an evacuation shelter.

6. Shelter managers need to accommodate the needs of diverse religious minority groups.

7. Shelter managers need to provide a prayer room for diverse faith groups.

8. Shelter managers need to provide food that is acceptable to diverse faith groups.

9. Shelter managers need to address cleanliness and sanitation needs of diverse faith groups.

10. Shelter managers need training in conflict resolution.

OPEN RESPONSE

Please answer the following question: "I used to think_____, but now I think_____."

(Use back of page if needing extra space.)

References

Aldrich, D. P. (2011). The externalities of strong social capital: Post-tsunami recovery in Southeast India. *Journal of Civil Society*, *7*(1), 81–99.

Bleich, E. (2012). Defining and researching Islamophobia. *Review of Middle East Studies*, *46*(2), 180–189.

Casey, P. M. (2018). Stigmatized identities: Too Muslim to be American, too American to be Muslim. *Symbolic Interaction*, *41*(1), 100–119.

Chan, E. Y., Kim, J. H., Lin, C., Cheung, E. Y., & Lee, P. P. (2014). Is previous disaster experience a good predictor for disaster preparedness in extreme poverty households in remote Muslim minority based community in China? *Journal of Immigrant and Minority Health*, *16*(3), 466–472.

Farmer, A. K., Zelewicz, L., Wachtendorf, T., & DeYoung, S. E. (2018). Scared of the shelter from the storm: Fear of crime and hurricane shelter decision making. *Sociological Inquiry*, *88*(2), 193–215.

Ganapati, N. E. (2012). In good company: Why social capital matters for women during disaster recovery. *Public Administration Review*, *72*(3), 419–427.

Ganapati, N. E. (2013). Downsides of social capital for women during disaster recovery: Towards a more critical approach. *Administration and Society*, *45*(1), 72–96.

Ghafory-Ashtiany, M. (2009). View of Islam on earthquakes, human vitality and disaster. *Disaster Prevention and Management*, *18*(3), 218–232.

Gianisa, A., & Le De, L. (2018). The role of religious beliefs and practices in disaster. *Disaster Prevention and Management*, *27*(1), 74–86.

Gorski, P. C. (2019). *Guide for setting ground rules*. Retrieved from www.edchange.org/multicultural/activities/groundrules.html

Joakim, E. P., & White, R. S. (2015). Exploring the impact of religious beliefs, leadership, and networks on response and recovery of disaster-affected populations: A case study from Indonesia. *Journal of Contemporary Religion*, *30*(2), 193–212.

López, F. B. (2011). Towards a definition of Islamophobia: Approximations of the early twentieth century. *Ethnic and Racial Studies*, *34*(4), 556–573, University Press.

Malik, A. M. (2011). Denial of flood aid to members of the Ahmadiyya Muslim community in Pakistan. *Health and Human Rights*, *13*(1), 70–77.

Mando, A. M., Peek, L., Brown, L. M., & King-Kallimanis, B. L. (2011). Hurricane preparedness and sheltering preferences of Muslims living in Florida. *Journal of Emergency Management*, *9*(1), 51–64.

Mohamed, B. (2018). New estimates show U.S. Muslim population continues to grow. *Pew Research Center*. Retrieved from http://pewrsr.ch/2lP2MKc

Paradise, T. R. (2005). Perception of earthquake risk in Agadir, Morocco: A case study from a Muslim community. *Global Environmental Change Part B: Environmental Hazards*, *6*(3), 167–180.

Peek, L. (2004). Backlash mitigation plan: Protecting ethnic and religious minorities following a terrorist attack. *The Journal of the American Society of Professional Emergency Planners*, *11*(1), 115–122.

Peek, L. (2011). *Behind the backlash: Muslim Americans after 9/11*. Philadelphia: Temple.

Said, E. W. (1978). *Orientalism*. New York: Pantheon Books.

Schenk, C. G. (2013). Navigating an inconvenient difference in antagonistic contexts: Doing fieldwork in Aceh, Indonesia. *Singapore Journal of Tropical Geography*, *34*(3), 342–356.

Smith, T. W. (2002). The Muslim population of the United States: The methodology of estimates. *Public Opinion Quarterly*, *66*(3), 404–417.

12

Teaching Preparedness, Warning, and Protective Action With a Social Vulnerability Twist

DeeDee Bennett and Emily MacNabb

Overview

"Social vulnerability" is a broad term used to highlight individuals, groups, or their situations, which may factor in identifying root causes for disaster risk. For example, research has shown that women are oftentimes easily convinced of a possible threat and take protective action sooner (Fothergill, 1996; Neal & Phillips, 1990). However, in many instances being a woman can prevent one from deciding on protective action, as a result of class, culture, situation, or socialization (Enarson & Chakrabarti, 2009). Families in and near poverty levels may or may not have the funds to take certain protective action measures (Fothergill & Peek, 2004). Misperceptions about (and credibility of) warning messages may also differ from person to person and group to group, depending on previous experiences (Fothergill, Maestas, & Darlington, 1999). This may increase risk for some people. Individuals who are blind, deaf, hard-of-hearing, or who have limited vision may require assistive technology or accessible communications in order to receive the information properly (National Council on Disability, 2009). Furthermore, in the business world, small businesses do not often fare as well as larger businesses. This can have major impacts in the communities in which smaller businesses serve (Phillips, Neal, & Webb, 2012).

The socio-political ecology theory allows us to consider how some individuals may be more at risk during disasters because of the social construction of society. This theory is concentrated on the interaction between the natural and built environments with the human environment. After a disaster, the theory assumes that scarce resources will cause competition, leaving those most socially vulnerable without access (Peacock & Ragsdale, 1997). These resources span a wide spectrum, including but not limited to food, water, information, finances, and shelter. Because many resources become scarce immediately following a disaster, the competition for these resources may intensify inequalities previously present (Phillips et al., 2012). The disparities, of course, differ in each society, region, neighborhood, and person. Therefore, individuals more at risk in one nation or context may not be as at risk in another. In this exercise, we focus on warning information as the resource, which needs to be disseminated to the public.

Warnings are a process that includes detection of the threat, content of the message, and the perception of the message itself (Drabek, 1999; Lindell & Perry, 1987, 2004; Mileti, 1995). In the dissemination phase, information about the threat is given to the public. The channels used to convey a disaster warning are equally as important as the content of the message itself (Lindell & Perry, 1987; Rogers & Sorenson, 1991). The final phase is based on the perceptions of the public about the warning information given. It is during this phase that individuals decide whether to take protective action (Mileti, 1999; Lindell & Perry, 2004).

However, other outside factors also influence individuals' decisions. These factors include environmental cues, social setting, social ties, socio-demographic characteristics, psychological characteristics, and pre-warning perceptions (Mileti & Peek, 2000). Subtle persuasion for many in the public also includes the actions of other community members. Some will wonder about the following: what are the neighbors doing? If there are many people, businesses, and organizations preparing for the disaster, people will probably follow suit. While these terms are briefly discussed in this case study, it is highly recommended that the facilitator become familiar with the concepts by reviewing the reading list mentioned in the facilitator's notes.

Taking these key lesson points in mind, this case study has four major topics of focus:

1. What are some factors that influence individual and household ability to prepare?
2. Why do people dismiss warning messages?
3. What factors influence one's willingness to heed warning messages?
4. What circumstances affect individual and household protective action?

Case Study: Preparedness, Warning, and Protective Action

Goals of the Case Study

This exercise presents a unique opportunity for participants to apply, discuss, and reinforce lessons learned about preparedness, warning, and protective action. Participation in this exercise enhances the synthesis of knowledge among preparedness activities, protective action decisions following warning messages, and socially vulnerable populations in the United States. When connected with related lessons on social vulnerability, the exercise can highlight the application of and the concept behind the socio-political ecology theory.

Learning Outcomes

This exercise has six overall desired learning outcomes based on the topics described earlier:

1. Reinforce the concepts on warnings, receiver characteristics, and protective action.
2. Understand the decision process for taking protective action.

3. Appreciate the costs and hindrances that accompany planning and preparedness.
4. Introduce and explain the socio-political ecology theory.
5. Sensitize participants to socially vulnerable populations.
6. Help participants synthesize information from multiple lessons.

Set-Up and Case Study Facilitation

For this case study exercise, you will need the following materials:

1. Map of the impact area
2. Description of the threat
3. Demographics information
4. Character cards
5. Test questions
6. Potential discussion questions

The following map can be utilized for the exercise, or you can generate your own.[1] The authors created this map utilizing Fantasy Maps, a free service, and added specific locations, including a Deaf and Hard-of-Hearing school, sports arena, infectious diseases laboratory, and zoo. Naming these locations (and potentially others) can provide unique concerns for participants to consider.

When it comes to character cards, you can generate your own to personalize the exercise to the participants or community. Sample character cards are presented later. The cards include individuals from various socially vulnerable populations. You should aim to create enough character cards for all participants. You can even allow participants to help in character creation. Sample citizen characteristics are shown in Table 12.1. The character cards can also link citizens together. For example, you may have two citizens who live in an apartment complex owned by a landlord who is in serious debt. It is important to provide context for each of the characters and include income and savings information, car issues (or lack thereof), location of children's schools, any illness, or medical concerns.

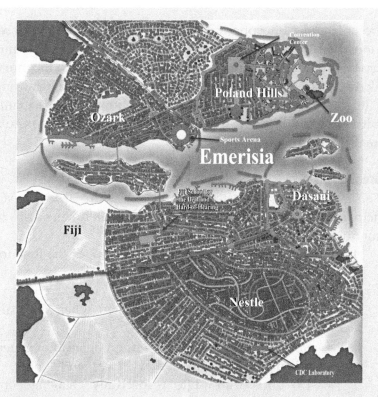

FIGURE 12.1 Example of Map Used in Exercise
Source: Bennett & MacNabb

TABLE 12.1 Sample Citizen Character Cards

A single mother of two school-aged children	A landlord of an apartment complex who is in debt	A conference visitor from a foreign country
A pregnant woman on bed rest	A family with four pets (two dogs, two cats)	A person with a sensory disability living independently
A retired senior dependent on social security	A tourist who does not speak English visiting the aquarium	A graduate student with limited income

Source: Bennett & MacNabb

An additional area of personalization is for the threat itself. The description of the threat is most important because it can impact the content of the message the emergency managers create. The facilitator can use information from the National

Oceanic and Atmospheric Administration (NOAA) on a pre-vious real threat (www.noaa.gov). Additionally, participants can be provided information on the types of damage the threat likely causes. For example, when doing an exercise regarding Category 4 hurricanes, the facilitator provided the participants with information on the wind speed, storm surge, and approx-imate infrastructure damage.

Breakdown

This exercise has been tested in classes with 30 to 40 par-ticipants. The facilitator should plan for the following steps to conduct this vulnerability exercise:

1. Discuss the following ground rules to set the tone for the exercise:
    Ground Rules (Gorski, 2019)
    - Listen actively – respect others when they are talking.
    - Speak from your own experience instead of gener-alizing ("I" instead of "they," "we," and "you").
    - Do not be afraid to respectfully challenge one another by asking questions but refrain from per-sonal attacks – focus on ideas.
    - Participate to the fullest of your ability – commu-nity growth depends on the inclusion of every individual voice.
    - Instead of invalidating somebody else's story with your own spin on their experience, share your own story and experience.
    - The goal is not to agree – it is to gain a deeper understanding.
    - Be conscious of body language and nonverbal responses – they can be as disrespectful as words.
2. Introduce the participants to the location; this is espe-cially important if using a fictional map. However, be mindful to provide a map for actual locations as well, because not all the participants may be familiar with

the area. Designate half the class as emergency managers and the other half as citizens.

3. Explain the roles. For the emergency managers, their role is to warn the other side of the class (or the citizens) of an impending threat. The emergency managers can use whatever channels they deem necessary and can create their group in whatever way they see fit. It is up to the emergency managers to decide which first responders, community groups, or public utility officials are in their group. It is also up to the emergency managers to decide what is in the content of their message. For the citizens, they are tasked with getting into character. They must determine what types of messages they will be able to hear or heed as well as anything that may hinder their ability to immediately take protective action. They also must determine the likelihood of their character having a preparedness kit.

4. Hand out materials. All participants can see the location in which the threat is to occur. Citizens will be able to identify the county in which they live, work, and/ or go to school. Only the citizens will have character cards. Only the emergency managers will have information about the impending threat and broad demographics information taken from the census.

5. (Optional) Provide the citizen side of the class with information about the impending threat, after approximately 10 minutes. This allows them to discuss what information they may need to make a clear decision and determine what transportation, sheltering, and protective actions they may want to consider. This step mimics the reality that information is provided to citizens through both official and unofficial groups, organizations, or individuals.

6. Provide participants 25 minutes to complete their tasks, after which time is up. Emergency managers will have to "warn" the citizens. They will provide the

content of their message, the channels they will use to warn, the frequency of their message, and a list of whom (what offices) they included to create the message. Allow them approximately 5 minutes to run down their warning list.

7. The citizens will determine whether they can heed the warning message and how likely it is that they have a preparedness kit; moreover, they should also discuss any other issues they had with the message as given. Allow the citizen side of the class approximately 5 minutes.

8. The facilitator will use broad discussion questions to encourage the two sides of the class to think about why some things worked or did not work with regard to warnings and protective actions. Allow for approximately 10 minutes to discuss the overall exercise and engage as many participants as possible. Once the activity has been completed, provide participants with five to seven minutes to take the test.

Discussion Questions

1. To those of you who were citizens, were you able to evacuate successfully with the information provided to you by the emergency managers?

2. To those of you who were emergency managers, what information did you take into consideration when crafting your warning messages?

3. To those of you who were emergency managers, did you anticipate most of your citizens would be able to heed your evacuation warning? Did their responses surprise you?

4. To those of you who were citizens, what could the emergency managers have done differently in designing their messages (if anything) that would have increased your ability to take the recommended protective action?

5. To all, why do you think social vulnerability impacts warning messages and someone's likelihood to heed them?

Pre-Test Assessment

PURPOSE OF THE SURVEY

This assessment survey is designed to demonstrate understanding of cultural competence–related aspects and establish a baseline of participant attitudes before the exercise.

DEFINITIONS

Directions: Please match the terminologies with their definitions.

_____ Protective Action   A.   A person receiving the emergency message and being able to evacuate, seek shelter, or move away from the threat, as requested in the warning message.

_____ Socially Vulnerable Populations   B.   A broad term used to highlight individuals, groups, or their situations that may factor in identifying root causes for disaster risk.

_____ Socio-Political Ecology Theory   C.   Allows us to consider how some individuals may be more at risk during disasters because of the social construction of society.

ATTITUDINAL SCALE

Directions: Please use the following scale to represent your reaction to the statements.

1	2	3	4	5
Strongly Agree	Agree	Neither Agree nor Disagree	Disagree	Strongly Disagree

1. Research shows that upon hearing a warning people take protective action immediately.

2. Your gender may influence the way you prepare for a disaster.

3. One of the major (most important) receiver characteristics for disaster warning is environmental cues.

4. Social vulnerability has no impact on ability to take protective action.

5. Immigration or transient status could influence disaster kit preparation.

6. Individuals' social vulnerability could influence their decision-making in response to warning messages.

MULTIPLE CHOICE

Directions: Please select the best answer to the following questions:

1. Warning myths include:

A. Withdraw: People need and want help from officials to make decisions, because they are helpless

B. Cry-wolf: If a warning message is false, people will ignore the next one

C. Less detail: Too much information will confuse the public

D. All of the above

E. None of the above

2. Warning is a process that includes all of the following, except:

A. Detection

B. Defense

C. Dissemination of information

D. Receiving the information

E. None of the above; these are all part of the warning process

3. Socially vulnerable populations can be categorized based on which of the following:

A. Gender

B. Ability

C. Residence

D. All of the above

E. None of the above

4. Disaster preparedness kits should include:

A. Money

B. Pet supplies (if you have a pet)

C. Copies of your ID

D. All of the above

E. None of the above

Post-Test Assessment

PURPOSE OF THE SURVEY

This assessment survey is designed to demonstrate understanding of culturally related impacts and establish a baseline of participant attitudes after the exercise.

DEFINITIONS

Directions: Please match the terminologies with their definitions.

_____ Protective Action

A. A person receiving the emergency message and being able to evacuate, seek shelter, or move away from the threat, as requested in the warning message.

_____ Socially Vulnerable Populations

B. A broad term used to highlight individuals, groups, or their situations that may factor in identifying root causes for disaster risk.

_____ Socio-Political Ecology Theory

C. Allows us to consider how some individuals may be more at risk during disasters because of the social construction of society.

ATTITUDINAL SCALE

Directions: Please use the following scale to represent your reaction to the questions.

1	2	3	4	5
Strongly Agree	Agree	Neither Agree nor Disagree	Disagree	Strongly Disagree

1. Research shows that upon hearing a warning people take protective action immediately.

2. Your gender may influence the way you prepare for a disaster.

3. One of the major (most important) receiver characteristics for disaster warning is environmental cues.

4. Social vulnerability has no impact on ability to take protective action.

5. Immigration or transient status could influence disaster kit preparation.

6. Individuals' social vulnerability could influence their decision-making in response to warning messages.

MULTIPLE CHOICE

Directions: Please select the best answer to the following questions:

1. Warning myths include:

   A. Withdraw: People need and want help from officials to make decisions, because they are helpless

   B. Cry-wolf: If a warning message is false, people will ignore the next one

   C. Less detail: Too much information will confuse the public

   D. All of the above

   E. None of the above

2. Warning is a process that includes all of the following, except:

A. Detection

B. Defense

C. Dissemination of information

D. Receiving the information

E. None of the above; these are all part of the warning process

3. Socially vulnerable populations can be categorized based on which of the following:

A. Gender

B. Ability

C. Residence

D. All of the above

E. None of the above

4. Disaster preparedness kits should include:

A. Money

B. Pet supplies (if you have a pet)

C. Copies of your ID

D. All of the above

E. None of the above

OPEN RESPONSE
Please answer the following questions:
"I used to think_____, but now I think_____."
How could individuals' social vulnerability influence their decision-making in response to warning messages?
What is the most important thing you learned during the exercise that you did not know (or realize the importance of) before?
(Use back of page if needing extra space.)

Note

1. The map of the impact area could be of the city and suburbs close to the class site. However, the map could also be of a fictitious place. Several websites offer free maps for educational use. It can be helpful to name important locations. One of these sites is http://fantasymapmaker.com/about/.

References

Drabek, T. E. (1999). Understanding disaster warning responses. *The Social Science Journal*, *36*(3), 515–523.

Drabek, T. E. (2013). *Human side of disaster* (2nd ed.). Boca Raton: CRC Press.

Enarson, E., & Chakrabarti, P. G. D. (2009). *Dhar women, gender and disaster: Global issues and initiatives*. Los Angeles: Sage Publications.

Fothergill, A. (1996). Gender, risk and disaster. *International Journal of Mass Emergencies and Disasters*, *14*(1), 33–56.

Fothergill, A., Maestas, E. G. M., & Darlington, J. D. (1999). Race, ethnicity and disasters in the United States: A review of the literature. *Disasters*, *23*(2), 156–173.

Fothergill, A., & Peek, L. (2004). Poverty and disasters in the United States: A review of recent sociological findings. *Natural Hazards*, *32*(1), 89–110.

Gorski, P. C. (2019). *Guide for setting ground rules*. Retrieved from www.edchange.org/multicultural/activities/groundrules.html

Lindell, M. K., & Perry, R. (1987). Warning mechanisms in emergency response systems. *International Journal of Mass Emergencies and Disasters*, *5*(2), 137–153.

Lindell, M. K., & Perry, R. (2004). *Communicating environmental risk in multiethnic communities*. Thousand Oaks, CA: Sage Publications.

Mileti, D. S. (1995). Factors related to flood warning response. In *U.S. Italy research workshop on the hydrometeorology, impacts and management of extreme floods*. Perugia, Italy. Retrieved from https://www.engr.colostate.edu/ce/facultystaff/salas/us-italy/papers/46mileti.pdf

Mileti, D. S. (1999). *Disasters by design*. Washington, DC: Joseph Henry Press.

Mileti, D. S., & Peek, L. (2000). The social psychology of public response to warnings of a nuclear power plant accident. *Journal of Hazardous Materials*, *75*, 181–194.

Neal, D., & Phillips, B. (1990). Female-dominated local social movement organizations in disaster-threat situations. In G. West & R. Blumberg (Eds.), *Women and social protest*. New York: Oxford.

National Council on Disability. (2009). *Effective emergency management: Making improvements for communities and people with disabilities*. Washington, DC. Retrieved from https://www.ncd.gov/publications/2009/Aug122009

Nohr, E. (2016, December 9). "A welcoming state": Nebraska led the nation in resettling most refugees per capita in the last year. *Omaha World-Herald*. Retrieved from www.omaha.com/news/metro/a-welcoming-state-nebraska-led-the-nation-in-resettling-most/article_b84f8b71-d374-5cda-ad33-afa9a923fb54.html

Peacock, W., & Ragsdale, A. K. (1997). Social systems, ecology networks, and disasters: Toward a socio-political ecology of disasters. In W. G. Peacock, B. H. Morrow, & H. Gladwin (Eds.), *Hurricane Andrew: Ethnicity, gender, and the sociology of disasters*. London, UK: Routledge.

Phillips, B. D. (2015). *Disaster recovery*. Boca Raton, FL: CRC Press.

Phillips, B., Neal, D., & Webb, G. (2012). *Introduction to emergency management*. Boca Raton: CRC Press.

Rogers, G. O., & Sorenson, J. H. (1991). Diffusion of emergency warning: Comparing empirical and simulation results. In *Risk analysis* (pp. 117–134). Boston, MA: Springer.

Appendix A

Previous Facilitation

The authors have conducted this in-class exercise to several undergraduate courses at both Oklahoma State University and the University of Nebraska at Omaha. The exercise takes approximately 45 minutes to conduct from start to finish. The instruction of the exercise complemented lessons learned from reading the *Introduction to Emergency Management* textbook by Brenda Phillips et al. (2012). Facilitators interested in using this exercise may also find it useful to review several other papers and books on warnings and human response to warnings, including *Disasters by Design* by Denis Mileti (1999), *Communicating Environmental Risk in Multiethnic Communities* by Michael Lindell and Ronald Perry (2004), or the *Human Side of Disaster* by Thomas Drabek (2013), as well as one book that provides an introduction to social vulnerability and related theories, *Disaster Recovery, Second Edition* by Brenda Phillips (2015); *Social Vulnerability to Disasters, Second Edition*, edited by Deborah S.K. Thomas, Brenda Phillips, William E. Lovekamp, and Alice Fothergill (2013); and *Dhar Women, Gender, and Disaster: Global Issues and Initiatives*, edited by Elaine Enarson and P.G. Dhar Chakrabarti (2009).

Finally, note that since the students conduct much of this exercise on their own in their groups, it is imperative to listen closely to the discussions among students to properly steer the exercise and keep them on topic. Progress can be easily derailed if students begin to consider other response-type activities such as long-term housing, debris removal, or financial assistance.

Results of Two Case Study Groups

Each time the authors have conducted this exercise, results have been glowing. Students were generally thrilled with a break from the normal lecture-type format and were equally excited that they actually "get" the material. Various other facilitators who have observed the class exercise in action thought it was very well thought out, scalable, and adaptable. In 2013, this exercise was presented at the 15th Annual Emergency Management Higher Education Conference for facilitators and practitioners. Both groups enjoyed the presentation and wished to adapt it for other disaster phases and activities.

Figure 12.2 displays the average for each test question from the two universities. Oklahoma State University consisted of upper-level undergraduate students, while University of Nebraska at Omaha students were freshmen. Results indicate high levels of understanding post-exercise for all topics, especially for social vulnerability, warning messages, and general protective actions – all of which received 100% correct responses.

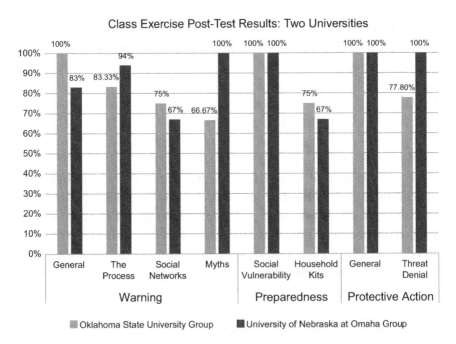

FIGURE 12.2 Percentage of Correct Answers for Preparedness and Warning Exercise Test Questions

Source: Bennett & MacNabb

We used the latest census information to provide information about the demographics of the community. We chose current demographics for cities with which students were most familiar; in Oklahoma, we used the demographics for Oklahoma City or Tulsa, and in Nebraska we used the demographics for Omaha. This helps to focus the students on areas they know well, but also provides information about various challenges faced by certain populations that they may not have previously noticed or been aware of. For example, many native Nebraskans in class were unaware that Nebraska was a national leader in refugee resettlement, with thousands settling in Omaha or Lincoln (Nohr, 2016).

Discussion

As designed, this exercise does not allow all students to experience both sides of the spectrum. They are either the emergency managers or the citizens. The exercise can be modified in several ways to give both sets of students a similar experience. Facilitators may want to compare how best to warn the citizens or compare the complexities of constituents to heed warning messages. The exercise can be split into two 30-minute sessions in which the class (in-groups) could practice warning the public based on a predetermined threat and location, thereby giving all students an opportunity to be emergency managers and compare results. During the second 30 minutes of the class, the students could explore the citizen side with the help of character cards and determine the complexities and considerations constituents may take in properly heeding warning messages. Following the second 30-minute segment the students could discuss social vulnerability and the warning process.

13

Cultural Competence and Disaster Management

Flooding in Coastalville

Frances L. Edwards

Overview

The United States is a heterogeneous[1] nation, whose disaster-prone communities need emergency managers with a high degree of cultural competency to effectively meet community needs (Edwards, 2012). Researchers have long noted that people of different ethnic groups and immigration statuses[2] respond to disaster events differently, often influenced by earlier experiences in their countries of origin (Basolo et al., 2009; Davidson, Price, McCauley, & Ruggiero, 2013; Lachlan & Rainear, 2017; Marlowe & Bogen, 2015; Wilson & Tiefenbacher, 2012). Also, community members have varying degrees of English language competency. Some native English speakers are illiterate or have limited English reading competency. People for whom English is a second language (ESL) may have limited literacy in English and/or may be illiterate in any language.

Most disaster shelters in the United States are run by the local government in cooperation with a non-governmental organization (NGO), such as the American Red Cross or Salvation Army. These

NGOs are typically run by volunteers who provide the food for the shelter residents based on nationwide menus that are designed to provide meals that will be acceptable to most Americans but may not appeal to people of all backgrounds, ages, and ethnicities. People whose origins are not in the United States or Europe may find some of the food unacceptable, such as cold cereal, peanut butter, and mayonnaise-based salads. Food is an important factor in the psychological care of disaster survivors, so developing community-specific menus can be an important part of community disaster preparedness.

Attaining a working knowledge of the cultural characteristics of stakeholders in the community will allow an emergency manager to anticipate community needs and concerns. By involving diverse community members in emergency planning, response challenges such as language interpretation needs, appropriate food for shelter residents, and anticipated access and functional needs accommodations can be arranged in advance (Andrulis, Siddiqui, & Purtle, 2011; Lloyd, Llorenz, & Schement, 2016; Storr & Haeffele-Balch, 2012; Nepal, Banerjee, Perry, & Scott, 2012).

In addition to ethnic diversity and literacy levels, immigration status divides many communities, influencing their responses to public programs and services. While citizens and green card holders may need assistance with post-disaster recovery paperwork (Edwards, 2012), people awaiting a decision on permanent residence status may be afraid that accepting any government assistance may make them a "public charge" and ruin their chances for permanent resident status or citizenship (Edwards & Wong, 2010). However, emergency assistance such as food, water, and shelter are offered to everyone who is impacted by a disaster, regardless of immigration status, including undocumented immigrants and foreign travelers (ImmigrationRoad.com, 2018). Under disaster circumstances, Supplemental Nutrition Assistance Program (SNAP) benefits ("food stamps") may be available to undocumented households (National Immigration Law Center, 2017).

The Federal Emergency Management Agency (FEMA) has a long-standing policy against providing cash assistance to undocumented residents (FEMA, 2004), but they provide guidance on getting community-based assistance from other sources. They also emphasize that only one member of the household must be in legal status to apply for disaster assistance, as they do not collect immigration status information about other household members (FEMA, 2009). Legal status includes green card holders, legal resident status because of asylum, refugee status, parole status, suspension of deportation status, or status as victims of domestic violence (FEMA, 2009). Undocumented parents can also apply for assistance for a minor child in their household who is an American citizen or otherwise in legal status, so long as the child has a Social Security card (FEMA, 2016, 2017).

Historically, the undocumented immigrant community has a fear of gathering in areas where La Migra (formerly the Immigration and Naturalization Service – INS, now Immigration and Customs Enforcement – ICE) may easily gather them up for deportation (Viva, 2017). In both the Loma Prieta and Northridge earthquakes, the Hispanic community did not go to American Red Cross (ARC) shelters for fear of being found by federal immigration officials (Kamel & Loukaitou-Sideris, 2004). The Department of Homeland Security (DHS) has a policy against enforcing immigration law during disasters and issued public announcements before Hurricane Isaac in 2012 and Hurricane Matthew in 2016. At that time DHS, the parent agency of both ICE and Customs and Border Patrol – CBP, stated immigration enforcement initiatives and evacuations or sheltering would not be associated. In addition, actions related to enforcement, such as checkpoints, would not occur within impacted areas (Cheng, 2017). During Hurricane Harvey in 2017, the moratorium[3] on enforcement in disaster areas lasted from August 29 through September 9, 2017. Storm evacuation sites, shelters, and food banks were specifically protected from routine, non-criminal enforcement by ICE and CBP (Kelly, 2017).

As federal agencies, ICE and CBP are part of the Emergency Support Function (ESF)–based response to disasters (DHS, 2017a). The ESF is the "primary federal coordinating structure for delivering response" (DHS, 2017b, p. 3). For example, more than 30,000 federal employees from multiple departments and agencies were deployed to assist victims of Hurricane Harvey in Texas and Louisiana. Their roles included supporting shelter operations and assisting with search and rescue operations (DHS,

2017a). In their role as ESF responders, CBP officers rescued 1,362 people and 29 pets during the Hurricane Harvey response (Kelly, 2017).

During the response to Hurricane Florence in 2018 the moratorium on immigration enforcement in the disaster area was renewed. ICE issued a statement specifically protecting shelters and evacuation areas from enforcement actions (Bowden, 2018). CBP provided "150 officers, aircrew members and agents to the Carolinas to help with air support missions, road clearing and security" (Molina, 2018, para. 9). They were part of the 800 federal employees deployed to Hurricane Florence disaster areas, supported by 550 federal law enforcement personnel serving in other states as part of the National Park Service, Federal Bureau of Investigation (FBI), and other agencies, but not ICE. The Coast Guard, North Carolina National Guard, and volunteer Cajun Navy also participated in the response effort. Residents of the disaster area, which is home to undocumented immigrants, expressed concern that the survivors may not know when the moratorium on immigration enforcement is lifted (Molina, 2018).

Case Study: Disaster Response

About the Activity
The goal of this exercise is to develop an understanding of the need for cultural competency in emergency management staff members as you confront some of the challenges faced when delivering disaster services to a heterogeneous population that includes undocumented residents, non–English-speaking residents, and diversity in age, race, and the level of assistance needed because of access and functional needs.

Group interactions: People will respond to the case study differently based on their life experiences. Refrain from becoming focused on your personal situation but instead focus on your role, and how you would manage service delivery to the disaster survivors.

Learning Outcomes

◆ Participants will develop an understanding of the role of cultural competency in emergency services delivery

◆ Participants will demonstrate the ability to integrate cultural competency concepts in emergency services delivery through the pre- and post-tests

Definitions

◆ Citizen: In the United States, a person who was born in the United States, a person who was born anywhere whose parents are American citizens, or a person who was granted citizenship through a system of immigration and naturalization (Davis & Donald, 1997).

◆ Green Card: An immigration document that grants the holder the permanent right to live in the United States. It may also be part of the path to naturalized citizenship.

◆ H-Visas: Visas that are issued to people who have job-related skills needed in the United States' industries' jobs that cannot be filled by citizens or residents; H1-A visas are for agricultural workers, and H1-B visas are for skilled workers such as high-technology company workers, doctors, nurses, and similar workers. The visas are issued for a specified duration, at the end of which the holders must return to their country of origin.

◆ Heterogeneous: A collection of people or items that are dissimilar, often specifically referring to people who have different racial and ethnic backgrounds.

◆ Residents: People living in the United States who are citizens or who have a green card or visa that permits them to live in the United States.

◆ Tourists: People visiting the United States for no more than six months who intend to return home after their visit.

◆ Undocumented Immigrants: People living in the United States without required permission and resident permit or work permit (Wilson & Tiefenbacher, 2012).

◆ Whole Community Approach: Under Presidential Policy Directive-8 (PPD-8), the responsibility for community resilience is with not only the local government but also the faith-based community, non-governmental organization (NGO) community, and the private sector (Edwards, 2015).

Breakdown

◆ Divide into groups of four to five people.
◆ Discuss the ground rules to set the tone.
◆ Review the scenario and the group's discussion questions
◆ Allow ample time for discussion (approximately 45 minutes).
◆ Facilitate group dialogue about responses to questions.
◆ Use supplemental questions if needed.

Ground Rules (Gorski, 2019)

1. Listen actively – respect others when they are talking.
2. Speak from your own experience instead of generalizing ("I" instead of "they," "we," and "you").
3. Do not be afraid to respectfully challenge one another by asking questions but refrain from personal attacks – focus on ideas.
4. Participate to the fullest of your ability – community growth depends on the inclusion of every individual voice.
5. Instead of invalidating somebody else's story with your own spin on their experience, share your own story and experience.
6. The goal is not to agree – it is to gain a deeper understanding.
7. Be conscious of body language and nonverbal responses – they can be as disrespectful as words.

Supplemental Questions

1. What are your first thoughts about this scenario? Did you have any emotional reactions to this scenario? If yes, why? If no, why?

2. Was there anything thought provoking about how your fellow participants reacted to this exercise? (Please use generalizations and do not target others.)

3. What would your reaction to this exercise be if you had been raised as a member of one of the ethnic groups whose members had been displaced by the flood?

4. How do you think this scenario relates to emergency management? Why was this exercise created?

5. Who would you contact for help in creating special needs evacuation centers and shelters?

Supplemental Information for Facilitator

1. The Asian language was Cambodian. The better-educated members of the community had dispersed throughout the metropolitan area, with the older immigrants remaining in the central neighborhood. One city policeman was Cambodian, and when he arrived at the command post he was fought over between the police and fire departments – was he needed to make the loudspeaker announcements in the community or to explain the situation to people arriving at the command post?

2. The Incident Command Post started the first emergency response to get three buses from the local transit agency to act as expedient shelters for the cold, wet residents until the ARC shelters at the high schools could be opened. The Salvation Army's disaster response vehicle brought hot chocolate, coffee, tea, and pastries to the command post for the residents and first responders.

3. The Emergency Operations Center (EOC) contacted the American Red Cross, which has standing contracts with the high school districts, and a community shelter was opened within four hours, with standard American food – cold cereal for breakfast, peanut butter or bologna sandwiches for lunch, and pasta or casseroles for dinner.

4. The Cambodian community members were all documented, green card holders. They went to the ARC shelter; the Cambodian community provided bilingual translators. Once they realized that they could not eat the ARC food, the Cambodian community also provided food at each mealtime that was culturally appropriate.

5. The Hispanic community members included American citizens and green card holders, but most were undocumented. The citizens and green card holders went to the ARC shelter, but the undocumented Hispanic residents refused formal shelter in fear of the federal agency.

6. The woman with the Seeing Eye dog was an American citizen who was blind. She was of Hispanic heritage and bilingual, and she spoke Colombian Spanish, but most of the neighborhood's Hispanic residents spoke the language of western Mexico, which has many indigenous words, so she was not able to interpret anything complicated for them.

7. The Cambodian people were very frightened of the Seeing Eye dog, who was a large German shepherd. After one night the ARC gave the woman and her dog a motel voucher and a comfort kit so that she and the dog could leave the shelter. The local NGO paratransit agency took her and the dog to the motel, and then to work every day.

8. Most of the Hispanic residents were undocumented, so they were unwilling to go to the ARC shelter, as they feared that the federal agency would target it. They were living in their cars in a city park, where overnight parking is illegal, and the bathrooms are locked at 10 p.m. The children were getting sick from the cold and damp living conditions. The EOC worked with the faith-based community to find alternatives. The Salvation Army offered tents, tarps, bottled water, and clothing vouchers for their thrift stores, and Catholic charities provided food and baby care items. Several churches offered their parking lots and bathrooms.

9. The undocumented residents would only communicate with Spanish-speaking volunteers and Spanish-speaking Hispanic clergy. They were afraid of all government staff and ARC volunteers, and they were distrustful of non-Hispanic volunteer staff.

10. County public health provided their mobile health van in the park to care for sick children and encouraged the parents to go to the ARC shelter, or to find new housing. They were afraid to go to the ARC shelter and had no money to get a new apartment. Slowly they left the area, and the rumor was that they were going to the Central Valley for the planting season.

11. Access to temporary housing and financial assistance for the shelter residents was organized at the ARC shelters using community volunteers who spoke the languages of the evacuees.

12. Access to temporary housing and financial assistance for those in informal shelters was offered through community centers and religious organizations, where community members who spoke the languages of the evacuees assisted them in completing financial assistance forms that they were willing to complete, and

in finding other resources for temporary housing and resources to re-start their households, such as gift cards and thrift shop vouchers.

13. The original ARC shelter had to be moved after the first day of school because the flooded community was on the gang turf of a rival gang. Although the other high school was farther away, it was not on rival gang turf. The police said that they could not keep the peace if the shelter was not moved.

14. One large, local home improvement store offered two small delivery trucks and drivers to move personal property from the flooded neighborhood to a new location within five miles. People in second-floor apartments seldom had interior damage, so they could retrieve their household goods and move them to a new dwelling in many cases.

15. One large law firm provided a free Saturday consultation on landlord-tenant rights. This helped people get their security deposits and balance of the month's rent so they could find a new apartment.

16. The county apartment owners' association created a list of available low-income apartments from their members, which helped speed re-housing.

Breaking News: Unexpected Flooding in Coastalville

The Situation

It is 9:30 p.m. on February 13. The Stone Creek neighborhood is unexpectedly flooding from the Eastern River. The population of the neighborhood is 3,000, many of whom do not speak English. The police department has established a command post at the neighborhood's entrance to prevent anyone from entering the flooded area. The fire department has two engines driving through the floodwater using loudspeaker systems to warn residents to evacuate. One fire captain is bi-lingual, making announcements in English and Spanish.

People speaking an Asian language are arriving at the police command post and are upset that they cannot go home. There is no one at the command post who can understand them; they do not speak English. The police incident commander is on the radio with dispatch to try to access the AT&T language line to find out what language they are speaking and what they need. The water is too deep for passenger cars, so people are wading out to the command post, and they are now wet and very cold. One family has an elderly family member in a wheelchair that they pushed through the floodwater. There are many children in the waiting group, at least two people with white canes, and one woman with a service dog,[4] both of whom are soaked.

The fire department is also responding to two flooded mobile home parks in an adjacent neighborhood with mostly elderly people. Streets are flooding the length of the Eastern River because the storm drains can no longer discharge water into the river since the flap gates are all closed because of the river's rise. No other residences are currently at risk, but the rain is still falling.

About Coastalville

Coastalville is a West Coast city of more than one million people that is one of the most heterogeneous cities in the United States. It has a strong local economy with a major role in the international supply chain. It sits in a valley with a river at the base of each mountain range.

The climate is Mediterranean, with dry summers and wet winters. After a wet, rainy season, a major winter storm arrived and stalled over the valley. Rain poured down on the already saturated mountains, creating large amounts of water run-off into the two rivers. It is at a bend in the river where the land was only three feet above the river's surface during most months, but with a higher river level during this rainy period. There has never been flooding in this area.

The Responders
- The fire department is touring the neighborhood, making announcements. More vehicles are coming to assist with evacuations, but available resources must be shared with the two mobile home parks.
- The police department is running the Incident Command Post, focusing on traffic management to keep people from entering the flooded area.
- The city's emergency operations center is open at Level 2, meaning that all five National Incident Management System (NIMS) functions – management, planning/intelligence, operations, logistics, and finance/administration – are staffed with at least one person coordinating community-wide response to the flooding.
- The Public Information Officer (PIO) Unit has three staff members, including one Spanish speaker.
- Mutual aid has been requested from other jurisdictions for water rescues.

Things to Know
- People prized the easy access to the river for fishing.
- Most of the residents lived in four-plex housing nearest to the river, with about 100 single family homes a few blocks away from the river.
- The four-plex apartments were occupied principally by two groups. About half of the population was non-English-speaking Asian ethnicity with green cards, while the other half was bi-lingual Hispanic ethnicity, principally undocumented, with mixed levels of English competency.
- Both groups included people of all ages, from infants to seniors, and people of varying functional and access needs.

♦ Both groups had specific cuisines that did not include typical American food that was on the shelter agencies' menus.

♦ Federal agency is active in the community, working against human trafficking and wage slavery, which was occurring in local food-processing establishments.

Your Role

You are a member of the city's emergency management staff. You are preparing for the action planning meeting to plan the response strategy for the next four hours.

Questions for Discussion

1. What is your top priority from a community perspective right now?
2. What five things do you have to do within the next hour?
3. What are the EOC Action Plan goals for the four-hour action planning period?
4. What city staff members need to be added to the basic EOC staff?
5. What other organizations should be invited to assist with the response? How would you find them?
6. What role could the private sector play in resolving the community flooding problem?

Pre-Test Assessment

PURPOSE OF THE SURVEY

This assessment survey is designed to demonstrate your knowledge of cultural competency applied to emergency planning and establish a baseline of participant knowledge before participating in the exercise.

DEFINITIONS

Directions: Please match the terminologies with their definitions.

_____ Heterogeneous A. Under Presidential Policy Directive-8, the responsibility for community resilience is with not only the local government but also the faith-based community, non-governmental organization (NGO) community, and the private sector.

_____ La Migra B. A community with several ethnic groups.

_____ Whole Community Approach C. A term used among immigrants to describe government immigration status enforcement.

ATTITUDINAL SCALE

Directions: Please use the following scale to represent your reaction to the questions.

1	2	3	4	5
Strongly Agree	Agree	Neither Agree nor Disagree	Disagree	Strongly Disagree

1. I believe that cultural competence is important for mass care and shelter staff.

2. I believe that emergency planners need to be culturally competent to create acceptable emergency plans.

3. I believe that a community should provide one standard of emergency assistance to all residents, regardless of gender, ethnicity, or access and functional needs.

4. I believe that only citizens and legal residents should receive emergency response services.

5. I believe that emergency managers should plan for and focus on permanent community members.

6. I have enough knowledge of applying cultural competency principles to mass care and shelter planning and delivery.

7. I have enough knowledge of applying cultural competency principles to write a community emergency plan.

8. I have enough knowledge to develop culturally competent standards of post-disaster assistance for a heterogeneous community.

9. I have enough knowledge about cultural competency to design emergency response services for a heterogeneous community.

10. I have enough knowledge about cultural competency to plan for all community members in a heterogeneous community with residents of differing immigration statuses.

Post-Test Assessment

PURPOSE OF THE SURVEY

This assessment survey is designed to demonstrate your knowledge of cultural competency applied to emergency planning and establish a baseline of participant knowledge after participating in the exercise.

DEFINITIONS

Directions: Please match the terminologies with their definitions.

_____ Heterogeneous

A. Under Presidential Policy Directive-8, the responsibility for community resilience is with not only the local government but also the faith-based community, non-governmental organization (NGO) community, and the private sector.

_____ La Migra

B. A community with several ethnic groups.

_____ Whole Community Approach

C. A term used among immigrants to describe government immigration status enforcement.

ATTITUDINAL SCALE

Directions: Please use the following scale to represent your reaction to the questions.

1	2	3	4	5
Strongly Agree	Agree	Neither Agree nor Disagree	Disagree	Strongly Disagree

1. I believe that cultural competence is important for mass care and shelter staff.

2. I believe that emergency planners need to be culturally competent to create acceptable emergency plans.

3. I believe that a community should provide one standard of emergency assistance to all residents, regardless of gender, ethnicity, or access and functional needs.

4. I believe that only citizens and legal residents should receive emergency response services.

5. I believe that emergency managers should plan for and focus on permanent community members.

6. I have enough knowledge of applying cultural competency principles to mass care and shelter planning and delivery.

7. I have enough knowledge of applying cultural competency principles to write a community emergency plan.

8. I have enough knowledge to develop culturally competent standards of post-disaster assistance for a heterogeneous community.

9. I have enough knowledge about cultural competency to design emergency response services for a heterogeneous community.

10. I have enough knowledge about cultural competency to plan for all community members in a heterogeneous community with residents of differing immigration statuses.

OPEN RESPONSE
Please answer the following question: "I used to think_____, but now I think_____."
(Use back of page if needing extra space.)

Notes

1. The term "heterogeneous" means that people of many ethnicities and races live within the United States.
2. Immigration status may include people who have become permanent residents and have a green card, people who have tourist visas, people who have student visas, people who have special work permit visas such as H1-A or H1-B, and people who are in the country with no documentation through the Immigration and Naturalization Service, sometimes referred to as "undocumented" or "illegal".
3. The term "moratorium" refers to a period of time when an action is stopped, or enforcement of a law is temporarily suspended.
4. According to the Americans with Disabilities Act, service animals are defined as dogs that are individually trained to do work or perform tasks for people with disabilities. This definition does not affect or limit the broader definition of "assistance animal" under the Fair Housing Act or the broader definition of "service animal" under the Air Carrier Access Act.

References

Andrulis, D., Siddiqui, N., & Purtle, J. (2011). Integrating racially and ethnically diverse communities into planning for disasters: The California experience. *Disaster Medicine and Public Health Preparedness, 5*(3), 227.

Basolo, V., Steinberg, L., Burby, R., Levine, J., Cruz, A., & Huang, C. (2009). The effects of confidence in government and information on perceived and actual preparedness for disasters. *Environment and Behavior, 41*(3), 338.

Bowden, J. (2018, September 12). ICE: No immigration enforcement in areas of hurricane shelters or evacuations. *The Hill*. Retrieved from https://thehill.com/homenews/administration/406717-ice-no-immigration-enforcement-in-areas-of-hurricane-shelters-or

Cheng, A. (2017, August 29). Undocumented and seeking safety during a disaster. *American Civil Liberties Union*. Retrieved from www.aclu.org/

blog/immigrants-rights/ice-and-border-patrol-abuses/undocumented-and-seeking-safety-during-natural

Davidson, T., Price, M., McCauley, J., & Ruggiero, K. (2013). Disaster impact across cultural groups: Comparison of Whites, African Americans, and Latinos. *American Journal of Community Psychology, 52*(1–2), 97–105.

Department of Homeland Security (DHS). (2016). *National response framework fact sheet*. Washington, DC: DHS. Retrieved from www.fema.gov/media-library-data/1466014682982-9bcf8245ba4c60c120a a915abe74e15d/National_Response_Framework3rd.pdf

Department of Homeland Security (DHS). (2017a). *Emergency support functions annex*. Retrieved from www.fema.gov/pdf/emergency/nrf/nrf-esf-intro.pdf

Department of Homeland Security (DHS). (2017b). *The road to recovery: The federal family's coordinated efforts to support survivors in the aftermath of Hurricane Harvey*. Retrieved from www.dhs.gov/news/2017/09/03/road-recovery-federal-family-s-coordinated-efforts-support-survivors-aftermath

Edwards, F. (2012). Doing good badly: The need for cultural competency in disasters. In K. A. Norman-Major & S. T. Gooden (Eds.), *Cultural competency for public administrators*. Amonk, NY: M.E. Sharpe.

Edwards, F. (2015). Presidential Policy Directive-8. In D. A. Bearfield, E. M. Berman, & M. J. Dubnick (Eds.), *Encyclopedia of public administration & public policy* (3rd ed.). London: Routledge.

Edwards, F., & Wong, Y. (2010). Silicon valley's elderly Chinese immigrants and disaster vulnerability. In J. Rivera & D. S. Miller (Eds.), *How ethnically marginalized Americans cope with catastrophic disasters*. Lewiston: The Edwin Mellen Press.

Federal Emergency Management Agency (FEMA). (2004). *Questions and answers for undocumented immigrants regarding FEMA assistance*. Retrieved from www.fema.gov/news-release/2004/06/17/questions-and-answers-undocumented-immigrants-regarding-fema-assistance

Federal Emergency Management Agency (FEMA). (2009). *How FEMA aid applies to undocumented immigrants*. Retrieved from www.fema.gov/news-release/2009/10/05/how-fema-aid-applies-undocumented-immigrants

Federal Emergency Management Agency (FEMA). (2016). *Non-US citizens can apply for FEMA assistance*. Retrieved from www.fema.gov/news-release/2016/11/15/non-us-citizens-can-apply-fema-assistance

Federal Emergency Management Agency (FEMA). (2017). *Citizenship status and eligibility for disaster assistance.* Retrieved from https://wildfirerecovery.org/wp-content/uploads/2017/10/DR-4344-CA-FAQ-Citizenship-Status-and-Eligibility-for-Disaster-Assistanc....pdf

Gorski, P. C. (2019). *Guide for setting ground rules.* Retrieved from www.edchange.org/multicultural/activities/groundrules.html

ImmigrationRoad.com. (2018). *Guidance on immigrants receiving government disaster aid.* Retrieved from https://immigrationroad.com/immigration-news/immigration-status-disaster-aid.php

Kamel, N., & Loukaitou-Sideris, A. (2004). Residential assistance and recovery following the Northridge Earthquake. *Urban Studies (Routledge), 41*(3), 533–562.

Kelly, C. (2017, September 12). Immigration enforcement resumes after pause for Hurricane Harvey. *Dallas Morning News.* Retrieved from www.dallasnews.com/news/politics/2017/09/12/customs-border-protection-resumes-operations-despite-ongoing-harvey-disaster-declaration

Lachlan, K., & Rainear, A. (2017). Intercultural crisis management. *The International Encyclopedia of Intercultural Communication,* (1–5).

Lloyd, M., Llorenz, J., & Schement, J. (2016). Understanding a diverse America's critical information needs (pp. 49–63). In M. Lloyd & J. Llorenz (Eds.), *The communication crisis in America, and how to fix it.* New York: Palgrave Macmillan.

Marlowe, J., & Bogen, R. (2015). Young people from refugee backgrounds as a resource for disaster risk reduction. *International Journal of Disaster Risk Reduction, 14*(125).

Molina, C. (2018, September 20). Why are immigration agents in area hit by Hurricane Florence? FEMA sent them. *News Observer.* Retrieved from www.newsobserver.com/news/politics-government/article218654785.html

National Immigration Law Center. (2017). *Disaster assistance.* Retrieved from www.nilc.org/wp-content/uploads/2017/10/disaster-assistance-2017.pdf

Nepal, V., Banerjee, D., Perry, M., & Scott, D. (2012). Disaster preparedness of linguistically isolated populations. *Health Promotion Practice, 13*(2), 265.

Storr, V., & Haeffele-Balch, S. (2012). Post-disaster community recovery in heterogeneous, loosely connected communities. *Review of Social Economy, 70*(3), 295.

Viva, R. (2017, January 14). "I left my tacos on the table and took off running": Immigrants remember the workplace raids of the 1980s. *Los Angeles Times*. Retrieved from www.latimes.com/local/california/la-me-immigration-trump-fears-20170109-story.html

Wilson, S., & Tiefenbacher, J. (2012). The barriers impeding precautionary behaviors by undocumented immigrants in emergencies: The Hurricane Ike experience in Houston, Texas, USA. *Environmental Hazards*, *11*(3), 194.

14

Response to Ebola Virus Outbreak in a Refugee Camp

Local Contexts vs. International Standards

Yoon Ah Shin and Jungwon Yeo

Overview of the Context

The Ebola virus disease (EVD) is a highly contagious and fatal viral hemorrhagic fever of humans (Davis, 2015; World Health Organization [WHO], 2014a, 2014b). The EVD is spread through direct contact with the virus that either is carried by an infected person's body fluids such as blood, breast milk, feces, mucus, tears, saliva, semen, sweat, or urine. It also can be transmitted through items recently contaminated by the infected bodily fluids. Therefore, the most significant strategies to prevent further contagion have been strict isolation of infected people and limiting their contact with individuals who are not infected.

In 2014, an outbreak of EVD in West African countries, including Guinea, Liberia, and Sierra Leone, became the worst global epidemic in history (Davis, 2015; WHO, 2014a, 2014b). These EVD-affected countries share borders and usually experience heavy traffic of people who cross borders to visit family, relatives, and friends in other countries. The open borders and free travels of people

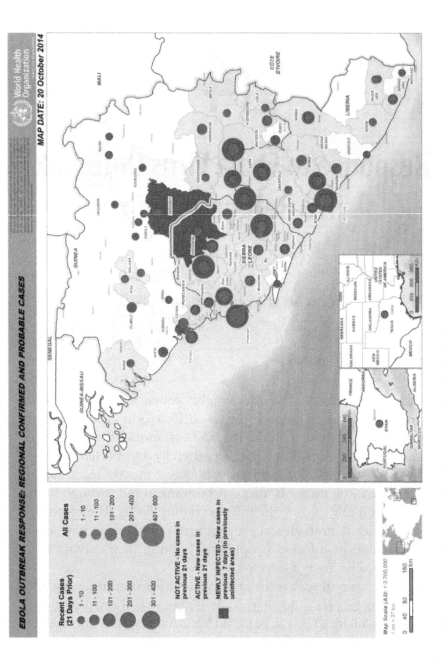

FIGURE 14.1 Ebola Outbreak Map 2014: Confirmed and Probable Cases

Source: (WHO, 2014b).

among these countries contributed to the spread of EVD across borders for the first several months of the EVD crises. People had traveled back and forth to attend funerals of families or friends who passed away as a result of EVD.

Compared with the other countries, the EVD outbreak in Sierra Leone was slow and silent at the beginning. However, by the end of the year, the country reported the highest suspected cases and became the deadliest country. The first and second cases were attributed to people's free travels to Guinea where the EVD index case was found. Then, EVD transmission was accelerated within the country, mostly because of traditional customs of handling infected people as well as the ones who died from the disease. Although there were substantial support and involvement of international societies through a massive disease response coordination in the country, it took nearly 22 months to clear the last case, resulting in 14,112 confirmed cases and 3,691 deaths (WHO, 2014a, 2014b).

Case Study: Ebola Virus Outbreak in a Refugee Camp

Goals of the Case Study

The 2014 Ebola crisis serves as the blueprint of the current international collaboration system in response to an international disaster (Table 14.1). By reviewing the Ebola crisis in a refugee camp, this case study aims (1) to analyze the gap between medical standard procedures and the refugees' response practices and (2) to discuss how to implement international response protocols effectively given the context. In particular, the goal of the scenario is to help international foreign-aid organizations work with local organizations and people to develop new strategies adapting to a local cultural context and assist people at risk to understand the standard procedures and adapt their behaviors to protect themselves from EVD.

TABLE 14.1 Medical Standard Procedures and Local Response to an Epidemic Crisis

	Medical Standard Procedure	*Local Response*
Membership	Experts group from relevant international organizations	Community residents with varying educational levels
Diagnosis of an epidemic outbreak	Assessment based on medical scientific knowledge	No in-depth medical understanding to judge a surrounding situation
Major strategy in response to EVD	Supply of medical preventive guidelines and medical resources	Improvising traditional treatment practices with local resources such as wild herbs
Working location	Working with national authorities at Emergency Operational Center (EOC)	Geographically isolated with limited fundamental infrastructures: transportation, communication, and health systems
Behavioral characteristics in decision-making	Lack of understanding of local context: culture, traditions, living conditions, and social norms	High value on social norms to be a member in a small network society; very defensive toward foreigners

Source: Shin & Yeo

Learning Outcomes

♦ Participants will demonstrate understanding of the strengths and weaknesses of diverse stakeholders with different levels of knowledge, resources, and cultural competency in a global emergency management practice

♦ Participants will demonstrate communication with multiple stakeholders with different views and approaches to the global emergency management practice

♦ Participants will demonstrate strategies development for work with diverse partners in global emergency management practices

♦ Participants will demonstrate comprehension of how the aforementioned process would influence their perspectives toward global emergency management

Definitions

♦ Index Case: Refers to the patient in an outbreak who is first noticed by the health authorities, and who makes them aware that an outbreak might be emerging (Last, 2008).

♦ (Foreign) Aid: In international relations, aid (also known as international aid, overseas aid, foreign aid, or foreign assistance) indicates a voluntary transfer of resources, including human, physical, technical, and financial support, from one country to another. In general, those resources are assigned to serve a specific purpose (Agarwal, 2019).

♦ Non-Governmental Organizations (NGOs): Non-governmental organizations, often called nonprofit organizations. Even though these organizations actively provide public services, such as humanitarian, educational, health care, public policy, social, human rights, environmental, and other areas, they are an independent entity from governments and international governmental organizations. These groups are founded and funded by citizens (U.S Department of State, 2017).

Breakdown

♦ Divide into groups of four to five people.
♦ Discuss the ground rules to set the tone.
♦ Review the scenario and the group's discussion questions.
♦ Allow ample time for discussion (approximately 45 minutes).
♦ Facilitate group dialogue about responses to questions.
♦ Utilize supplemental questions if needed.

Ground Rules (Gorski, 2019)

♦ Listen actively – respect others when they are talking.
♦ Speak from your own experience instead of generalizing ("I" instead of "they," "we," and "you").
♦ Do not be afraid to respectfully challenge one another by asking questions but refrain from personal attacks – focus on ideas.

- Participate to the fullest of your ability – community adaptation depends on the inclusion of every individual voice.
- Instead of invalidating somebody else's story with your own spin on their experience, share your own story and experience.
- The goal is not to agree – it is to gain a deeper understanding and adapt response processes to be more effective in practice.
- Be conscious of body language and nonverbal responses – they can be as disrespectful as words.

Supplemental Questions (for the facilitator)

- What types of communication would be effective to embrace different and sometimes conflicting ideas and opinions among stakeholders?
- What kind of leadership roles are you going to delegate?
- How do you reach out to listen to community people's perspectives?

Outbreak in a Refugee Camp

Scenario

Several asylum seekers from previous Ebola-affected regions have been relocated to a refugee camp in a West African country. The asylum seekers established a strong community as they settled in the refugee camp. Most of them brought their national culture and social norms into the camp.

One day, an Ebola outbreak occurs and begins to spread through the refugee camp. The case has the potential to spread throughout Africa and requires a quick response. A group of international medical experts, coordinators from international non-governmental organizations (NGOs), and the national government of the camp's hosting country focused on a prevention approach entered the camp to address the outbreak. In particular, to prevent widespread infection of the Ebola virus, the medical experts disseminated standard protocols of preventive behaviors. Those protective behaviors included the following:

◆ Washing hands frequently
◆ Eliminating contact with potential patients or contaminated goods
◆ Reporting any potential cases to government officials who would then quarantine the individuals
◆ Banning traditional funeral practices at private places
◆ Cremating the bodies of deceased persons infected with EVD

Regardless of the initial prevention efforts, the number of Ebola-affected cases keeps increasing in the refugee camp. The major challenge is that people continue their regular practices of following tradition and culture regardless of the known risk of exposure and refuse to adopt preventative measures.

Things to Know

◆ In their home country, there is a shortage of water and sanitation systems, and people were not accustomed to the regular practice of hand washing. In addition, the camp does not have enough water and sewer systems because of limited financial and human resources.
◆ According to West African beliefs, sickness is a result of natural and metaphysical (spiritual) causes like witchcraft and/or punishment from ancestral spirits (Manguvo & Mafuvadze, 2015).
◆ Even though healthcare providers are sent by the government regularly to visit the camp, the refugees rely on traditional methods for their health issues. When they are sick, they prefer to seek wise people (e.g., faith healers or chief) in their community rather than the medically trained healthcare providers whom they

were unfamiliar with. These healers would utilize traditional methods, such as salt baths or herb rubs into small incisions, to try and cure the illness.

♦ In addition, strong communal culture encouraged people's cohabitation and collective care for their sick families and friends. The culture and tradition contrasted with Western medical procedures for an epidemic crisis, such as isolation of people for quarantine or hospitalization.

♦ People's deep respect for rituals and family prevents ceasing traditional funeral practices. Traditionally, people believe that the deceased become their ancestors who take care of their welfare during their lifetime. During the funeral, people show their respect to the deceased by washing, touching, and kissing the dead bodies.

Responders Roles

♦ International Organizations: These are major health organizations that develop global health policies, having medical knowledge and various resources for responding to the situation. This list includes the World Health Organization (WHO), Doctors Without Borders (MSF), International Federation of Red Cross (IFRC), United Nations Office for the Coordination of Humanitarian Affairs (UNOCHA), and World Food Programs (WFP). They are legitimate and trusted partners of the national government. However, neither have enough knowledge of the local contexts nor have local contacts. Locals do not trust the foreign organizations. In addition, because of the high turnover rate and rotations, the coordinators are only in Sierra Leone for a limited time (about one month).

♦ National Government of the Camp Host Country: They are the official leader of the national response operation and include the president, Ministry of Health, and other relevant ministries. They have authority to allocate public resources to field operations. They are well connected to international organizations and have a good understanding of international health protocol standards. However, they have neither enough medical knowledge of EVD nor cultural backgrounds of this refugee group.

◆ Local Non-Governmental Organizations (NGOs): These are local community organizations that support refugee camps. They work closely with leaders or households in the refugee camps. Hence, they have more or less trusted relationships with the refugee communities. With their presence in the community, they have been observing EVD situations and have been trying to help communities during the EVD epidemic. However, they do not have proper medical knowledge or resources to intervene in the situation. In addition, they have not been included as a part of formal response operations.

◆ Local Community Leaders: The local leaders include the chiefs, elders, teachers, pastors, and/or faith healers; they are well respected by community members. These include chiefs, elders, teachers, pastors, and/or faith healers. Community people usually visit them whenever they need some information and advice. They have actual influence to mobilize residents. However, they do not have any medical knowledge or understanding of the situation.

Your Role

You are a local community leader of the refugee camp. You are familiar with refugees and their culture and social norms. You, also, fully understand the standard protocol provided by the international medical experts and coordinators because you studied abroad to pursue a higher education. You have learnt about the seriousness of the previous and current Ebola cases. The international medical experts and coordinators, as well as the national government of the camp hosting country, encourage you to facilitate the dissemination and education of standard behavior protocol in your community. The medical experts and coordinators have organized a coordination meeting to listen to your ideas concerning why people in the refugee camp continue their tradition and rituals even after distributing the prevention protocol. You need to help these international experts understand your community's situations and collaborate with the rest of the group to discuss the next steps.

To Be Specific, You Need to Address:

1. How to modify the prevention protocol, including burial practices, quarantining Ebola patients in medical facilities, and adapting to refugees' culture and tradition.
2. How to promote people's behavioral changes.
3. What avenues of communication can be utilized to encourage the behavioral change policy in the refugee communities?
4. Which kinds of resources are needed to help people's behavioral changes in your community?
5. Alternative ways to trace suspicious Ebola-affected cases and to isolate the Ebola-confirmed cases in the refugee camp.

Questions for Discussion

1. What are the core issues to deal with?
2. What are tasks you need to accomplish?
3. Who are your stakeholders?
4. Who do you assist first? Who do you assist next?
5. How do you divide your resources?

Pre-Test Assessment

PURPOSE OF THE SURVEY

This assessment survey is designed to demonstrate understanding of cultural competence–related aspects and establish a baseline of participant attitudes before the exercise.

DEFINITIONS

Directions: Please match the terminologies with their definitions.

_____ Index Case   A. Organizations that provide public services and are an independent entity from public organizations.

_____ Foreign Aid   B. A voluntary transfer of resources from one country to another.

_____ Non-Governmental C. A patient in an outbreak who is first noticed by the health authorities.
Organizations
(NGOs)

ATTITUDINAL SCALE

Directions: Please use the following scale to represent your reaction to the questions.

1	2	3	4	5
Strongly Agree	Agree	Neither Agree nor Disagree	Disagree	Strongly Disagree

1. I believe personal culture influences my role(s).

2. I believe cultural groups influence my role(s).

3. I believe stereotypes influence my role(s).

4. I believe I have adequate knowledge of how my own cultural identities influence my role(s).

5. I believe I have adequate knowledge of other cultures and their influence on my role(s).

6. I believe I have adequate knowledge of stereotypes and their influence on my role(s).

7. I believe I have adequate knowledge of my cultural identities and their influence on emergency and crisis management.

8. I believe I have adequate knowledge of other cultural identities and how they influence emergency and crisis management.

9. I believe I have adequate knowledge of stereotypes and how they influence emergency and crisis management.

Post-Test Assessment

PURPOSE OF THE SURVEY

This assessment survey is designed to demonstrate understanding of culturally related impacts and establish a baseline of participant attitudes after the exercise.

DEFINITIONS

Directions: Please match the terminologies with their definitions.

_____	Index Case	A.	Organizations that provide public services and are an independent entity from public organizations.
_____	Foreign Aid	B.	A voluntary transfer of resources from one country to another.
_____	Non-Governmental Organizations (NGOs)	C.	A patient in an outbreak who is first noticed by the health authorities.

ATTITUDINAL SCALE

Directions: Please use the following scale to represent your reaction to the questions.

1	2	3	4	5
Strongly Agree	Agree	Neither Agree nor Disagree	Disagree	Strongly Disagree

1. I believe personal culture influences my role(s).

2. I believe cultural groups influence my role(s).

3. I believe stereotypes influence my role(s).

4. I believe I have adequate knowledge of how my own cultural identities influence my role(s).

5. I believe I have adequate knowledge of other cultures and their influence on my role(s).

6. I believe I have adequate knowledge of stereotypes and their influence on my role(s).

7. I believe I have adequate knowledge of my cultural identities and their influence on emergency and crisis management.

8. I believe I have adequate knowledge of other cultural identities and how they influence emergency and crisis management.

9. I believe I have adequate knowledge of stereotypes and how they influence emergency and crisis management.

OPEN RESPONSE

Please answer the following question: "I used to think_____, but now I think_____."

(Use back of page if needing extra space.)

References

Agarwal, P. (2019). Foreign aid. *Intelligent Economist*. Retrieved from www.intelligenteconomist.com/foreign-aid/

Davis, P. (2015). *Ebola in Sierra Leone: Economic impact & recovery*. Sierra Leone Opportunities for Business Action (SOBA), DFID, Adam Smith International. Retrieved March 9, 2018, from www.adamsmith international.com/documents/resource-uploads/Ebola_in_Sierra_Leone.pdf

Gorski, P. C. (2019). *Guide for setting ground rules*. Retrieved from www.edchange.org/multicultural/activities/groundrules.html

Last, J. M. (2008). *A dictionary of epidemiology*. Oxford: Oxford University Press.

Manguvo, A., & Mafuvadze, B. (2015). The impact of traditional and religious practices on the spread of Ebola in West Africa: Time for a strategic shift. *The Pan African Medical Journal*, *22*(Suppl 1).

U.S. Department of State. (2017). *Non-Governmental Organizations (NGOs) in the United States*. Retrieved from https://web.archive.org/web/20170122211029/www.state.gov/j/drl/rls/fs/2017/266904.htm

World Health Organization (WHO). (2014a, December 10–11). *Health systems situation in Guinea, Liberia and Sierra Leone*. Proceedings of the Ebola and Health System Meeting, Geneva, Switzerland. Retrieved from www.who.int/csr/disease/ebola/health-systems/health-systems-ppt1.pdf

World Health Organization (WHO). (2014b). *Ebola outbreak response: Confirmed and probable cases*. Retrieved from www.who.int/csr/disease/ebola/ebola-geographic-map-20-oct-2014.png?ua=1

World Health Organization. (2015). *Ebola situation report 17 June 2015*. Retrieved from http://apps.who.int/ebola/current-situation/ebola-situation-report-17-june-2015

Additional Sources

Shin, Y., Yeo, J., & Jung, K. (2018). The effectiveness of international non-governmental organizations' response operations during public health emergency: Lessons learned from the 2014 Ebola outbreak in Sierra Leone. *International Journal of Environmental Research and Public Health*, *15*(4), 650.

15

Cultural Competence Training for International Response and Recovery Workers

Christa L. Remington

Overview of the Context

In the aftermath of the 2010 Haitian earthquake, thousands of untrained aid workers were hired in a short time span and deployed to Haiti. Because of many high-profile intercultural blunders, such as distributing health information in French, rather than the local language Haitian Kreyòl, mistrust between international aid workers and Haitian beneficiaries was widespread. This suspicion caused many initiatives to fail and the relationship between beneficiaries and aid worker to deteriorate. In the months following the initial disaster, a cholera epidemic spread rapidly through the camps of those who had been displaced by the earthquake. Mistrust of aid workers caused many Haitians to become wary of the health clinics managed by the non-governmental organizations (NGOs). As a result, many did not seek lifesaving medical care and refused to follow the health instructions on preventing the spread of cholera.

According to the Centers for Disease Control (2013), more than one million had contracted the disease and at least 8,000 had died by the end of 2012.

While there are many definitions of culture, it broadly refers to norms, roles, belief systems, laws, and values that are interrelated in meaningful ways (Triandis, Vassiliou, Vassiliou, Tanaka, & Shanmugam, 1972). Culture has both overt and hidden components. Overt culture refers to easily observed aspects such as demographics, food, language, and religion. Hidden culture, such as social structures, humor, and body language, is equally as important as the overt, yet all too often overlooked (Hall, 1976; Hofstede, 2001; Zweifel, 2003). Many foreigners inadvertently cause misunderstandings by focusing solely on the overt culture, which presents barriers to effective cross-cultural communication to those unwilling or untrained to recognize it.

A growing body of research suggests that cultural competence increases trust and communication between aid workers and beneficiaries, leading to more effective emergency response efforts (Ditzler, Hastings, & Deleon, 2009; Grandey, 2003; Paton, 1996). In the aftermath of a disaster, this means lives saved. Research also shows that the most effective way for aid workers to gain cultural competence is by exposure to the host culture, cultural exchange through conversation, and being mentored by an experienced employee (Remington, 2017). Despite this, NGOs seldom provide opportunity for these activities and often outright prohibit their practice because of safety concerns and the lack of importance placed on cultural competence.

This case study introduces participants to the tradeoffs and values hierarchy in NGO leadership that is inherent to postdisaster response efforts. It also emphasizes the need to make cultural competence a central part of an organization's plan of action before an emergency. This case emphasizes that, while having to quickly train aid workers in cultural competence is not ideal, it is still critical to the success of emergency response and recovery operations, especially when cascading disasters may occur.

Case Study: Haiti Nonprofit Organization Response and Recovery

Goals of the Case Study

The goals of the case study are as follows:

- To introduce participants to the ways that intercultural issues can cause conflict and harm during post-disaster relief efforts
- To introduce participants to the tradeoffs and critical decisions that must be made in an emergency response situation
- To give participants an opportunity to brainstorm solutions to complex intercultural issues
- To help participants think about the importance of making cultural competence an integrated part of organizational policies and training before an emergency

Learning Outcomes

Upon completion of this exercise, participants will:

- Be able to demonstrate a better understanding of the importance of cultural competence in an international post-disaster context
- Be able to reflect on the elements of a cultural competence training program

Definitions

It is suggested that facilitators provide the following definitions for participants to enhance their understanding of the case study's context:

- Compound: Large, secure NGO buildings surrounded by high walls.
- Tent City: A settlement of displaced persons residing in makeshift tents made of material such as cardboard, canvas, fabric, and plastic.

◆ Manifestation: Protests or riots, which sometimes turn violent. Manifestations often block roadways using large rocks or burning tires.
◆ Haitian Kreyòl: The language spoken by the majority of Haitians.
◆ Beneficiaries: Those receiving aid from a non-governmental organization.
◆ Culture: Norms, roles, belief systems, laws, and values that are interrelated in meaningful ways.
◆ Overt Culture: Easily observed aspects of culture such as demographics, language, and religion.
◆ Hidden Culture: Less easily observed elements of culture such as social structures, humor.

Breakdown

The following steps are intended to help the instructor guide the participants through this activity. The suggested time for completion is 90 minutes.

Step 1. Distribute the pre-test and allow participants time to complete it.

Step 2. Divide into groups. Discuss the ground rules for the activity. Decide who will record the group's ideas and who will be responsible for presenting this information to the other groups after the activity.

Step 3. Distribute the case study and give participants a chance to read it. Give time for them to ask the instructor any questions they may have.

Step 4. (30 minutes) Allow participants to design their training program as a group, using the discussion questions given later. The instructor should announce the remaining time in five-minute increments to simulate the pressure, panic, and chaos of the scenario.

Step 5. Bring all the groups together and allow each group to briefly present the main points of their training program. Next, follow up by selecting some of the discussion questions to explore as a class.

Step 6. Distribute the post-test and ask participants to reflect on what they learned about cultural competence and its importance in international post-disaster contexts.

Ground Rules (Gorski, 2019)

Ground rules exist to ensure that all voices are heard and that there are respectful and successful interactions among participants.

1. Listen actively – respect others when they are talking and avoid engaging in side conversations.
2. Speak from your own experience instead of generalizing ("I" instead of "they," "we," and "you").
3. Do not be afraid to respectfully challenge one another by asking questions but refrain from personal attacks – focus on ideas.
4. Participate to the fullest of your ability – community growth depends on the inclusion of every individual voice. Everyone in the group is required to participate.
5. Instead of invalidating somebody else's story with your own spin on their experience, share your own story and experience.
6. The goal is not to agree – it is to gain a deeper understanding.
7. Be conscious of body language and nonverbal responses – they can be as disrespectful as words.
8. No technological devices (i.e., cell phones, laptops, tablets) may be used during this activity.

Non-Governmental Organizational Response in Haiti

Scenario

A 7.0 earthquake has devastated the nation of Haiti, destroying the nation's limited infrastructure and creating a large scale humanitarian crisis. Hundreds of thousands are dead, and millions are without access to food and water. Families are separated, and countless people are injured.

You are a training manager for a large emergency relief non-governmental organization (NGO) that initially responded with food, water, and medical care to those immediately impacted. Now, three months later, more than 30,000 displaced individuals made homeless by the quake have gathered in makeshift tents and shelters, creating a "tent city" near your organization's compound. Your organization has taken on the task of managing the camp, providing immediate sanitation, food, water, and emergency medical care, while also helping to craft long-term solutions. Most of your experienced disaster workers have now left – on to their next assignment – and you have been tasked with training 200 new aid workers from a variety of nations and backgrounds, including 50 that are Haitian nationals. Few of the international aid workers have emergency management experience or been trained in the elements of cultural competence, and none speak Haitian Kreyòl, which limits their ability to communicate effectively. Already, violent conflicts, called manifestations, have erupted between Haitian beneficiaries and some international aid workers. At the same time, the Haitian aid workers and international aid workers are struggling to work together. Tensions are running high, and day-to-day operations are not being effective.

Some beneficiaries have started to complain that international aid workers are evil, exploitative, and immoral, while some of the Haitian aid workers are concerned that the international aid workers are not acting "professionally". Many of the beneficiaries are deeply offended by the tattoos, piercings, and dress of the international aid workers (i.e., shorts and sleeveless shirts for women) and feel personally disrespected by their body language and mannerisms (e.g., greeting children before elders). As these rumors spread, they undermine the credibility of the aid workers, causing beneficiaries to ignore their warnings and fail to follow health information or seek medical aid.

International aid workers, on the other hand, view the general demeanor of their Haitian counterparts as unprofessional and untrustworthy. The failure of international aid workers to understand Haitian cultural norms for professionals, such as not looking superiors in the eye or neither smiling nor laughing much while on duty, has led to numerous misunderstandings and frustrations on both sides.

Your own intercultural experience tells you that these areas of miscommunication are born out of a lack of specific cultural knowledge among both parties and a lack of the skills needed to culturally adapt among your new employees. Differences in everything from body language to cultural appropriateness vary widely across cultures and influence how communication signals are interpreted and received.

You are responsible for ensuring that your new hires rapidly acquire the cross-cultural competencies they need to effectively work on an intercultural team and communicate care, competence, and comfort in a form that is culturally understood. If given the opportunity, you would choose to develop a comprehensive cultural competence training program. However, time is not on your side. Because of unsanitary conditions, a cholera outbreak is starting to sweep through the tent city, and Haitian beneficiaries are reluctant to seek help or follow sanitation procedures from the international aid workers, which can have deadly consequences.

As you reflect on your own cultural competence training, you remember that you found that opportunities for interaction with those in your host culture, chances to ask reflective questions, and mentoring by those already in the field to be highly effective in helping you develop intercultural skills, but your current situation is complicated. Your new hires must acquire these skills in an environment that is constantly changing, chaotic, and even dangerous. Some of your colleagues suggest that this is neither the time nor place to provide such training and that both sides just need to "get over it," while others suggest that the best solution is to simply provide assigned reading material that can be reviewed when not on duty.

Roles and Tasks

You are a training manager for a large emergency relief NGO. Your international staff and Haitian staff are at odds. Conflict and mistrust caused by cultural misunderstandings between the beneficiaries and the aid workers are hindering the effectiveness of life-saving programs. You have decided to start cultural competence training with your international aid workers. What will this program look like? Use the questions that follow to guide your decisions.

Questions for Discussion

1. What will your training program look like? What will it include (e.g., reading material, videos, field trips, immersion, mentoring)? What will it not include?
2. How do you get your international employees on board and drive home the importance of this training?
3. What steps can you take to improve trust and cooperation between the different groups?
4. Do you require your employees to change their appearance, such as removing piercings, covering tattoos, and wearing clothing that is considered more conservative? Where do you draw the line on this?
5. Knowing that this rushed training is not ideal and that there are already negative consequences occurring, what could the organization have done to avoid this?
6. How can you communicate need to take cultural competence seriously to the organization's headquarters? What policies would you suggest?
7. What could be a negative or unintended consequence of trying to undertake this project? What would your reaction to this exercise be if you had been raised as a Haitian?

Supplemental Questions

Facilitators may consider asking the following supplemental questions for the scenario provided later:

- ◆ What are your first thoughts about this scenario? Did you have any emotional reactions to this scenario? If yes, why? If no, why?
- ◆ Was there anything thought provoking about how your fellow participants reacted to this exercise? (Please use generalizations and do not target others.)
- ◆ How do you think this scenario relates to emergency management? Why was this exercise created?

Pre-Test Assessment

PURPOSE OF THE SURVEY

This assessment survey is designed to demonstrate understanding of cultural competence–related aspects and establish a baseline of participant attitudes before the exercise.

DEFINITIONS

Directions: Please match the terminologies with their definitions.

_____ Culture   A.   Less easily observed elements of culture such as social structures, humor.

_____ Overt Culture   B.   Norms, roles, belief systems, laws, and values that are interrelated in meaningful ways.

_____ Hidden Culture   C.   Easily observed aspects of culture such as demographics, language, and religion.

ATTITUDINAL SCALE

Directions: Please use the following scale to represent your reaction to the questions.

1	2	3	4	5
Strongly Agree	Agree	Neither Agree nor Disagree	Disagree	Strongly Disagree

1. I believe personal culture influences my role(s).

2. I believe cultural groups influence my role(s).

3. I believe stereotypes influence my role(s).

4. Cultural competence is important to post-disaster response and recovery operations.

5. After a disaster, intercultural skills can be put on hold until things calm down.

6. Cultural competence is a personality trait and cannot be taught.

7. Cultural competence is only important for people who are easily offended.

8. Cultural competence can enhance lifesaving programs.

9. Cultural competence increases trust between groups of people.

Post-Test Assessment

PURPOSE OF THE SURVEY

This assessment survey is designed to demonstrate understanding of culturally related impacts and establish a baseline of participant attitudes after the exercise.

DEFINITIONS

Directions: Please match the terminologies with their definitions.

_____ Culture   A. Less easily observed elements of culture such as social structures, humor.

_____ Overt Culture   B. Norms, roles, belief systems, laws, and values that are interrelated in meaningful ways.

_____ Hidden Culture   C. Easily observed aspects of culture such as demographics, language, and religion.

ATTITUDINAL SCALE

Directions: Please use the following scale to represent your reaction to the questions.

1	2	3	4	5
Strongly Agree	Agree	Neither Agree nor Disagree	Disagree	Strongly Disagree

1. I believe personal culture influences my role(s).

2. I believe cultural groups influence my role(s).

3. I believe stereotypes influence my role(s).

4. Cultural competence is important to post-disaster response and recovery operations.

5. After a disaster, intercultural skills can be put on hold until things calm down.

6. Cultural competence is a personality trait and cannot be taught.

7. Cultural competence is only important for people who are easily offended.

8. Cultural competence can enhance lifesaving programs.

9. Cultural competence increases trust between groups of people.

OPEN RESPONSE

Please answer the following question: "I used to think_____, but now I think_____."

(Use back of page if needing extra space.)

References

Centers for Disease Control and Prevention. (2013). *Outbreak notice: Cholera in Haiti*. Retrieved from wwwnc.cdc.gov/travel/notices/outbreak-notice/haiti-cholera.htm

Ditzler, T. F., Hastings, P. R., & Deleon, R. B. (2009). Sustainable community mental health: Psychological first aid in humanitarian emergencies. *Journal of Human Security, 5*(2), 35+.

Gorski, P. C. (2019). *Guide for setting ground rules*. Retrieved from www.edchange.org/multicultural/activities/groundrules.html

Grandey, A. A. (2003). When "the show must go on": Surface acting and deep acting as determinants of emotional exhaustion and peer-rated service delivery. *Academy of Management Journal, 46*(1), 86–96.

Hall, E. T. (1976). *Beyond culture*. Garden City, NY: Anchor Press.

Hofstede, G. H. (2001). *Culture's consequences: Comparing values, behaviors, institutions, and organizations across nations* (2nd ed.). Thousand Oaks, CA: Sage Publications.

Paton, D. (1996). Training disaster workers: Promoting wellbeing and operational effectiveness. *Disaster Prevention and Management: An International Journal, 5*(5), 11–18.

Remington, C. (2017). *The cultural competence of response and recovery workers in post-earthquake Haiti* (PhD Dissertation). Miami, Florida International University.

Triandis, H. C., Vassiliou, V., Vassiliou, G., Tanaka, Y., & Shanmugam, A. (1972). *The analysis of subjective culture*. New York, NY: Wiley.

Zweifel, T. D. (2003). *Culture clash: Managing the global high-performance team*. New York, NY: SelectBooks.

Additional Resources

Dale, J. M., & Dulaimi, M. F. (2016). Cultural competence: A success factor in NGO projects? *Built Environment Project and Asset Management, 6*(2), 232–246.

Global Affairs Canada. (2018, September 19). *Cultural information: Haiti: Centre for intercultural learning*. Retrieved from www.international.gc.ca/cil-cai/country_insights-apercus_pays/ci-ic_ht.aspx?lang=eng

Institute for Disaster Mental Health. (n.d.). *Tip Sheet on Haitian Culture*. New York: State University of New York. Retrieved from https://www.in.gov/isdh/files/Hatian_Culture_tip_sheet-IDMH.pdf

Simkhovych, D. (2009). The relationship between intercultural effectiveness and perceived project team performance in the context of international development. *International Journal of Intercultural Relations, 33*(5), 383–390.

16

Disaster Relief in a Conflict Zone

The Case of Syria

James D. Ramsay

Overview

Human civilization is characterized by migration, or consistent mobility within or between countries, for millennia. For example, there were multiple pathways of mass movements of people during the Roman Empire, 100 to 500 CE (Cornell & Matthews, 1982). One form of migration is immigration – the movement out of one's native land to live in another land. People immigrate because of famine, war, governmental failure, or persecution. These immigrants are referred to as *refugees*. In contrast, people may also migrate to another country to pursue personal and professional aspirations. Individuals who migrate to pursue seasonal work or other recurring professional opportunities are referred to as seasonal migrants (i.e., "migrant workers").

At times migration is motivated by opportunity, while at other times it is relatively involuntary. History offers hundreds of motivations for migration. Migration can be facilitated by economic opportunities, political oppression, the opportunity to improve religious freedom, to own land, or to self-govern, which motivated many to immigrate to the "New World" in the 1600s and 1700s.

Alternatively, poor access to natural resources, social prestige, crop failure, civil conflict, and natural disasters have also operated alone or in combination to motivate migration.[1] Worldwide, the numbers of displaced people, asylum seekers, and refugees are staggering. The United Nations (UN) estimated recently up to 258 million international migrants (3.4% of the global population). To put this in context, this means one in every 300 people is a refugee at any given moment each year (UN, 2017a).

One of the most pressing social issues today, which is intimately tied to both natural disasters and to migration, is climate change. Indeed, climate change is a forcing function for natural disasters and migration. Climate change can have both purely natural causes as well as anthropomorphic causes. In fact, climate change has been a regular component of life on earth for hundreds of thousands of years. According to the National Aeronautics and Space Administration (NASA) (2019):

> Just in the last 650,000 years there have been seven cycles of glacial advance and retreat, with the abrupt end of the last ice age about 7,000 years ago marking the beginning of the modern climate era – and of human civilization.
>
> (para. 1)

In contrast to naturally occurring climate change, anthropomorphic causes include changes from activities of human living, such as fossil fuel combustion, which maximizes carbon dioxide in the lower atmosphere. Anthropomorphic climate change is also implicated as a root cause for more frequent and more severe natural disasters (e.g., hurricanes and wildfires) (U.S. Geological Survey, 2019). That is, changes can heighten food or water vulnerabilities in geographic regions already prone to chronic resource shortages, such as the Middle East. When such environmental changes occur in regions with weak and/ or ineffective governments, resource scarcity can cause, force, or motivate populations to move to seek safety (i.e., political asylum) or higher living standards – or become displaced – because of conflicts that arise because of insufficient resources, or both.

While extreme-weather events (e.g., wildfires or floods) cause a direct and urgent movement of people, climate change events that emanate from slower-moving events (e.g., drought and erosion) are increasing in frequency and severity – and becoming persistent. Even as natural disasters have immediate displacement effects and can disrupt established migration patterns, climate-related emergencies – combined with a host of socioeconomic factors – are forcing increasing numbers to migrate both within their own countries as well as across borders. Though often connected, the implications and consequences of such disasters vary considerably across governments and regions. This in turn affects migration patterns and international policy-making. Ultimately, these implications combine to influence the degree and effectiveness of disaster relief operations. Interestingly, populations forced to flee or migrate because of extreme weather patterns or food or water shortages resulting from climate change are referred to as "climate refugees".

Connecting Security to Migration via Climate Change

Human security is the concept that individuals are collectively the basis of national security – as opposed to the security of state being the imperative as it is in most nations today. Human security includes several dimensions, which can be affected by the drivers of migration. Dimensions of human security include economic security, food, water, energy security, community, and gender security, as well as political security. The UN characterizes human security as:

> The right of people to live in freedom and dignity, free from poverty and despair. All individuals, in particular vulnerable people, are entitled to freedom from fear and freedom from want, with an equal opportunity to enjoy all their rights and fully develop their human potential; and further that human security recognizes the inter-linkages between peace, development and human rights, and equally considers civil, political, economic, social and cultural rights.
>
> (UN Resolution 66/290, 2012)

There has been a nexus between human security and changes in climate or the local/political/military environment and subsequently migration for centuries. Appreciating that for scholars of conflict studies it is not always a simple matter to establish causal linkages between conflict and resource shortages and then migration, or between changes in climate to resource shortages to conflict. Such connections are studied constantly, and linkages have been established. For instance, climate-induced migration was identified as a key security concern at the 2015 UN Climate Change Conference (known as COP21) that took place in early December 2015 (COP21, 2015). Interestingly, Walter Kaelin of the Nansen Initiative said, "Disaster displacement represents one of the biggest humanitarian challenges of the twenty-first century," (Nansen Initiative, 2015, para. 1). From a human security perspective, humanitarian challenges present several security challenges for individuals and nations (if not for regions).

Syrian Immigration: A Case of Conflict, Immigration, and the Need for Culturally Competent Emergency Management Expertise

Relating conflict to climate change and disaster displacement provides a logical explanation for how conflict may arise in many parts of the world. Perhaps one of the best-known situations of a refugee crisis brought on by both conflict and climate change is the Syrian crisis.[2] The five-year drought in Syria is suspected to be a significant factor in the ethnic tensions that ultimately produced the civil war and subsequent flow of refugees (Migration Policy, 2015). It may seem relatively obvious that when migration occurs as a result of changes in climate, food, or water supply, or civil conflict – or even all these working together – there could be deeply serious security implications. Mixtures of language, culture, and ethnicities not only stress response capabilities of even more developed countries, but they also combine in the context of extreme stress to form a volatile combination and complex security scenario.

On March 15, 2011, protests broke out in Syria against the Assad regime, which had been in power for more than 40 years and was widely thought to be oppressive, secretive, and brutal toward opposition. The protests in Syria followed similar uprisings in Tunisia, Libya, and Egypt – a collective phenomenon known more widely as the "Arab Spring". Fueled by five years of drought and conflict, more than 350,000 have died over the past eight years in the Syrian conflict (Infomigrants, 2018). According to the UN Refugee Agency (UNHCR) (2018), more than 5.6 million Syrians have fled their country since 2011, with another 6.6 million people displaced internally. Regionally, there are approximately 3.6 million Syrian refugees in Turkey, 950,000 in Lebanon, 670,000 refugees in Jordan, 250,000 in Iraq, and 132,000 in Egypt (UNHCR, 2018). However, nearly one million Syrian refugees have continued their odyssey to Europe to seek better economic opportunities and political stability from more developed countries (i.e., the U.K., Germany, the Netherlands, France, Belgium, and Scandinavia) than would be possible from the less developed nations (i.e., Jordan, Lebanon, and Egypt) (Conner, 2018).

When refugees are placed in host nations, they tend to cluster. Such clusters of refugees occur because of the desire to bond with those like themselves in terms of language, diet, customs, belief systems, etc. Since there tends to be a general lack of adequately trained and culturally competent relief/emergency workers, host nations often face the bitter reality of wanting to do the right thing but being unable to do so because of the inability to reeducate, retrain, or even teach a new language skill to large numbers of individuals. As these social/communal clusters grow in size and number, fear and resentment can occur among native populations. Though studies indicate that most refugees and immigrants do not engage in criminal activity or pose security challenges, some society members still believe this out of fear. According to RAND, the 2016 Pew Research Center's global attitudes survey found that most respondents in Germany, Greece, Italy, and the U.K. believed the presence of Syrian refugees increased terrorism and took jobs from citizens (Amaral, Woldetsadik, & Armenta, 2018). As refugees increase, collective poverty results from makeshift shantytowns built from sub-standard housing that deepens isolationism and memorializes poverty. Over time, those who are either uneducated or predisposed to being xenophobic or racist increase the fear and suspicion, producing a cycle that can continue for successive generations. Such stereotypes and ethnic biases worsen security, delay movement up the social ladder for immigrants, and extend the processes required to adequately integrate refugees into peaceful and contributing members of society.

Final Thoughts

Climate change and conflict seem to be persistent centerpieces of modern life on earth. Exacerbating matters, population demographers believe the human population will continue to grow for another 100 years, expected to reach 9.8 billion by 2050 and 11.2 billion by 2100 (UN, 2017b). This global population growth will greatly affect less developed countries where governments are poorer and weaker and have less surge capacity than wealthier, more developed countries. It seems logical to suspect human beings will continue to compete for scarce resources, territory, and wealth, and the use of fossil fuels will worsen anthropomorphic climate change. Such conditions can be expected to continue to cause huge numbers of climate or other sorts of refugees seeking asylum and better lives. For instance, applications for asylum are expected to increase because of climate change. As Missirian and Schlenker (2017, p. 1,610) state:

> Holding everything else constant, asylum applications by the end of the century are predicted to increase, on average, by 28% (98,000 additional asylum applications per year) under representative concentration pathway (RCP) scenario 4.5 and by 188% (660,000 additional applications per year) under RCP 8.5 for the 21 climate models in the NASA Earth Exchange Global Daily Downscaled Projections.

In less developed countries where climate crises and conflict seem to strike hardest, and that have the largest populations, persistent migration will continue to plague, weaken, or cause those governments to fail. At the same time, migration pressures will continue to over-burden the response and placement capabilities of even more developed governments that tend not to maintain adequate capacity to absorb immigrants or an adequate workforce of culturally competent emergency/relief workers. Further complicating matters are persistent stereotypes and ethnic biases around refuges. Hence, there is a pressing need for more culturally and linguistically competent emergency/relief workers to be able to respond to climate change and the many existing and near-term conflicts and security needs across the globe.

Case Study: Culturally Competent Planning for Refugees

Goals for the Study

The goal of this case study is for participants to exercise their cultural competency knowledge, skills, and abilities to a migration crisis occurring in a conflict zone.

Learning Outcomes

- Define migration and discuss several factors that cause migration.
- Relate the concepts of climate change and human security to conflict and migration.
- Describe how Syrian refugees might be the cause of heightened security concerns in Europe.
- Define the term "cultural competence" in the context of disaster relief and how it is related to security.
- Compare and contrast types of migration and how climate change acts as a forcing function to cause conflict and migration.

Definitions

- Anthropomorphic Climate Change: Refers to climate change that is brought about, enhanced, or worsened by human activities. This contrasts with natural climate change and is believed to be the main type of climate change in the past 150 years.

- Climate Change: According to the National Geographic Society (n.d.), climate change refers to a broad range of longer-term global phenomena created predominantly by burning fossil fuels, which add heat-trapping gases to Earth's atmosphere. These phenomena include the increased temperature trends described by global warming, but also encompass changes such as sea level rise; ice mass loss in Greenland, Antarctica, the Arctic, and mountain glaciers worldwide; shifts in flower/plant blooming; and extreme weather events. To the degree that such changes are due to human activities, this is referred to as "anthropomorphic climate change."

- Disaster Relief: Typically regarded as immediate aid provided for alleviating the suffering of domestic disaster victims.

- Human Security: According to the UN (2018), "human security is an approach to assist Member States in identifying and addressing widespread and cross-cutting challenges to the survival, livelihood and dignity of their people" (para. 2). It calls for "people-centered, comprehensive, context-specific and prevention-oriented responses that strengthen the protection and empowerment of all people" (para. 2). Security of the individual encompasses economics, gender, food, water, energy, environment, political, and the community.

- Immigration: Coming to live permanently in a foreign country.

- Less Developed Country (LDC): According to the UN (2019), "least (or less) developed countries (LDCs) are low-income countries confronting severe structural impediments to sustainable development." LDCs are highly vulnerable to economic and environmental shocks and have low levels of human assets. They are low-income countries that face significant structural challenges to sustainable development. There are

47 countries on the UN'S list of LDCs, such as Malawi, Lesotho, and Cambodia.

◆ More Developed Country (MDC): Are in direct contrast to LDCs. An MDC is an economically advanced country, the economy of which is characterized by large industrial and service sectors, technology and widespread literacy, and a high gross national product, such as the United States, Britain, Germany, etc.

◆ Migration: Human migration is the movement by people from one place to another with the intentions of settling, permanently or temporarily, in a new location. The movement can be either over short or long distances, within a country or from one country to another.

◆ Refugee: According to the UN Refugee Agency (2019), "refugees are people who cannot return to their country of origin because of a well-founded fear of persecution, conflict, violence, or other circumstances that have seriously disturbed public order, and who, as a result, require international protection" (para. 5). For example, "climate refugees" is a general term referring to those who become refugees because of extreme climatic shifts that cause water, food, or energy insecurity, precluding the ability to support themselves or their families.

Breakdown

◆ Divide into groups of four to five people.
◆ Discuss the ground rules to set the tone.
◆ Review the scenario and the group's discussion questions.
◆ Allow ample time for discussion (approximately 45 minutes).
◆ Facilitate group dialogue about responses to questions.
◆ Utilize supplemental questions if needed.

Ground Rules (Gorski, 2019)

1. Listen actively – respect others when they are talking.
2. Speak from your own experience instead of generalizing ("I" instead of "they," "we," and "you").
3. Do not be afraid to respectfully challenge one another by asking questions but refrain from personal attacks – focus on ideas.
4. Participate to the fullest of your ability – community growth depends on the inclusion of every individual voice.
5. Instead of invalidating somebody else's story with your own spin on their experience, share your own story and experience.
6. The goal is not to agree – it is to gain a deeper understanding.
7. Be conscious of body language and nonverbal responses – they can be as disrespectful as words.

Supplemental Questions

Facilitators may consider asking the following supplemental questions for the scenario provided herein:

♦ What are your first thoughts about this scenario? Did you have any emotional reactions to this scenario? If yes, why? If no, why?
♦ Was there anything thought provoking about how your fellow participants reacted to this exercise? (Please use generalizations and do not target others.)
♦ How do you think this scenario relates to emergency and crisis management? Why was this exercise created?

Scenario

Following a five-year drought, Syrian refugees have started migrating into southern Turkey, which is stressing the local government's capacity to manage the impending crisis. Providing adequate food, water, shelter, and sanitation is becoming increasingly difficult. There are not enough local resources to house and feed everyone, and there is not adequate expertise to provide proper preparation for relief workers. In addition, the sheer number of refugees is increasing each week. These stressors combine to overwhelm the local government's capability, and hence they are struggling to keep people safe, healthy, fed, toileted, housed, and secure. In turn, the refugees are in duress, and it is becoming clear that overall tension among refugees, relief workers, and local citizens is understandably and possibly dangerously increasing. Some refugees are showing signs of anger and frustration, and some are even acting out. Although such tension, uncertainty, and stress are understandable as the number of refugees grows, local citizens are expressing concern for their own safety. Each week, more refugees arrive.

There is a distinct sense among the relief workers that they are not comfortable anticipating or responding to even basic emergencies in the refugee camp. Most relief workers express only "hope" that "nothing bad happens to anyone." At this early stage of the relief effort, no one among the staff seems to have a background in security operations, military tactics, law enforcement, or even basic emergency management. Sheltering in place, medicine, and food distribution are the primary competencies. In addition, most staff do not speak the dialect of the typical Syrian refugee, the number of physicians and nurses cannot keep pace with the weekly additions of refugees, medicines are in short supply, and power seems to come and go. Gunfire and bombings can be heard most days and nights. Fear is palpable among both staff and refugees. All this complicates relief efforts and compromises security. As the numbers of refugees increases, the Turkish government has requested assistance from international relief organizations and other countries, resources, and military personnel to manage the crisis and to be on guard lest the Syrian Civil War spreads to Turkey.

To offer logistical support as well as a show of security, both the Turkish and the U.S. militaries have been deployed to the relief camp. However, there are rumors the U.S. military is planning to set up a base on ancient burial grounds known to the local citizens. Unfortunately, the local citizenry recalls that this has happened before during the first Gulf War against Saddam Hussein. Even though the locals realize and appreciate the role the U.S. military played then, and now, such actions resulted in the locals feeling disrespected. Ultimately, the U.S. military failed to successfully work with local governments, hurting efforts to gather actionable intelligence and generally leaving a poor impression of the United States in the hearts of local citizens. Today, 15 years later, as the U.S. military arrives in the region, word has spread from among the locals to the relief workers that, once again, culturally inappropriate actions may be taking place. This apprehension has fueled distrust among the locals.

Role
You are part of a task force that is about to be deployed to assist with local relief efforts. Although you are an expert relief worker, you realize that you and perhaps many on your team do not fully understand local customs, dialects, foods, attitudes toward healthcare, and even the local political structure. You are justifiably concerned how this may hinder your relief efforts. Because one does not currently exist, you are also responsible for creating an emergency response plan for the refugee camp. Your plan needs to accommodate how best to manage the continuous flow of refugees from Syria, emergencies that arise from medical or health issues, from violence, and other concerns that are part of life in a conflict zone.

Questions for Discussion
1. What are the sorts of capabilities you need to have on your team of relief workers?
2. Who are some of the stakeholders of the relief effort?
3. What are some of the security issues that may arise when managing refugees?
4. Where do security and cultural issues come together in supportive roles? In conflicting roles?
5. What are the major elements of your emergency response plan for the refugee camp? What are cultural issues you need to consider when creating this plan?

Pre-Test Assessment

PURPOSE OF THE SURVEY

This assessment survey is designed to demonstrate understanding of cultural competence–related aspects and establish a baseline of participant attitudes before the exercise.

DEFINITIONS

Directions: Please match the terminologies with their definitions.

_____ Migration   A.   Leaving one's country to move to/live permanently in another country.

_____ Immigration   B.   An approach to assist Member States in identifying and addressing widespread and cross-cutting challenges to the survival, livelihood, and dignity of their people.

_____ Human Security   C.   The movement by people from one place to another with the intentions of settling, permanently or temporarily, in a new location.

ATTITUDINAL SCALE

Directions: Please use the following scale to represent your reaction to the questions.

1	2	3	4	5
Strongly Agree	Agree	Neither Agree nor Disagree	Disagree	Strongly Disagree

1. I believe personal culture influences my role(s).

2. I believe cultural groups influence my role(s).

3. I believe stereotypes influence my role(s).

4. I believe I have adequate knowledge of how my own cultural identities influence my role(s).

5. I believe I have adequate knowledge of other cultures and their influence on my role(s).

6. I believe I have adequate knowledge of stereotypes and their influence on my role(s).

7. I believe I have adequate knowledge of my cultural identities and their influence on emergency and crisis management.

8. I believe I have adequate knowledge of other cultural identities and how they influence emergency and crisis management.

9. I believe I have adequate knowledge of stereotypes and how they influence emergency and crisis management.

Post-Test Assessment

PURPOSE OF THE SURVEY

This assessment survey is designed to demonstrate understanding of culturally related impacts and establish a baseline of participant attitudes after the exercise.

DEFINITIONS

Directions: Please match the terminologies with their definitions.

_____	Migration	A.	Leaving one's country to move to/live permanently in another country.
_____	Immigration	B.	An approach to assist Member States in identifying and addressing widespread and cross-cutting challenges to the survival, livelihood, and dignity of their people.
_____	Human Security	C.	The movement by people from one place to another with the intentions of settling, permanently or temporarily, in a new location.

ATTITUDINAL SCALE

Directions: Please use the following scale to represent your reaction to the questions.

1	2	3	4	5
Strongly Agree	Agree	Neither Agree nor Disagree	Disagree	Strongly Disagree

1. I believe personal culture influences my role(s).

2. I believe cultural groups influence my role(s).

3. I believe stereotypes influence my role(s).

4. I believe I have adequate knowledge of how my own cultural identities influence my role(s).

5. I believe I have adequate knowledge of other cultures and their influence on my role(s).

6. I believe I have adequate knowledge of stereotypes and their influence on my role(s).

7. I believe I have adequate knowledge of my cultural identities and their influence on emergency and crisis management.

8. I believe I have adequate knowledge of other cultural identities and how they influence emergency and crisis management.

9. I believe I have adequate knowledge of stereotypes and how they influence emergency and crisis management.

OPEN RESPONSE

Please answer the following question: "I used to think_____, but now I think_____."

(Use back of page if needing extra space.)

Notes

1. In this case study, note that "disaster" refers to natural hazards such as tornadoes, drought, flood, fires, or those that are human-made as a result of conflict, civil war, etc. Hence "disaster relief" refers to operations to stabilize localities and comfort victims of either natural or human-made disaster.
2. The onset and role of ISIS in the Syrian conflict, as well as the roles of Russia and Iran and the proxy war with the United States, cannot be overstated. However, a responsible treatment of this long-term and complex interplay and how that has impacted migration is beyond the scope of this case study.

References

Amaral, E., Woldetsadik, M., & Armenta, G. (2018). *Europe's greatest challenge: Integrating Syrian refugees*. Retrieved from www.rand.org/blog/2018/04/europes-great-challenge-integrating-syrian-refugees.html

Conner, P. (2018). Most displaced Syrians are in the Middle East, but about 1 million are in Europe. *Pew Research Center*. Retrieved from www.pewresearch.org/fact-tank/2018/01/29/where-displaced-syrians-have-resettled/

Cornell, T., & Matthews, J. (1982). *Atlas of the Roman world*. New York, NY: Facts on File, Inc.

Gorski, P. C. (2019). *Guide for setting ground rules*. Retrieved from www.edchange.org/multicultural/activities/groundrules.html

Infomigrants. (2018). Retrieved from www.infomigrants.net/en/post/8077/the-syrian-conflict-and-its-impact-on-migration

Migration Policy.org. (2015). *Climate change and natural disasters displace millions*. Retrieved from www.migrationpolicy.org/article/top-10-2015-%E2%80%93-issue-7-climate-change-and-natural-disasters-displace-millions-affect

Missirian, A., & Schlenker, W. (2017). Asylum applications respond to temperature fluctuations. *Science, 358*(6370), 1610–1614.

National Aeronautics and Space Association (NASA). (2019). *Climate change: How do we know?* Retrieved from https://climate.nasa.gov/evidence/

National Geographic Society. (n.d.). *Climate change*. Retrieved from www.nationalgeographic.org/encyclopedia/climate-change/

Nansen Initiative. (2015). *More than 100 governments affirm broad support to better protect people displaced across borders by disasters and the effects of climate change*. Retrieved from www.nanseninitiative.org/more-than-100-governments-affirm-broad-support-to-better-protect-people-displaced-across-borders-by-disasters-and-the-effects-of-climate-change/

United Nations. (2017a). *Population facts*. Retrieved from www.un.org/en/development/desa/population/publications/pdf/popfacts/PopFacts_2017-5.pdf

United Nations. (2017b). *World population projected to reach 9.8 billion in 2050, and 11.2 billion in 2100*. Retrieved from www.un.org/development/desa/en/news/population/world-population-prospects-2017.html

United Nations. (2018). *What is human security?* Retrieved from www.un.org/humansecurity/what-is-human-security/

United Nations. (2019). *Least developed counties*. Retrieved from www.un.org/development/desa/dpad/least-developed-country-category.html

United Nations Climate Change Conference (COP21). (2015). *COP-what it's all about*. Retrieved from www.cop21paris.org/about/cop21

United Nations Refugee Agency (UNHCR). (2018). *Syria emergency*. Retrieved from www.unhcr.org/syria-emergency.html

United Nations Refugee Agency (UNHCR). (2019). *Asylum and migration*. Retrieved from www.unhcr.org/en-us/asylum-and-migration.html

United Nations Resolution 66/290. (2012, September 10). Resolution adopted by the general assembly. Retrieved from www.un.org/en/ga/search/view_doc.asp?symbol=A/RES/66/290

U.S. Geological Survey. (2019). *What are the signs of climate change?* Retrieved from www.usgs.gov

Additional Resources

The European Parliament. (2019). *The concept of "climate refugee": Toward a possible definition*. Retrieved from www.europarl.europa.eu/RegData/etudes/BRIE/2018/621893/EPRS_BRI(2018)621893_EN.pdf

Hamid, S. (2015, October). Islamism, the Arab Spring, and the failure of America's do-nothing policy in the Middle East. *The Atlantic*. Retrieved from www.theatlantic.com/international/archive/2015/10/middle-east-egypt-us-policy/409537/

Intergovernmental Panel on Climate Change. (2018). Retrieved from www.ipcc.ch/

National Public Radio. Arab Spring, a Year of Revolution. (2011). Retrieved from www.npr.org/2011/12/17/143897126/the-arab-spring-a-year-of-revolution

Scott, J. (2007). *Concept paper: The importance of cultural competence in disaster relief.* Retrieved from www.hsdl.org/?view&did=6108

Schwartzstein, P. (2017). Climate change and water woes drove ISIS recruiting in Iraq. *National Geographic.* Retrieved from https://news.nationalgeographic.com/2017/11/climate-change-drought-drove-isis-terrorist-recruiting-iraq/

UNHCR Climate Change and Disasters. (2019). Retrieved from www.unhcr.org/climate-change-and-disasters.html

United Nations – Department of Economic and Social Affairs. (2019). Retrieved from www.un.org/development/desa/en/

United Nations Framework on Climate Change. (2019). Retrieved from https://unfccc.int/

United Nations – Refugees and Migrants. (2019). Retrieved from https://refugeesmigrants.un.org/

U.S. Department of Health and Human Services. (2017). *Cultural and linguistic competence in disaster preparedness planning and crisis response.* Retrieved from www.phe.gov/Preparedness/planning/abc/Pages/linguistic.aspx

About the Editors and Contributors

About the Editors

Claire Connolly Knox, Ph.D., is an associate professor and the director of the Master of Emergency and Crisis Management program in the School of Public Administration at the University of Central Florida (UCF). She holds a joint appointment with UCF's National Center for Integrated Coastal Research. Her research interests include environmental vulnerability and disaster response, environmental policy and management, Habermas Critical Theory, and the scholarship of teaching and learning. She has published in multiple journals, including *Public Administration Review, Coastal Management Journal, Disaster Prevention and Management, Journal of Environmental Policy and Planning, Environmental Politics, Administration & Society, Journal of Emergency Management*, and *Journal of Public Affairs Education*. She is Chair of ASPA's Section on Emergency and Crisis Management, associate editor of Emergency Management for *Public Administration Review*, editorial board member for the *International Journal of Security, Preparedness and Resilience Education*, and is the past chair for FEMA's Scholarship of Teaching and Learning special interest group. She has won multiple awards for her research and teaching, including the 2015 Florida Emergency Preparedness Association's Gary Arnold for her dedication to improving Florida's emergency management community through higher education.

Brittany "Brie" Haupt, Ph.D., is an assistant professor at Virginia Commonwealth University. Her previous educational achievements contributed to developing her passion for increasing her cultural competency and becoming trained in diversity education and multiculturalism, as well as intercultural dialogue and community development. Her research interests include cultural competency, emergency management communication, community resilience, and competency-based education. She is on American Society for Public Administration's board for the Section on Emergency and Crisis Management and serves as co-chair for the Social Media Committee. In addition to being a part of an early career editorial board program member for Natural Hazards Review, she has published in *Public Administration Review, Journal of Public Affairs Education, Disaster Prevention and Management, Risk, Hazards, and Crisis in Public Policy, Journal of Emergency Management, and Frontiers in Communication* section on *Disaster Communications*. In addition, she has presented at the American Society for Public Administration, PA Theory conference, the Association for Public Policy Analysis and Management, the Public Administration Research conferences, as well as presented for the Federal Emergency Management Agency on a case study created for diversity education–related training. Her professional efforts were acknowledged via selection as the American Society for Public Administration's Founders Fellow in 2017, as well as an International Scholar Workshop participant in Chennai, India.

About the Contributors

DeeDee Bennett, Ph.D., is an assistant professor in the College of Emergency Preparedness, Homeland Security, and Cyber Security at the University at Albany – SUNY. Her primary research areas include emergency management, socially vulnerable populations during disasters, emergency communications, disaster policy, and mobile wireless communications. She has taught at both the undergraduate and graduate level; some of her classes include disaster response and recovery, intergovernmental and cross-sector collaboration during disasters, and vulnerable populations. Dr. Bennett has secured several internal and external research grants from the National Science Foundation and the Department of Homeland Security. She has published in various journals and presented at several conferences related to emergency management, disability, wireless technology, and future studies. Her previous appointments include assistant professor and director of the Emergency

Management and Disaster Science program at the University of Nebraska at Omaha (UNO) and research scientist at the Center for Advanced Communications Policy at Georgia Institute of Technology. Dr. Bennett received her Ph.D. from Oklahoma State University in Fire and Emergency Management. In addition to bringing expertise in emergency management, she has a unique academic background, having received both her M.S. in public policy and B.S. in electrical engineering from the Georgia Institute of Technology.

Thomas Carey, Ed.D., teaches at both Monmouth University and Metropolitan College of New York. He instructs undergraduate students in the foundations of intelligence in homeland security policy and practice at Monmouth University. At the Metropolitan College of New York, Dr. Carey develops curriculum and instructs graduate students in the applications of hazard analysis, disaster preparedness, and recovery procedures. His research interests include the utilization of client-based service learning and experiential learning pedagogies in emergency management and homeland security curricula. Additionally, he serves as a reviewer for authors and publishing companies producing emergency management and homeland security textbooks. Dr. Carey has spent 23 years in the NYPD as a supervisor in various investigative and training assignments. His combined military service includes 27 years in the New York Army National Guard and U.S. Army, achieving the rank of sergeant major. He is also a combat veteran of the Operation Iraqi Freedom campaign. Professional certifications held include the Certified Protection Professional (CPP) awarded by the American Society of Industrial Security and the Certified Emergency Manager (CEM) awarded by the International Association of Emergency Managers.

Stephen Stuart Carter, M.S., is a consultant and educator with more than 50 years of experience in public safety, emergency services, emergency management, industrial safety, leadership training, and higher education. He is an instructional coordinator and adjunct faculty for the Mid-Atlantic Center for Emergency Management & Public Safety at Frederick Community College, assigned to special projects and the apprenticeship program. In 2014, he retired as the program chair and associate professor for the Public Safety

Administration, Emergency Management, Fire Service Administration, and Homeland Security in the University of Maryland
University College (UMUC) School of Undergraduate Studies. He
joined the full-time colligate UMUC faculty in 2006 after serving
more than three years as an adjunct associate professor. He served
as a senior staff member for Johns Hopkins University assigned to
the Maryland Emergency Management Agency in Exercise, Training, and Strategic Analysis. For 19 years, he was a faculty member
of the University of Maryland College Park, Maryland Fire and
Rescue Institute, including two years as the manager of the Field
Programs Section, coordinating the delivery of the statewide emergency services training program through a network of six regional
offices. From 1998 until 2004 he was the manager of the Logistical
Support Section (LSS) of the institute that maintains its statewide
facilities, vehicles, and equipment, along with coordinating EPA
and OSHA compliance for the institute. From 1993 to 1998, he
served as manager of MFRI's Special Programs Section, a revenue-
generating unit, which provides consulting and training to both
industry and government around the world in fire, rescue, emergency care, safety, and OSHA regulatory compliance. Steve was an
adjunct faculty member of the National Fire Academy from 1981
until 2008, teaching in the leadership and management programs.
His experience includes administering a national training effort for
Indian Health Service, coordinating Maryland's emergency medical technician program for five years, and serving as the chief executive officer for an Arizona fire district. He has a B.A. in psychology
from Thiel College, Greenville, Pennsylvania (1968), and a master
of science in management, state and local government, from the
University of Maryland University College (1998). He is a graduate
of the Executive Fire Officer program of the National Fire Academy,
Federal Emergency Management Agency.

Frances L. Edwards, M.U.P., Ph.D., C.E.M., is professor and director
of the Master of Public Administration program at San Jose State
University. She is also deputy director of the National Transportation Security Center at the Mineta Transportation Institute (MTI).
She is a certified emergency manager with more than 20 years'
experience in California. She is editor of *Housing Recovery After*

Disasters, co-author with Dan Goodrich of *Introduction to Transportation Security*, and of two books with Fritz Steinhausler on terrorism, 12 major publications for MTI, and more than 40 articles and book chapters. She was an early researcher in cultural competency in emergency management, writing a chapter for the National Center for Earthquake Engineering Research's school emergency preparedness publication in 1991. Recent work in the area includes "Doing Good Badly: The Need for Cultural Competency in Disasters," in Norman-Major and Gooden's (eds.) book *Cultural Competency for Public Administrators*. Dr. Edwards provides emergency management plan writing, review, and training for Caltrans, and the Santa Clara Valley Transportation Authority, and gives frequent media talks, conference presentations, and public education seminars in Silicon Valley.

N. Emel Ganapati, Ph.D., is the director of the Laboratory for Social Science Research at the International Hurricane Research Center, Extreme Events Institute, Florida International University. She is also an associate professor of public policy and administration in the Steven J. Green School of International and Public Affairs. She received her Ph.D. in planning from the University of Southern California in Los Angeles. Her research interests include disaster management, international development administration, and citizen participation/community empowerment. She has received multiple grants from the National Science Foundation, including funding to study resilience in South Florida and post-disaster recovery after the 2015 Nepal Earthquake and 2010 Haiti Earthquake. She has published in multiple journals, including *Public Administration Review, Journal of the American Planning Association, Administration and Society, Disasters, Natural Hazards Review, Natural Hazards*, and the *International Journal of Mass Emergencies and Disasters*.

Jerry V. Graves, Ph.D., M.P.A., is an environmental and urban planning consultant based in New Orleans. He previously served in the public sector for more than a decade. Dr. Graves is also an adjunct professor at Tulane University and the University of New Orleans. He earned a doctorate in urban studies and master's degree in public administration from the University of New Orleans. He also earned a bachelor's degree in political science from the University of Louisiana at Lafayette.

Alessandra Jerolleman, Ph.D., M.PA., C.F.M. is an assistant professor of emergency management at Jacksonville State University. She is the co-founder of Hazard Resilience, a United States–based consultancy providing leadership and expertise in disaster recovery, risk reduction, and hazard policy. She is currently an assistant professor in Jacksonville State University's Emergency Management Department. Dr. Jerolleman is one of the founders of the Natural Hazard Mitigation Association (NHMA) and served as its executive director for its first seven years. She is a subject matter expert in climate adaptation, hazard mitigation, and resilience, with a long history of working in the public, private, and nonprofit sectors. She is involved in various aspects of planning and policy at the national and local levels, including participation in several workshops each year. Her experience includes the following: conducting independent research on disaster risk reduction and hazard mitigation for various organizations such as the National Wildlife Foundation; working as the lead grant writer and emergency planner for the First Peoples' Conservation Council, through her role with the Lowlander Center on coastal community resettlement; community-based resilience planning across the United States; working with Save the Children USA along the Gulf Coast following hurricanes and tornadoes, on a resilience initiative relating to children's needs in emergencies; hazard mitigation planning at the local, state, and campus level; community education and outreach regarding mitigation measures and preparedness; development of collaborative networks and information sharing avenues among practitioners; and delivery of training and education to various stakeholders. She speaks on many topics, including: hazard mitigation and climate change; campus planning; threat, hazard, and vulnerability assessments; hazard mitigation planning; protecting children in disasters; and public/private partnerships.

Mark Landahl, Ph.D., C.E.M., currently serves as the emergency manager for the city of Rockville, Maryland. Before this position, he served at the Frederick County (Maryland) Sheriff's Office where he retired as a lieutenant. Dr. Landahl has held several positions over his law enforcement career, including his last assignment as homeland security commander. He also served as supervisor of the School Resource Program, supervisor of the Sheriff's Office Homeland Security Section, and as an investigator assigned to the Maryland-Delaware Joint Terrorism Task Force. Dr. Landahl received his master's degree from the U.S. Naval Postgraduate School Center for Homeland Defense and Security and holds a graduate certificate in Law Enforcement Intelligence Analysis from Michigan State University. He earned his Ph.D. in emergency management from Oklahoma State University in 2015 and has published in multiple journals, including the *Journal of Homeland Security and Emergency Management*, *Homeland Security Affairs*, and the *Journal of Urban Management*. Previous to his law enforcement career, Dr. Landahl served as a public school history and government teacher and worked on the congressional staff of a member of the U.S. House of Representatives.

Emily MacNabb is a doctoral student in public administration and disaster policy at the University of Nebraska at Omaha. As an undergraduate student, she completed three semesters at the University of Haifa in Israel and while there focused her studies on counterterrorism and nuclear proliferation, later completing both her bachelor's and master's degrees in political science at the University of Nebraska at Omaha focusing in Middle East politics. Emily's research includes a variety of disaster-related topics, including the impact of disasters on both long- and short-term food insecurity in socially vulnerable communities. Her focus pertains to citizen trust in public emergency management officials and first responders, considering how negative police-community relationships impact disaster response capabilities. She has also collaborated on a project to better understand the inclusion of the FEMA Next Generation Core Competency of Sociocultural Literacy, in particular, social vulnerability and community capacity building on college campus emergency management. Emily teaches the undergraduate level Introduction to Emergency Management course.

James D. Ramsay, Ph.D., M.A., C.S.P., is a professor of security studies, coordinator of the Homeland Security program, and the founding chair of the Department of Business, Politics, and Security Studies at the University of New Hampshire. Before UNH, he created one of the first undergraduate programs in homeland security in the United States in 2006 at Embry-Riddle. Dr. Ramsay serves on the editorial boards for *Homeland Security Affairs Journal* and the *Journal of Homeland Security and Emergency Management*. He also co-founded and serves on the advisory/editorial boards for the *International Journal of Security, Preparedness and Resilience Education*, and the *Journal of Human Security and Resilience*. Current research interests include climate security, homeland security, intelligence and law enforcement education, and the relationship between environmental and human security and national security strategy. Books include *Introduction to Homeland Security* and *Critical Issues in Homeland Security: A Casebook* and *Foundations of Environmental Security: Integrating Resilience into National Security*. His current book is with Routledge entitled *Homeland Security Theory, Concepts and Cases* and is expected to be available in winter 2019.

Christa L. Remington, Ph.D., is an assistant professor of public administration at the University of South Florida. She holds a bachelor's degree in sociology/anthropology, a master's degree in public administration, and a Ph.D. in public affairs from the Steven J. Green School of International and Public Affairs at Florida International University. Her research focuses on cultural competence, program effectiveness, and post-disaster response and recovery. She has completed field work at international NGO headquarters, hospitals, internally displaced persons (IDP) camps, and prisons in Haiti. Dr. Remington is also a nonprofit consultant and project manager. In 2003, she co-founded The Mission Haiti Inc., a nonprofit organization that focuses on education and community building in rural Haiti, and currently serves as its project director.

Keith Douglas Revell, Ph.D., is an associate professor of public administration at Florida International University. He received his M.A. and Ph.D. in American history from the University of Virginia. Dr. Revell is the author of *Building Gotham: Civic Culture and Public*

Policy in New York City, 1898–1938 (Johns Hopkins University Press, 2003), which won the Urban History Association's prize for Best Book in North American Urban History in 2002. He has published on zoning, skyscrapers, railroad regulation, fiscal development in Latin America, and nightclubs in Miami Beach. He is currently writing a book on the history of Miami Beach. He has taught leadership and public policy at FIU since 1996 and won a Faculty Senate Teaching Award in 2006.

Abdul Samad is a doctoral student in the School of International and Public Affairs at Florida International University (FIU). His research primarily focuses on issues related to race, religion, social equity, and public participation of marginalized communities. At FIU, he serves as the leader of the Public Affairs Student Association and is currently the president of the International City and County Management Association (ICMA). Abdul was the recipient of the 2019 American Public Policy and Management Association (APPAM) Equity and Inclusion Fellowship, American Society for Public Administration (ASPA) Founders' Fellows Award (2015), ASPA International Young Scholar Award (2018), Muslim Public Service Network Fellowship Award (2018), and the Dewey W. Knight, Jr., Memorial Scholarship (2019). Outside of his research, he enjoys playing tennis, cooking, traveling, and, most of all, learning new languages. In addition to his experience and educational background, Abdul has a strong passion for youth leadership development. He is fascinated by language. He is fluent in English, Urdu, Punjabi, and Hindi and can speak basic Arabic. He is also an enthusiastic beginner in Chinese and Farsi.

Yoon Ah Shin, M.P.A., is a Ph.D. candidate of the Graduate School of Public and International Affairs (GSPIA) at the University of Pittsburgh. Her research interests are in inter-organizational collaboration, the decision-making process in a dynamic situation, civic participation, public health policy, and disaster management systems. She has participated in the Hazard SEES inter-disciplinary project supported by the National Science Foundation, establishing sustainability and resilience of coastal cities exposed to near-field tsunami hazards in Indonesia. Her dissertation is "Network

Coordination of Relief Logistics and Its Impact on Field Operations in Emergency Health Services: The Ebola Crisis in Liberia in 2014." She is an awardee of the 2018 dissertation award hosted by the Section on Emergency and Crisis Management of the American Society for Public Administration.

Susan Spice, Ph.D., is a visiting assistant professor in the Department of Government at New Mexico State University. She has also taught at the University of Central Florida and Auburn University. Her interest in emergency management developed during her M.P.A. program, and her thesis focused on sheltering and evacuation practices of three memory care facilities in Tallahassee, Florida. The topic was deeply personal as her mother had been a resident of one of those facilities for a short time. It was a natural progression for her dissertation research to look beyond memory care facilities to the larger world of special needs sheltering in Florida. In addition to emergency management, Spice's other research interests include nonprofit management, organizational behavior, and human resource management.

Jungwon Yeo, Ph.D., is an assistant professor of public administration, and emergency management and homeland security in the School of Public Administration at the University of Central Florida. Her research and teaching interests include behaviors, communication, and decision-making for collective action across sectors and jurisdictions, operating in the context of emergency and crisis management, immigrant integration, and border management. She has published in high-impact journals such as *American Review of Public Administration, Safety Science, Disaster Prevention and Management, Journal of Homeland Security and Emergency Management*, and *International Journal of Public Administration*. She has served on ASPA's Section on Emergency and Crisis Management as the membership chair as well as a board member since 2017. She has also been serving as an associate editor for the *Natural Hazards Review* journal.

Index

Page numbers in bold indicate a table on the corresponding page.

Made in the USA
Monee, IL
20 December 2023

50240015R00155